Remembering Carlsbad
& caving in

Adventure of Caving

The Guadalupes

David

3/88

About the Author

David McClurg began caving in 1956 while on assignment as a Foreign Sevice Officer in Curacao (Netherlands West Indies), and has remained an active caver ever since. Following a tour of duty in Germany, he spent over 25 years exploring the caves and lava tubes of California, other parts of the United States, Mexico, and Yugoslavia. In 1986, he and his wife—and constant caving companion—Janet, relocated to Carlsbad, New Mexico. Here they continue to explore and photograph some of the most beautiful caves in the world, those of the Guadalupe Mountains.

Active in the National Speleological Society since 1958, Mr. McClurg has served as administrative vice president, public relations chair, program and activites chair, and as chair and co-chair of two annual conventions, Sequoia National Park (1966, California) and Frog Town (1975, Angel's Camp, California). In 1983, he was given the society's highest honor, the Outstanding Service Award. *Adventure of Caving,* represents a complete revision and updating of the author's two previous books, *Exploring Caves* (1973), and *Amateur's Guide to Caves and Caving* (1980).

Adventure of Caving

A Practical Guide for
Advanced and Beginning Cavers

DAVID R. McCLURG

Photos by David and Janet McClurg

D&J Press

The Adventure of Caving

Published by
D&J PRESS
1610 Live Oak
Carlsbad, New Mexico 88220

D&J Press, 1610 Live Oak, Carlsbad, NM 88220. Phone
505/887-5761.

Library of Congress Catalog Card Number   86-71024
ISBN 0-937757-00-4 (pbk)

Liability Disclaimer. WARNING: Serious injury or death
could result from the use of the equipment or techniques set
forth in this book. It is your responsibility to get qualified
instruction in safe caving including equipment, techniques,
safety measures, and back up systems. This book is sold
with no liability to the author or publisher, expressed or
implied, in case of injury or death to the purchaser or reader.

Contents

About
Adventure of Caving

This book—like my two previous volumes— describes the equipment and techniques needed for safe and responsible cave exploration.

This means that if you follow the recommendations given here concerning proper training and joining a club, you stand a good chance of going caving without hurting yourself or the cave.

Both you and the cave are fragile, particularly the cave. Both of you need all the help you can get to be sure that a visit to a cave is a rewarding one—one that leaves the cave the way you found it and leaves you in full command of mind and limb. Before you go on, however, please think about this.

No book—this one included—can teach you caving all by

itself. The best way to learn is to join an organized caving club or find a group of experienced cavers. That way you can get hands-on, practical experience above and below ground. Never forget that caving is a strenous and potentially dangerous sport.

Above all, **never go caving alone**. The worst thing you could do is buy a book on caving and rush out to explore a wild cave all by yourself. Any wild cave.

Caving alone isn't safe. You'll see why in some detail later.

But for now, if you don't do anything else except close the cover and put this book back on the shelf, promise me you won't forget the warning about caving alone. It could save your life.

A final note—my wife and I have been exploring caves, both horizontal and vertical, for nearly thirty years. (Some non-caving friends accuse us of never growing up.) I mention this to bring out an important point.

Instead of trying to cover everything, this book centers on the equipment and methods I have found succcessful in my years of active field use. My caving style has changed and evolved over the years, but I remain a very active caver.

Rest assured that what you'll learn here in the way of equipment and techniques is:

• The latest available.
• What we consider the best (and the safest).
• In current use by organized cavers.
• Available from commercial sources (with one or two exceptions, which you may need to make yourself).

So if we haven't scared you off, let me finish with this hope—That this book will be the first step towards your own wonderful adventures in caving. Adventures that will be both safe and environmentally responsible.

Acknowledgements

Drawings in this book are by David Belski. My thanks also to the following for information and review: Gary Bush, Dr. Denny Constantine, Boh Ehr, Steve Hudson, Carl Kunath, Dick Newell, Doug Rhodes and many others too numerous to list here.

1

A Real Life
Caving Adventure

In caving,we have three levels of lost— off route, momentarily confused, and totally lost. This time,we were totally lost.

"Are we lost?
"It looks like it."
"Are you sure?"

I hated to admit it, but if being lost means that nothing seems familiar, then we were lost. And we had been for about thirty or forty minutes.

We were in a part of the cave called the Lower Maze. I leave it to your imagination as to what kind of cave it's going to be if one section is labelled the Lower maze. Not just the maze pure and simple, but the Lower Maze. Complete with Capital L and Capital M.

That could only mean the cave has other mazes. And indeed it has. The Upper Maze, the Green Lake Maze, the Intermediate Level Maze, and for all I know, three or four others as well. Oh yes, in case I forgot to mention it, this cave is called Endless Cave.

It got that name because local folks here in Carlsbad, New Mexico used to get lost in this cave regularly. It's close enough to town so that when it was discovered in the years after World War 1, it soon became a popular Sunday afternoon excursion. Later, it was gated to protect it from further vandalism—and to keep folks from getting lost all the time.

Nowadays, to visit the cave you need a permit from the Bureau of Land Management office in Carlsbad. Besides the combination to the lock, the rangers there are nice enough to provide a map of the cave and some valuable advice on equipment and caving in general.

At this point on our little cave trip, we were on the way out of the cave. In accordance with good caving practice, I had gone ahead of the others a bit to see if something— anything—looked familiar. A passage, the floor, the ceiling, a formation. Once you've been in a certain part of a cave, you can nearly always remember it later. It's like driving. Once you've been on a certain road, later—even years later—it somehow seems familiar.

But not this time.

"You mean we're really lost?"

"Yep. I'm afraid so."

About this time, the others caught up with us and said in chorus

"We're not lost again are we?"

It seems several of them had been lost on an earlier trip.

"No," I said indignantly, "We're not lost again. As a matter of fact, this is the **first** time I've ever been lost in Endless."

First time or tenth time, we were really lost.

Three Levels of Lost: Off Route, Momentarily Confused, and Really Lost. I should explain that in caving there are actually three levels of the condition of being lost. In truth, cavers seldom get lost. Despite what many non-cavers think, this isn't one of the really serious caving dangers. There are plenty of others, but getting lost isn't usually one of them. Anyway, back to the three levels.

The first level is when you're simply "off route." You have chosen, by accident or maybe on purpose, to traverse a certain part of the cave using passages or rooms different from the usual route. In the process, you perhaps have strayed into some less familiar territory. This degree of getting lost is so trivial that most cavers seldom even speak of it, unless it progresses to the next level, which is almost universally known as "momentarily confused."

All experienced cavers (the honest ones anyway) will admit to being momentarily confused or momentarily disoriented several times in their caving careers. It's a kind of in joke in the caving world. The humorous part is, that by tacit agreement, the word momentarily really means anywhere from about a few minutes to an hour. If it goes much longer than that, you've slid down the lost scale to level three. In other words, you're really lost.

And take my word for it, that's what we were this time—really lost.

Now, you have to understand that we didn't start out that day with the idea of getting lost in Endless. Or anywhere else, for that matter. I mean, this was Thanksgiving Weekend and Endless was supposed to be a sweetness and light trip.

We had just tucked six days of border-line hard-core caving under our hard hats, braving wind and weather up on Guadalupe Ridge. At this point, I and the twelve visiting firemen from the San Francisco area (where we lived until August of that year) were looking forward to an easy trip.

"Three hours tops," I assured them, "if we can just keep the damn photographers moving."

On the way out to the cave, I told them all about how it was mostly walking, with only a few short hands-and-knees crawls. Truly a piece of cake. I didn't dwell on why the cave is called Endless. Or mention the Upper Level Maze or the Lower Level Maze or the Easy Chair maze or any of the little bitty mazes either. I'd been to Endless many times before, and I was sure I could get in and out of there blindfolded.

Oh that it were true that day.

Figure 1.1. While still beautiful, the Venus Room in Endless Cave is now only a shadow of its former glory due to heavy vandalism.

A Marginal Beginning. We started out OK. At least for the first two hundred feet of the Entrance Passage! But when we hit the Canyon (a wet flowstone climbdown), we all of a sudden took off in a left hand passage about a third of the way down. That's not the way I had gone before, but one of the other cavers knew that way, so we plunged on. I had always gone further into the canyon towards the Mud Crack Room, then climbed to the bottom and popped out of a hole directly into the Lower Level Maze.

It turned out that taking off higher up put us at an intermediate level (you guessed it, the Intermediate Level Maze).

Here we crawled and huffed and puffed, and stoop-walked and huffed and puffed, and duck-walked and huffed and puffed, and eventually got into the Expressway where we really got to trucking right along for quite a way.

We were trucking so good that when we got down to the Lower Level Maze, we boogied right past the small hole that I knew as the connection to the back of the cave.

Instead, we went around a couple of corners or more, then found a different tiny hole and squeezed into a little passage that took us into—HELLO—into the Venus room.

Familiar Ground for a Moment. Well, this was the first time in an hour or more that I could honestly say I knew where we were. After catching my breath, I scouted around the room and located the other connection, the one I knew from earlier trips. Then after getting everybody pointed toward Green Lake and the parts beyond, I told the others where I was going, grabbed my cave pack, and took off to find the short way out of the cave.

I didn't find it. But, I did find the Commode (a gypsum formation that looks like you know what). I found it by moving slowly and following the old rule about stopping regularly to look back to see what the route looks like when you're coming from the other direction.

And what's more, despite the fact that I got mixed up and was really (you know level three) lost in the Lower Maze for about 15 minutes, I was sure I could get from the Venus Room connection back to the Commode.

From there, I figured with a dozen or so seasoned (and hungry) cavers, we'd find that hole in the bottom of the Canyon and be out of the cave in jig time. As I was making my way back to the rear area connection, one of the cavers I had taken the precaution of telling where I was going, was just coming to see if I was lost, bless his soul.

So, we made it to Commode without incident. Then we proceeded slowly and carefully, checking out every possible lead (or so we thought). For the next hour or so, another caver and I climbed up into some really interesting (and hairy) chimneys. We made not one but three very scenic but

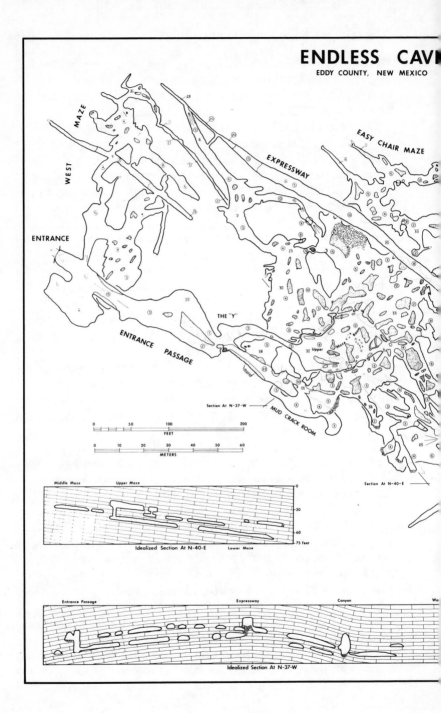

ENDLESS CAV

EDDY COUNTY, NEW MEXICO

WEST MAZE

WEST

ENTRANCE

ENTRANCE PASSAGE

THE "Y"

EXPRESSWAY

EASY CHAIR MAZE

Upper Maze Room

Section At N-37-W

MUD CRACK ROOM

Section At N-40-E

0   50   100   200
FEET

0   10   20   30   40   50   60
METERS

Middle Maze   Upper Maze
0
30
60
75 feet
Idealized Section At N-40-E   Lower Maze

Entrance Passage   Expressway   Canyon   Wa
Idealized Section At N-37-W

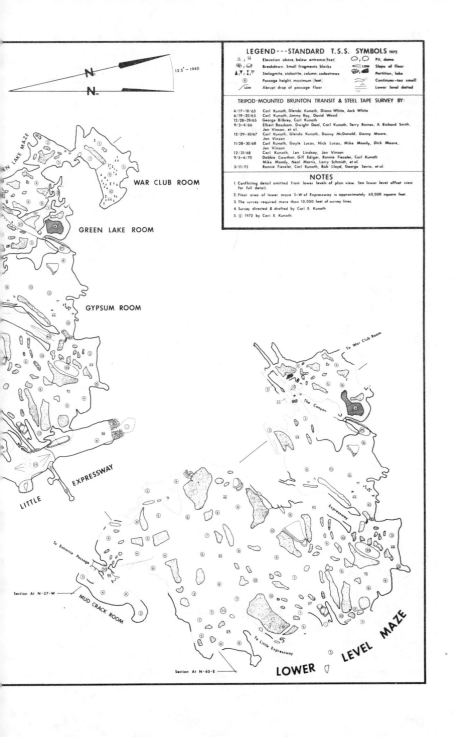

N

N_m

12.5° — 1940

LEGEND---STANDARD T.S.S. SYMBOLS 1972

Elevation above, below entrance (feet)   Pit, dome

Breakdown. Small fragments, blocks   Slope of floor

Stalagmite, stalactite, column, sodastraws   Partition, lake

Passage height, maximum (feet)   Continues—too small

Abrupt drop of passage floor   Lower level dotted

TRIPOD-MOUNTED BRUNTON TRANSIT & STEEL TAPE SURVEY BY:

4/17-18/65   Carl Kunath, Glenda Kunath, Diana White, Jack White
6/19-20/65   Carl Kunath, Jimmy Ray, David Wood
12/28-29/65   George Bilbrey, Carl Kunath
9/3-4/66   Elbert Bassham, Dwight Deal, Carl Kunath, Terry Raines, A. Richard Smith, Jan Vinson, et al.
12/29-30/67   Carl Kunath, Glenda Kunath, Danny McDonald, Danny Moore, Jan Vinson
11/28-30/68   Carl Kunath, Gayle Lucas, Nick Lucas, Mike Moody, Dick Moore, Jan Vinson
12/31/68   Carl Kunath, Len Lindsay, Jan Vinson
9/5-6/70   Debbie Cawthon, Gill Ediger, Ronnie Fieseler, Carl Kunath, Mike Moody, Neal Morris, Larry Schmidt, et al.
3/11/72   Ronnie Fieseler, Carl Kunath, Bob Lloyd, George Sevra, et al.

NOTES

1. Conflicting detail omitted from lower levels of plan view. See lower level offset view for full detail.
2. Floor area of lower maze S-W of Expressway is approximately 60,000 square feet.
3. The survey required more than 10,000 feet of survey lines.
4. Survey directed & drafted by Carl E. Kunath.
5. © 1972 by Carl E. Kunath.

GREEN LAKE MAZE

WAR CLUB ROOM

GREEN LAKE ROOM

GYPSUM ROOM

EXPRESSWAY

LITTLE

To Entrance Passage

Section At N-37-W

MUD CRACK ROOM

To War Club Room

The Canyon

Expressway

Section At N-40-E

To Little Expressway

LOWER   LEVEL   MAZE

very unsuccessful excursions into the Upper Level Maze.
Never realizing of course, that a couple of times we were
within 100 feet of the Entrance Passage without knowing it.

The rest of the group was having a swell time waiting
down below (as they should be instead of running around
getting even more lost) reminiscing about the great week of
caving that was just closing. Eventually, we got the idea to
try a little further back in the Lower Maze. This provided us
with a real nice tour of the Little Expressway—a place I
hadn't been to before and had always wanted to see. But not
on this trip.

Finally, we sat down and studied the page-size map the
BLM provides. I'm sure you recognize this kind of ploy.
It's known as "If all else fails, read the directions." It shows
how desperate we were getting.

Believe it or not, we were actually able to figure out where
we were on the map. One of the women in our party—a
geologist as it happens—managed to decipher the snake fight
that the map of Endless becomes when it's reduced to a
standard page.

So this time, one of the other cavers and I (in the tradition
of sending fresh replacements into the Endless battle) began
to check the leads on the left hand wall of the cave.

"We need a passage with flowstone walls, like a canyon,"
I told him.

And hidden away there in that low-ceilinged gypsum-
coated section where I'd swear the first guy and I had carefully checked, he yelled back he'd found a little hole that
looked promising. I squirmed over, climbed through,
checked a ways ahead just to be sure, then yelled for
everybody to get moving—dinner at the local steak house
was awaitin'.

What a relief.

P.S. A postscript to this trip is that on Christmas Day,
Janet and I went back again to Endless, this time with our
son Dai, who was visiting during his holiday break from
the University of Washington.

Guess what. We didn't get lost. But we didn't see as
much of the cave either. Or maybe have as much fun.

After all, getting lost in Endless—**really lost**—not just off-route or momentarily confused, is part of the fun.

Isn't it?

LOST LESSONS

So what can you learn from this story about a Thanksgiving trip to Endless when a dozen or more seasoned cavers managed to get themselves lost.

First. Getting lost is not necessarily a serious problem if you cave with a group. This is one more example that proves how you should never go caving alone. I don't want to be tiresome on this point, but it can't be emphasized too strongly. What becomes an amusing anecdote if it happens to a team can so easily end in tragedy for a solo caver.

Never forget—Floyd Collins was a solo caver.

Second. If you do get lost, send one or two cavers ahead to scout it out and see if they see anything familiar. Be sure they take their packs. Spares and second and third sources of light are needed above all when you're away from the group. If you're one of those looking ahead, tell the others what you're doing and don't go too far afield. Try to stay within earshot. The rest of the group should stay together in a comfortable spot so the advance party can get back to them by sighting on their lights or the sound of their yells.

Third. Don't panic. Sit down and take stock. Study the map. Try to reconstruct where you've been and how to get back that way. Even if that way is longer, it's probably better than trying an unfamiliar route.

Sooner or later, one of your party will find a friendly landmark. Then you'll be back on route after your first adventure with being lost in caving.

———————

2

Conservation

Inside a cave, we are the outsiders. We must move with care and caution. Natural beauty that has taken countless thousands of years to create can be destroyed in a second by a careless or thoughtless action.

Have you ever visited a commercial cave like Carlsbad Caverns or Mammoth Cave? Anyone who loves caves can't help but be awed by the huge rooms, beautiful formations, and tunnels large enough for a speeding subway train. For the most part, commercial caves seem to be either very beautiful or at least very impressive.

One of the reasons they remain so is that they have been singled out in order to preserve them or make them into tourist attractions. Put another way, they were made into show caves (often at great expense) because their unique qualities made them worth preserving or worth showing to others for a fee.

In fact, commercialization is probably the most successful way of protecting a beautiful cave over the long term. After all, the owners—whether private or public—willingly

Fig. 2.1 The Inkwell,   Soldier's Cave, California.

assume the responsibility for keeping their property in the
best condition. It's in their best interest to do so.

Protecting Wild Caves. But how about the wild or
undeveloped caves—the kind that cavers like you and I go
into. Who's responsible to protect them? You guessed it.
It's got to be us. We're the ones who visit wild caves the
most. Potentially we can cause the most damage. Furthermore, we go to a cave on our own. We don't have a guide
regulating or modeling behavior as in a show cave.

Even if the cave has a nearby owner, an impressive gate,
or a complicated procedure for getting a permit, we cavers
are the ones that are most likely to do damage to it. The best
cave management plan—whether it assumes the form of a
simple "Sure you fellas can visit my cave" or a signed
three-part government release—can only protect the cave
if we are so committed.

So, if we don't behave responsibly to save wild caves, no
one else will. And this responsibility extends beyond our
own actions underground. Many of us have come to realize
that we must try to educate even casual cave visitors about
how their visit can damage the delicate cave environment.

Caves are Fragile. Caves are fragile, extremely fragile.
Speleothems (cave formations[1]) like delicate soda straws or
eccentric helictites that took untold thousands of years to
grow can be destroyed in an instant by an accidental or
thoughtless act on our part.

To get a glimmer of understanding about how easily you
can damage a cave, try the conservation obstacle course
described next. Although its purpose is deadly serious, it's
also a lot of fun , and it's guaranteed to improve your
conservation awareness.

Conservation Awareness Course

Cover part of a floor in your house (or at a club meeting)
with an obstacle course of easily disturbed objects. These
can be ping pong balls, aluminum cans, bottles standing on

end, plastic straws, or packing materials like styrene chips. Make a narrow winding path on the floor through these delicate cave formations for participants to walk or crawl through. Add interest by finding a big carton, like a refrigerator box, to double as a cave passage. Cut off the ends, lay it down and hang some plastic straws inside from the top. Finish off with some more straws on the side sticking out into the passage.

The point of the game is to go through the entire course without knocking over or touching a single thing. Have a referee complete with clipboard and pencil to record the number of hits.

Usually no one will be able do it perfectly the first time through. But that's one of the lessons you learn so dramatically from this game. You can do the course as many times as it takes until you learn that it's possible to move through a delicate area of a cave without breaking anything. You can move as slowly as you like, just as we want you to move in a highly decorated section of a cave.

My wife and I have run this obstacle course with great success as a conservation speleolympics at annual con- ventions and regional meetings of the National Speleological Society. Everyone who does the course gets a ribbon or certificate or something to show they tried. Those who disturb the fewest delicate objects get prizes and recognition. The more winners the better.

Try this game. You'll like it and other cavers will too. And it teaches careful cave movement better than anything else we've ever used[2].

Conservation Rules

If you tried the obstacle course, you now have some idea of how you should move in a pretty area of a cave. I hope it convinced you that it's possible to do zero (or almost) zero damage if you move slowly and carefully, always alert to the damage you can do.

For those who also like to learn from lists of helpful hints here are a few handy rules that will help you remember some

Fig. 2.2 Multi-banded crystaline draperies.

good conservation practices.

Keep in mind though, that cave conservation is really more a state of mind than a set of rules. If you remember to always take the action that will cause the least damage to the cave, I believe your own common sense can be as good as any rule.

CONSERVATION RULES

• **Don't take anything, don't leave anything.**
• **Don't break or remove cave formations.**
• **Don't collect cave life.**
• **Choose a route that minimizes damage.**
• **Don't smoke arrows or names on the wall.**
• **In other words,**
   Take nothing but pictures,
      Leave nothing but footprints (on trails),
   Kill nothing but time.

• **Don't take anything, don't leave anything**. Anything means anything and everything. On the **don't take** side it means don't take cave formations, cave animals, or cave debris of any kind. Archaeological remains are a special case. To be of real value, they must be examined in place, right where they were found. It's your responsibility to let qualified researchers know about your find, and let them prescribe the next action.

On the **don't leave** side, it means take everything out. Candy wrappers, carbide, empty cans, old batteries, everything. Take them out of the cave and throw them away in a safe disposal area. Above all, don't dump them outside the cave entrance. Spent carbide is toxic to humans and animals. Even if you bury it, it may find its way into the water supply. It's best to put it in a sealed container and be sure it ends up in a proper disposal site.

• **Don't break or remove speleothems** (cave formations). Speleothems—stalactites, stalagmites, columns,
draperies, helictites—all of them have this in common with
pebbles glistening in a stream. They're very beautiful in
their natural setting. But outside in the daylight, they seem
drab and dull. So don't try to take them home as a souvenir.
It will be a disappointment, I guarantee it.

Worst of all, it ruins the cave for everyone else. For all
practical purposes, when you break a cave formation, you
have destroyed it forever. It certainly won't grow back in
your lifetime, or tens of thousands of our kind of lifetimes.

Don't remove broken formations either. Try not to even
disturb them. Some might be worth reconstructing, but
you'll need all the pieces. This prohibition extends to natural
cave debris too. Branches, leaves, and other organic material
are part of the food chain.

• **Choose a minimum damage route.** Always choose a
route that will cause the least damage. Be especially careful
when you're tired at the end of a trip. It's so easy to brush
against a wall or ceiling and sweep away forever a priceless
cluster of soda straws or helictites. Stay on established
trails—particularly when they're already flagged to mark the
boundaries.

Your responsibility is even heavier if you discover a new
cave or new passage. The route or path you select will most
likely be the one others follow, so choose carefully for
minimum damage. Avoid completely any beautiful section if
it's necessary to destroy speleothems to enter. You may
want to mark the area with flagging tape or a sign to
encourage protection by others. And don't think you have to
do the whole cave on the first trip. It's best to slow down
and save the cave.

• **Don't collect cave life**. Even if your intention is to
take it to a scientist, don't collect cave life except under a
scientist's direct supervision. The chances are, the specimen

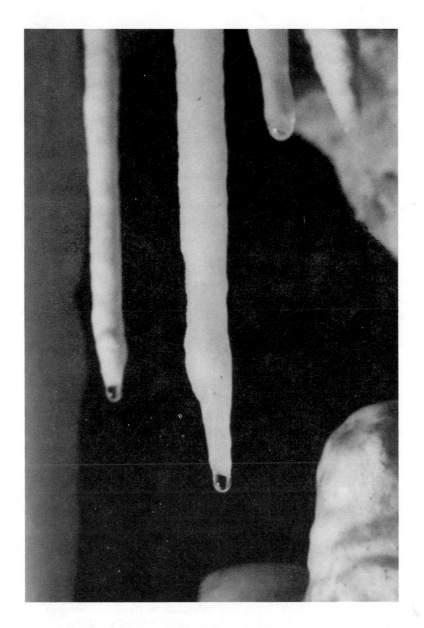

Fig. 2.3 Soda straws with water drops on ends.

has already have been studied and you are unnecessarily depleting the colony. Instead, take notes or a photo and show these to the researcher. If they want a sample, they'll probably be delighted to have the information and the offer of your help. They'll provide the right containers and will be able to instruct you on proper handling and storage, so the specimen will have eventual value.

One safety precaution: don't attempt to handle bats. You can easily injure them. In particular, avoid any that have fallen to the floor of the cave. (This is not common, except in caves with large bat colonies, where you probably shouldn't be intruding anyway.) Fallen bats could be sick and infectious to humans. Contrary to superstition, normal bats are harmless and quite beneficial to us. But bats are mammals too and any sick mammal could make us sick.

• **Don't smoke arrows or names on the wall.**
If you've done any wild caving at all, you'll know what we mean when we strongly advise against any further smoking of arrows on cave walls. In the good old days (which probably means before anyone thought about it), cavers rather freely smoked directional arrows on cave walls with their carbide lamps. The idea was that the arrows always pointed out.

Besides being unsightly, another more practical problem has arisen. In many parts of the country, cave exploration has progressed way beyond those early days and a lot of caves have been connected together. We now have not just simple names like Bat Cave and Crystal Cave and so on, but real tongue twisters like the Bat/Crystal/Smith/Deep Hole and so forth Cave System.

So which way is out? There can be several outs and the arrows can be essentially meaningless or could take you out the wrong exit.

Thus besides being ugly, arrows aren't even useful any-more as a practical means of navigation. In fact, conflicting directions and multiple colors do nothing but confuse a situation that more arrows could hardly improve.

In really complex mazes during the discovery phase,

Fig. 2.4 Tear drop shaped passage in lava tube.

removable markers like reflective tape may in rare cases be justified. Just be sure you're willing to follow our Golden Rule Number One and take out everything including those markers when you leave. Sometimes that may be more difficult that you imagine, so weigh the alternatives before you leave anything in a cave—removable markers included.

Heavily traveled caves haven't escaped from the burning need some people feel to spray or scrawl their names on any reasonably smooth surface. Caves seem to get their share of senseless and ugly obscenities too. If you're inclined to these excesses, please save your drawing urge for a more suitable canvas and more appreciative audience.

Cave Clean Up Projects

Did you ever wonder why Disneyland and other privately owned amusement parks are so clean and no one throws trash on the ground. Visitors often talk about it and marvel at how nice it is, compared, presumably, with publicly owned parks.

Well, I'm sure there are several reasons for this, not the least of which is that you paid to get in and someone may boot you out if you get caught littering. Or the fact that just as soon as you toss a gum wrapper, a Mouseketeer or such like appears from nowhere and whisks it invisibly away. However, I don't think that these are the only reasons, or the most important.

I believe that to a large extent it's because the place is clean to start with. And when most people find a place neat and tidy, I think (I'm known as an optimist) that except for the real slobs among us, they simply don't want to mess it up.

But—and this is a biggy—by the opposite token, when they find a place already trashed up, they don't seem to hesitate to add their beer cans and fast-food containers to the growing pile.

I mention all this because in the cave cleanups I have participated in, I have observed this effect. When you get in there with fifteen or twenty eager cleaner-uppers and remove 179 pounds of trash (as we did in a cave near a college campus), it stays clean for a surprisingly long time afterwards.

By that I mean, it's six months or a year, before it begins to become a dump again, and the sophomoric types, who have to prove their manhood by smashing beer bottles, start throwing them against the cave walls again. (A lot of that 179 pounds was brown glass embedded in the mud.) And it can be years and years if your caving club has the time and energy to regularly (every month or two) haul out the small amount of trash that will inevitably accumulate.

Just seeing your bunch in there sweating away digging out glass with a garden trowel and vigorously throwing unpleasant aluminum, plastic, and rubber objects into large heavy-duty garbage bags can have a salutary effect.

You may even get some volunteers to help right on the spot. It's the Tom Sawyer-Help-Whitewash-the-Fence effect. Believe it or not, it seems as deeply embedded in the American character today as it was in the 1840's and 50's of Mark Twain's world.

Removing Graffiti. Cavers of the National Speleological Society and cave management personnel, among others, have come up with some good tools and techniques in the fight against graffiti. For those of you who want to go beyond the trash removal phase and try cleaning walls and formations, here are some basic ideas for consideration.

One caution—before removing any graffiti, it's best to evaluate names and dates for authenticity and historical significance

As with a trash removal project, you're going to need manpower to remove graffiti. Figure on a minimum of a dozen to twenty or more eager souls for a wall and formation washing session. Arm each volunteer with a nylon bristle scrub brush and a small spray bottle full of the magic cleaning solution.

For the main cleaning job, a weak hydrochloric acid solution (5 to 10%) delivered under pressure from a hand carried garden sprayer will clean most cave graffiti. Plain water under pressure is also effective. You might be advised

to try plain water first on a scouting trip before using
hydrochloric acid, especially if cave animals are a factor.
Some cave managers have used diluted muriatic acid with
success also.

With the hydrochloric solution or water in the garden
sprayer, give the affected areas a general spraying. Then
your troopers with their smaller spray bottles and brushes
at ready can zero in on particularly tough items like felt pen
and spray paint markings.

Stronger chemicals like lye or paint remover are not a
good idea, either for you or the cave. Another caution—
before using the sprayer and spray bottles be sure to rinse
them thoroughly to remove any insecticides or cleansers.

Restoring Formations. Restoring broken speleothems is
a bit like all the king's horses and all the king's men trying to
put Humpty Dumpty together again.

Fortunately, repairing broken speleothems is often more
successful than the king's mighty forces were. To cement
the pieces together, two-part epoxy is usually effective. It
seems to adhere well, and is good at filling in open spots if
the pieces don't fit together too well.

Be sure to keep the glue joint and nearby area dry during
application and drying. It may be necessary to divert dripping or running water with rags during this process.

Sometimes, one or more pins of stainless steel (or other
material not subject to rust or water deterioration) will be
needed to reinforce the joint. To prepare holes for the pins, a
carbide tipped bit in a battery operated drill is a lot easier to
use and less likely to cause additional damage than a star drill
and hammer

Speleothem restoration is not easy, but it's very rewarding.
It makes a good club project—one that puts conservation on
a participation basis, rather than being just a lot of slogans.

1.Specialized terms are defined in the Glossary.
2. Our special thanks to Rob Stitt, who as NSS Conservation Chairman back in the 1970's, first suggested to us
the idea of a conservation obstacle course.

3

Cave Safety

Going caving without getting hurt depends on you. Reduce your risk by caving with an experienced group, getting the proper training, and choosing the right equipment.

You can hurt yourself in a cave—make no mistake about that. But compared to other high risk sports (like rock climbing, scuba diving, or hang gliding, to cite a few), caving has an enviable safety record. I believe this is due in no small part to the excellent training that almost any new caver can get from caving clubs just for the asking.

These clubs include many of the 100 plus chapters of the National Speleological Society, as well as local groups at colleges and outing clubs in certain areas. See the next chapter for information about how to get started in caving with an organized club.

What's in Caves? What's in wild caves that makes them dangerous to visit unless you're properly prepared? First of all, the large rooms and passages we mentioned in Carlsbad

Fig. 3.1. Caver cautiously examines a pit before chimneying.

Caverns and Mammoth Cave are the exception rather than the rule in wild caves. Sure there are booming trunk passages in wild caves and you'll get to see some of them if you cave in the areas where they're common.

But more than likely, what you'll encounter is a fast changing succession of small to medium sized rooms and passages. Some will be big enough to walk upright or shuffle along in a stooping position. Some will be so low you'll need to get down on your hands and knees or even your belly and crawl like a baby.

Some will meander along following a stream, so you'll be sloshing in and out of ankle to knee deep water regularly. Some passages are going to be muddy and nasty, some very narrow and snug. You'll have to scramble up and down slippery, muddy slopes, slide over wet boulders, and pick your way carefully around the edges of bottomless pits(they all seem bottomless in the dark).

Sounds great doesn't it? The point is, caving doesn't lack in physical challenges. But caving isn't just thrill seeking— always trying for the deepest or the tightest or the nastiest. Using good technique so you can overcome hazards and penetrate the unknown is what provides the satisfaction that most cavers seek, at least in my view.

Adventure, not Thrill Seeking. I used the word adventure in the title of this book because that's what I believe many of us get from caving. A sense of adventure, the satisfaction of exploring in a place that few others have explored before (or may care to).

Cavers always want a cave to go. When checking for new passages, we're constantly asking each other "Does it go?" Embodied in this query is the hope that a new or previously unnoticed passage may be a lead into new cave.

And when that lead is blowing air, you've got a going, blowing lead. In that case, cavers will come hundreds, even thousands of miles to push leads that go and blow. For those are the ones that might lead us into more adventures in caves unknown.

Getting Lost and Stuck. Besides slipping and sliding, what are some other minor cave hazards? We covered getting lost in Chapter 1. You'll recall that it's really not thought of as much of a problem if you stick together as a group. If you do get off route (remember? it's level one of being lost), try sending a couple of people ahead to see if they can find anything familar. (Be sure they take their packs and spare light sources with them.)

The trick to staying on route is to turn around often to see how the passage or junction will look from the opposite direction when you're coming back. Look for distinctive shapes, speleothems, flat ceilings or floors, or other features that can be easily recognized on your return. Watch for obvious signs of traffic that could put you back on trail: footprints, survey markers, out arrows, or (regretably) trash.

If you accidentally get separated from the group, don't panic. Sit down and listen for the others. Try giving a loud yell every few minutes to see if you can make audible contact. Turn off your helmet lamp and light a candle (one of the three light sources we'll describe later in Chapter 7) to conserve your main light supply. Above all, don't go rushing ahead. You could hurt yourself and turn the whole incident from a laughing matter into an ugly accident. Be calm. You'll be found sooner than you think.

And by the way, forget the Tom Sawyer ball of string trick. Most balls of string are only a couple of hundred feet long and even a bunch of intrepid first time flashlight cavers would have a hard time getting lost in a cave that small.

How about getting stuck. We all do it now and again. But to echo the same refrain, it's not a big deal if you're with a group. In caving, being small is a real asset. (Cave clubs love it when small people show up and want to get into caving.) We have some specific hints later in Chapter 8 to help you and your fellow cavers get unstuck.

Caving is a Team Sport. As you may have surmised, caving is one of the quintessential team sports. Everyone is in it together, so whether you know it or not, you need each other. This has some implications you might have thoutht of.

For example, if someone is hurt, it's the responsibility of the others to get the injured party out of the cave. You might think that doesn't sound so special—many outdoor sports have that implied responsibility.

But rescuing someone from a cave is a major undertaking. It could require dozens of additional people and some very specialized skills and equipment. Furthermore, the news media always seem to find cave accidents of fascinating if not morbid interest.

So what does this mean to you as an individual caver? It means the first rule of safe caving is:

1. Don't go caving alone. And the second rule is:

2. Don't hurt yourself. When you do something dumb or reckless, you involve not just yourself, but the entire group. Think about that. Think about it before you try something beyond your skills or training. No one is pushing you (or should be) to do anything you're not comfortable with.

3. Choose the Safer Alternative. Earlier, I said you should always choose the action that will help protect the cave.Seems only fair to recommend the same for you.

Fig. 3.2. Two cavers ask the question "Does it go?"

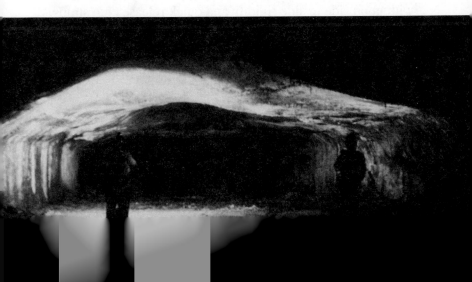

Always ask: which is the safer way to do it. Then go with
the safer alternative. We want you to live to tell about it—
rather than having you become another statistic in American
Caving Accidents.

4. Three Sources of Light. One of any kind of light, no
matter how high tech or special, isn't any good by itself.
Nor is two. Three is the minimum. It may be three of those
very same high tech lights or three low tech carbide lamps
(and nothing is quite so low tech as a carbide lamp—that's
why cavers put up with them). But as a practical matter,
most cavers pack a carbide or electric helmet lamp, a small
but powerfully beamed flashlight on a cord around the neck
or in the cave pack, and a candle or two with waterproof
matches. In addition, some carry a chemical light stick. Full
details are in Chapter 7.

5. Four Cavers. I recommend four as the minimum
number in a caving party. Three is OK a lot of times, but
four is safer in case of an accident. Two should always go
for help in an emergency, and the fourth needs to stay with
the hapless victim to provide succor and warmth.

6. Wear a Hard Hat. Every caver must wear a hard
hard. Recently, vertical cavers in particular have become
sold on the virtues of the newer style hard hats now
available. These helmets are made of high impact plastic
with good side to side rigidity and quick release chin straps.
They're not as cheap as the construction type bump helmet,
but they're much better. Again, see Chapter 7.

7. Wear Proper Clothing. The possibility of hypothermia is always there in cold, wet caves. Be prepared
with woolen or polypropylene clothing instead of cotton.
Wear several layers instead of one. Carry a garbage bag in
your helmet to use as an emergency poncho or shelter. If
you're going to get immersed in water, wear a wet suit.
Hypothermia is covered in detail in Chapter 4. Chapter
6 discusses the proper clothes.

Fig 3.3 A beautifullly decorated New Mexico cave.

8. Always Leave Word. Just as you might do when you go away on vacation, it's a good idea to tell someone about your caving plans. Include what section you're going to if it's a big cave, and when you expect to return. Always be very conservative about return times. Pad the figure with at least a couple of hours to cover weather or other problems.

You don't want people to call out the national guard just because the service was slow in the pizza parlor on the way home. Who should you tell? A neighbor, a fellow caver, a family member, or the owner of the cave if you need to stop by for permission to visit the cave. As a final precaution, like on an especially tough trip, you might want to leave a note at the entrance summarizing your plans and exit time.

Summarizing our cave safety rules in a tidy form:

Rules for Safe Caving

1. **Don't go caving alone.**
2. **Don't hurt yourself.**
3. **Choose the safer alternative.**
4. **Carry three sources of light.**
5. **Always have four cavers.**
6. **Wear a Hard Hat.**
7. **Wear the Right Clothes.**
8. **Always Leave Word.**

4

Hazards

Most cave accidents are minor. Serious ones come from flooding, loose rocks, falling, and hypothermia. Reviewing these accidents can help keep you from becoming a statistic yourself.

For almost 20 years the National Speleological Society has been compiling accident reports and publishing them in American Caving Accidents. From this wealth of information, it is now possible to generalize a bit about cave accidents and hazards.

First off, the good news is that most cave accidents are quite minor—scrapes, bruises, and sprains. There are serious accidents too. They usually result from drowning, loose rocks, falling, or hypothermia,.

But the record also seems to prove that a great many of the serious accidents happen to inexperienced people, those with little or no training in cave skills. Presumably, since you're reading these words, you at least have the desire to learn about good training and we trust you will not add your name to the list of serious or fatal accidents.

Knowing Your Limitations. Knowing your own limitations is often brought up at this juncture when discussing hazards in sports and outdoor activities. In caving, needing to know your limitations is true in spades. Remember Safety Rule No.2?— Don't Hurt Yourself. Sure, this primarily means don't do something foolhardy and hurt yourself that way.

But it also means not letting yourself get talked into something that your training or skills haven't prepared you for. Like climbing a wall or chimney without a belay line, when you really want one. Never be afraid to ask for a safety when you feel the situation is dangerous or beyond your capability.

Or maybe you're tired or ill that day. Play it cool. An accident in a cave always involves the whole group. Everybody has to get you out of the cave if you get hurt. In a large sense, knowing that your fellow cavers will do this is very comforting. It is in fact an article of faith among experienced cavers.

But the flip side is your responsibility to know your limitations and not get hurt in the first place.

Enough said.

Cave Flooding

Do you share the nightmarish fear about being trapped in a room that's slowly filling with water until you're finally dispatched to a watery grave? Believe me this can happen in a cave. It fact, it's one of the really scary things that cavers in the midwest and eastern parts of the United States worry a lot about during the rainy season. And with good reason.

This hazard is so real that in flood prone caves, explorers often stash survival food and supplies in safe areas well above the high water level .

Trapped for Three Days. This foresight proved its value in April 1983 in Kentucky's Precinct No.11 Cave. This five and one half mile cave was being extensively studied by a National Speleological Society grotto from Cincinnati. A

group of eight experienced Precinct No. 11 cavers had
entered the cave on an April Saturday morning at about
11:00 am. Two other members of the group remained
outside to work on a surface survey.

It was raining lightly and the weather was unsettled. But it
apparently didn't seem any worse than it had been on some
of their other trips, so it was not considered a cause for
alarm. As a precaution, they had checked a weather forecast
in Cincinnati before leaving and the weather was supposed
to clear up by afternoon

They noted that the cave seemed to be handling the rain
water pretty well. In particular, the entrance stream, which
would trap them if it rose, looked about normal. Knowing
that the entrance flooded and sometimes closed the cave for
months at a time, they had earlier placed a water level
gauge inside the entrance. This gauge indicated 18 inches,
the normal level for the entrance pool. This left an air space
of about three inches, which was typical during their two
previous years of experience with the cave. At 21 inches,the

Fig. 4.1.   Supplies and stranded cavers were at point X.

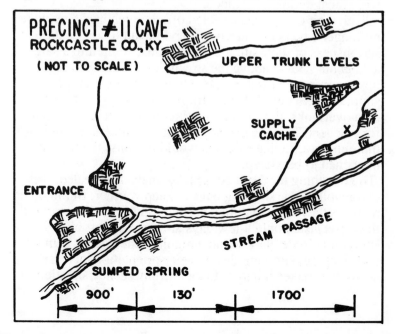

cave was known to sump (flood from floor to ceiling).

With no inkling of the ordeal that lay ahead of them, they proceeded without delay through the entrance section. This is the 200 foot low-level stream section of the cave (the so called base level) that must be traversed to reach the big, booming trunk passages in the upper level of the cave.

At some parts of this lower section, the air space is less than three inches. To head off the threat of hypothermia, they followed their usual practice of removing as much clothing as possible before sloshing through the water. On the other side, they changed into dry clothes brought through the water in waterproof plastic bags.

Retreat to High Ground. After some time underground, they began to notice a few warning signs that their previous stream cave experience had told them to be alert for. Things like a rising sound level, changes in the air flow, and increased foam and debris in the stream. Periodically, one of them would check the entrance area to see what the water level looked like. On late Saturday afternoon, to their horror it became clear that the stream had already sumped. They were most definitely trapped.

With their escape route sealed off, they realized they were no longer cavers but survivors, and began to assess the seriousness of their situation. They hustled up into a safe area about 25 feet above the stream level and 1800 feet upstream from the sump. Here they and their cached supplies were out of danger from the flooding. This safe area overlooks the stream, making it an ideal spot to watch for rescuers. They placed a glowing Cyalume light stick at that juncture, so that rescuers would not miss them if they happened to be asleep.

The one thing they lacked, as later analysis revealed, was extra clothing or sleeping bags to keep warmer. But in other respects they had what they needed to wait out the storm, if the crisis lasted only a few days at most. As part of their survival attitude, they set up a regular schedule for eating and sleeping, knowing that time disorientation increases stress and makes it harder to handle emergency situations.

Fig. 4.2. Base level entrance to an active stream cave in New York (Schoharie Cave).

Leaving on only a single candle to conserve light, they huddled together to get as warm as possible and settled in for what they prayed would not be too long a wait. In a situation like this, it's important to keep your spirits up and have faith in your eventual rescue. The question was who would win the race to save them—the rescue party or the receding flood waters. As it eventually turned out, it was both, though the water needed a healthy assist from some pumps and personnel voluntarily supplied by the LeeCo Coal and Mountain Clay Coal Companies of KANEB Corporation.

Cave Rescue Alert. Meanwhile, on Saturday afternoon, the two Cincinnati cavers who had remained on the surface returned to the cave entrance. They were shocked to find that the high water level had already sumped the entrance passage. They decided to wait in the hope that the water would drop enough to allow the trapped cavers to exit. With the entrance still flooded on Sunday morning, they called Cincinnati and alerted the Kentucky Cave and Rock Rescue Team, which later called the National Cave Rescue Commission of the National Speleological Society.

The rescue alert brought emergency personnel, cavers, and cave divers from far and wide. It also brought the inevitable gawkers and news reporters hoping for a sensational story.

A full scale rescue was mounted. Despite some initial difficulties with crowd control and relations with the news media, the effort proved eminently successful. Critical to its success was the use of the water pumps generously loaned by the two local coal companies. Volunteer amateur radio operators also contributed significantly to the effort with their communications facilities.

Divers Find A Note. On Monday, cave divers successfully penetrated the sumped entrance passage. These were divers qualified by the National Association for Cave Diving or the Cave Diving Section of the National Speleological Society. Their diving methods followed the prescribed techniques of adequate back up air supply, laying a diving guideline for other divers to follow, and using lighting and backup lights specifically designed for caves. Earlier, some open water scuba divers, who were not cave qualified, had wanted to enter the cave. Their offers, though well intentioned, were turned down (not without some ruffled feathers), until a properly trained and equipped team could be assembled.

Meanwhile, the pumps arrived and began moving great quantities of water. Based on previous experience with pumps in cave rescue, it was never certain that the pumps would really be able to lower the water enough to let the trapped cavers out. But after many hours of pumping away, the effort paid off and about 1 1/2 to 3 inches of air space appeared between the top of the water and the ceiling of the passage.

Although the trapped cavers weren't located during the initial penetrations of the sump, divers later found a note left by the stranded cavers attached to the diving guideline. It read:

HELP
8 CAVERS WAITING
ON DRY LEDGE 1800 FEET
UPSTREAM FROM HERE.
LEAVE DIVING TANKS HERE.
ONLY NEEDED FOR ENTRANCE.
BEEN HERE SINCE 11:00 AM SAT (4/23)
NOW NOON 4/25

Safe at Last. Immediately, the divers exited to spread the good news to the rescue team (and to the waiting world, as it happened by now). Soon after, two other divers reentered the cave with warm clothes and supplies and quickly located the trapped cavers. It was Monday evening by now and since the cavers were reasonably comfortable, it was decided to wait until Tuesday to bring them out, so they could rest and the water might recede more.

By Tuesday, the pumps had lowered the water enough so

Fig. 4.3 Caver wading in knee deep water in a cave in California's Mother Lode Country.

that four wet suited cavers (instead of fully equipped Scuba divers) were able to enter to assist the victims. One by one they slid into the water. With helmets scraping and necks straining to keep their heads within the precious air space, they half walked and half swam through the 200 foot long base-level passage to their freedom. It is worth noting that the air space disappeared soon after the last caver had cleared the cave and the pumps were turned off.

Three days of anguished waiting was over, thanks to the coordinated efforts of many people and organizations: The Kentucky Cave and Rock Rescue Team, the pumps from KANEB corporation , the National Cave Rescue Commission of the National Speleological Society, and the divers of the NSS Cave Diving Section and the National Association for Cave Diving, among so many others.

Analysis. In analyzing the whys and wherefors of this incident certain valuable lessons can be learned. The more obvious ones are summarized below in the heading Flooding Dangers. But what went wrong in this case? Why did eight experienced cavers get caught? Did they make any mistakes?

Probably their only error was going in the cave at all, especially through a base level area, when it was raining and had been on and off for a month or so in Kentucky. They wisely got a weather forecast before leaving. But unfortunately it was in Cincinnati, some two hundred miles from the cave (and who believes weather forecasts anyway). A late afternoon update after they had entered the cave reported heavy rain in southern Kentucky.

With hindsight the direct cause of the cave flooding now seems fairly easy to grasp. However, the details of a similar event would be very hard to predict beforehand, since so many interrelated factors affect the hydrology of a karst area (a limestone terrain riddled with many caves).

In typical karst, a cave often functions as a vital part of the underground water system. In other words, some caves are little more than storm sewers, capturing run off and carrying it away. This is apparently what happened in Precinct No. 11 Cave. Because the ground was saturated from earlier

rain, it couldn't soak up any more. The extra rain pooled
and became runoff that flooded the cave.

And it came into the cave not just through the entrance, but
through a complex system of cracks (joints) small and large
in the surrounding limestone, through sinking streams, and
through sink holes. Water in cave streams can rise more than
50 feet in Kentucky caves, surely a terrifying phenomenon if
you happened to be unlucky enough to be inside a cave and
see it happen.

The moral is clear, and becomes point number one in our
list of flooding dangers: Stay out of base level caves in rainy
weather.

Below are some more.

Flooding Dangers

In Rainy Weather:

- **Stay out of:**
  - **Base level stream passages.**
  - **Caves with active entrance streams.**
  - **Caves with steep sinkhole entrances.**
  - **Passages with leaves or debris high on walls.**

- **Check caving area weather forecast before entering.**

- **If Inside a Cave:**
  - **Watch for these warning signals:**
    - **Sudden changes in air movement.**
    - **Rising stream or lake levels.**
    - **Increased mud or debris in the water.**
    - **More foam in waterfalls or new waterfalls.**
    - **Noise or rumblings from water or moving air.**

- **If any of those warning signals are seen:**
  - **Leave the cave, if route to entrance is clear.**

- **If entrance is cut off, head for a high area above stream level.**
    - **Assume a survivor mentality**
    - **Conserve your light and food.**
    - **Huddle together to stay warm.**
    - **Wring out wet clothes, put back on to dry.**
    - **Keep spirits up, keep track of time.**
    - **Check stream levels regularly for receding water.**
    - **Leave notes with location, date, time, and needs.**

Survival in a Cave. After the Precinct No.11 rescue, two of the survivors wrote a very helpful article (NSS NEWS June 1984) on survival in a cave. Many of their suggestions are embodied in the account just related. Here is a summary of their pre trip advice.

Pre-Trip Precautions
For Flood Prone Caves

- **Leave word about your trip plans**
- **Wear layered polyprop and wool.**
- **Carry garbage bags, one space blanket.**
- **Bring extra water, food, heat tab stove.**
- **Carry first aid kit, watch, Ensolite pad.**
- **Bring candles, matches, lighter.**
- **In project caves, cache supplies.**

Scuba Diving Deaths. Despite the successful use of scuba diving in the Precinct No.11 rescue, you should know that deaths from underground scuba diving out number all other cave fatalities many fold. These deaths occur mostly in Florida and invariably claim open water scuba divers inexperienced and untrained in cave diving.

In point of fact, divers qualified by the Cave Diving Section of the National Speleological Society have a perfect safety record—no fatalities to date.

This seems to bear out our point about high risk sports. Cave diving—although certainly a magnitude or two more hazardous than caving itself—can be engaged in safely. But you must be willing to train properly, use the right gear, and keep up your proficiency with regular practice.

New Caves and Passages. Discovering a new cave (or a new section in an old one) is surely one of the stellar events in any caver's life. I think all of us dream of stumbling into another Carlsbad Caverns or a huge new river system in Mexico. (True cavers nod sagely when we tell them we recently relocated to New Mexico after 25 years in relatively cave poor California.)

But a new discovery carries with it some rather weighty responsibilities too, both to yourself and to the cave. You must tread with caution when you first enter a previously unexplored cave or passage. Floyd Collins' grave stone, placed above his coffin in the cave that bears his name, dubs him "The Greatest Cave Explorer Who Ever Lived."

Floyd died the kind of death, at least in the words of the news media, that many people fear above all others—that of being buried alive. Actually, he was trapped in a crawlway by rock weighing only thirty pounds and eventually succumbed to hypothermia. This happened on a solo trip to a new cave. (I'd like to believe his pap told him not to go in those dang caves alone—But I'll never prove it.) It was back in the 1920's and the whole nation, figuratively heard every creak of poor Floyd's death rattle via a new communications marvel called radio. Today we'd call it a media event.

Sixty years later, we continue to have serious accidents in new caves, averaging one or more a year. Mostly they're from cave ins and falling rocks. The problem with newly discovered passages is that by definition they haven't had any traffic.

Furthermore, many new caves and passages are entered by digging or removing rocks to enlarge a small hole that's blowing air. Thus you must be very alert for unstable boulders or breakdown that could be dislodged by your movements. Floors or boulders under which mud or gravel have washed away leaving them loose or unstable are additional hazards.

So is the danger of causing irreparable damage to the cave by a careless move in a delicate area. Never forget the need to choose the alternative that preserves the new cave as well as you.

Mines. Some of the manifold ways to get hurt in old mines

Fig.4.4 Floyd's Casket in Floyd Collins Crystal Cave.

are from falling timbers, bad air, and collapsing passages. Avoid particularly old ladders, ropes, and cables.

Compared to mines, caves are considered geologically stable (for the most part). Caves were formed tens of thousands of years ago and have lived through the twisting and wrenching of countless mountain building forces like earthquakes and volcanos. Mines measure their age in tens or hundreds of years at most. Play it safe. Explore caves, not mines,

Incidentally, some parts of the country have both mines and caves. When you make local inquiry (as we like call it) to find new caves, folks may direct you to a mine instead. Maybe the distinction between the two is not altogether clear in their minds, but it should be in yours.

Just remember this. Mines are always dangerous. Caves are not dangerous—usually. As I keep repeating, if you're properly trained and equipped, caves are only as dangerous as you make them.

Unstable Rocks and Slabs. A minute ago, I said that caves are geologically stable, for the most part. Until recently, I wouldn't have felt it necessary to add "for the most part." But in the last couple of years two freak accidents have tragically claimed the lives of three experienced cavers when huge pieces of the cave moved and crushed them to death. All three were taking actions that all of us do all the time. That why I'm going to summarize the incidents here—then suggest a couple of precautions to take in similar situtations instead of automatically doing certain things the way we've always done them before.

Valhalla Claims Two Victims. The first accident was in Valhalla, a 227 foot (low side rigging) free-fall pit in Alabama, justly famed for its beauty. It's a favorite of vertical cavers from all over the country who make regular pilgrimages to TAG Country. TAG is a region formed at the corner common to Tennessee, Alabama and Georgia (see Figure 13.1). Here over a thousand vertical pits, large and small, have been located. TAG and the deep pits of Mexico,

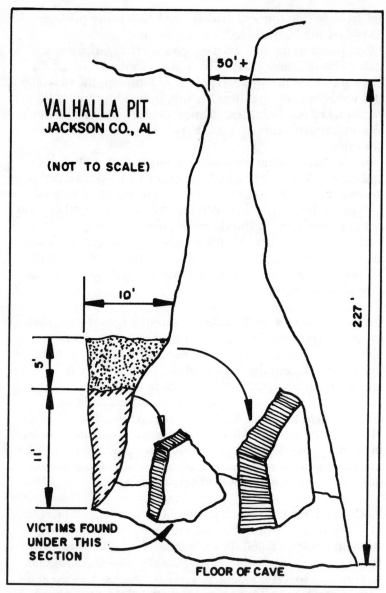

VALHALLA PIT
JACKSON CO., AL

(NOT TO SCALE)

50'+

10'

5'

11'

227'

VICTIMS FOUND
UNDER THIS
SECTION

FLOOR OF CAVE

Fig. 4.5 Vahalla Pit where two cavers waiting in the usual sheltered alcove were killed when a school-bus sized slab came off the wall.

are considered the twin birthplaces of American vertical techniques.

In June 1984, three experienced vertical cavers from Georgia Tech dropped Valhalla and were beginning their ascent out. It was about 7:30 PM and one of the three was already on the rope about half way up. Earlier that day some 15 other cavers had already visited the cave, and these three were the last.

While the first caver was on the rope, the other two waited at the bottom under a sheltered overhang. This was a concave undercut alcove, which they purposely selected to be out of the line of fall in case the first caver dropped anything or kicked any rocks loose. This wasn't too likely, because the pit is free (no contact with the wall) except for the top 50 feet. None the less, they waited in this protected alcove just as hundreds of other Valhalla cavers have over the years. It was the prescribed safety practice.

Without warning, a school bus sized slab above the two cavers suddenly broke loose from the wall and fell over splitting in two as it hit the floor. Both cavers had no time to react and were killed instantly. Meanwhile, still ascending the rope, the first caver heard the terrible noise of the crashing slab. He reported that it sounded like an earthquake. Stopping immediately, he repeatedly called down to his friends. Sensing disaster, he completed his ascent and went immediately for help.

Later analysis estimated the weight of the slab at over 50 tons. No one can say with certainty why it peeled off. It simply decided to do that at the precise instant that two unlucky cavers were under it. Had it happened an hour later, it would only have caused idle curiosity on future trips as to where the two big rocks came from.

Tragedy in Culverson Creek System. Another freak accident exhibited some similarities. On Thanksgiving Weekend in 1985, a caver was crushed by a six to nine ton boulder that chose that second in eternity to tilt over a few feet farther and crash into the wall. It happened just at the fateful moment that the unfortunate caver was squeezing between the boulder and the wall. It pinned his head and arms and—mercifully—killed him instantly .

His companions, all fully experienced cavers as he was, immediately took action to save him. Since they were just inside the entrance, (the Fuller's Cave entrance), they were able to quickly get a car jack and free him. But despite first aid and CPR (Coronary Pulmonary Resuscitation), they couldn't revive him.

The boulder that trapped him somewhat resembles a large pear (see Figure 4-6). It leans toward one side of a stream passage and partially blocks the way. This is one of those times when you can go high (climb over it) or low (crawl under or squeeze by it), depending on which you favor.

After the tragic accident, it was postulated that recent storms and flooding may have washed away some of the gravel and mud underpinning it. This could have inclined it more to the left causing a portion of the upper part to suddenly contact the wall.

A Personal Note. My wife Janet and I were fellow grotto members of the young caver killed in this freak accident. We and many others were shocked and saddened by his death. Caving fatalities are so rare that the loss of a caver is always deeply felt by every one in the caving community.

As the impact of his untimely death has finally sunk in, we have been reminded repeatedly of Janet's song "We'll Miss Him." It was written to express sympathy with a 1981 accidental cave death.

He was a caver,   *And we'll miss him,*
Among the best.   *He was a caver.*
He took the challenge,   *Yes, we'll miss him,*
He passed the test.   *He was a caver.*

From time to time in the soft darkness that he loved so well, we'll pause and quietly sing those lines. Somehow, we know he'll hear us.

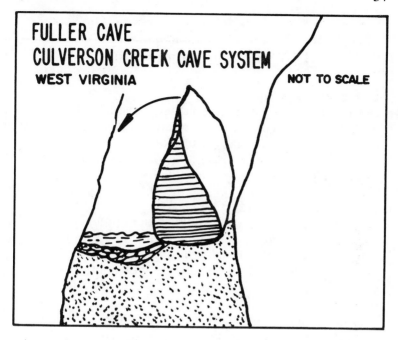

Fig. 4.6.Position of boulder in Fuller Cave passage. (After a February 1986 NSS NEWS drawing. Used with permission.)

Moving Cave Lessons. These two tragic accidents are a concern to all cavers, because any of us could say:

"There but for the grace of God go I."

All of us have ducked under overhangs to get out of the drop area. All of us have decided to go low under a boulder or break-down rather than staying high and scrambling over the top.

But after the Valhalla and Culverson Creek tragedies, I have these suggestions as a starting point for rethinking about how stable some caves really are.

Life Saving Suggestions

1. Check Overhangs.
Don't automatically assume a sheltered overhang that every-body says is ok is ok. Instead, examine it to see if it at least looks like it's really bomb proof. For example, try to choose a shelter that's firmly wedged in by other rocks or one that would slide the other way if it came loose.

2. Go over not under.
When you have a choice (I know, a lot of times you don't, but if you do)—Prefer to stay high and climb over rather than going low and squeezing through. If you have to go under a big rock or alongside a leaning boulder, try to go on the side that would not pin you if something suddenly decided to move without warning.

Also, when you're preparing to feed yourself through a snug crawlway—in breakdown or boulder chokes particu-larly— wiggle or kick those rocks on the ceiling or wall to see if they move. Cavers routinely test climbing holds. I'm suggesting we do the same in tight spots too. Maybe you already do. I'll tell you this, since learning about Culver-son Creek, I've started doing it too.

Bad Air. Although bad air is found sometimes in mines, it occurs in only a tiny fraction of caves (estimated to be less than1%). This is because many caves breath in and out in response to changes in atmospheric pressure.

But you can run into bad air in some situations. For example, in tight dead end passages, cavers themselves may start to use up the air supply before they realize the problem. Or sometimes, gas from decaying vegetation, leaking chemicals, or high concentrations of carbon dioxide or hydrogen sulphide from thermal water can replace the oxygen supply.

So what do you do to protect yourself against the rare

threat of bad cave air? One thing you shouldn't do is trust your carbide lamp or a candle to let you know if there's bad air. Both will continue to burn beyond the danger point to yourself.

If you run into any stale or foul smelling air, or any one gets short of breath or drowsy for no apparent reason, the best thing to do is to get the hell out of there right away. Don't wait for an engraved invitation to your wake.

Move out!

Fires and Stoves. Lighting a fire in a cave is not an especially bright thing to do. It uses up the air supply and can asphyxiate you. It also leaves black smudgy deposits on the walls and formations. Most cave fires are lit by people who don't know better in the entrance area where leaves and branches collect. In some parts of the country dry tumble weed and brush are occasionally found in or near the entrance. These can catch fire very easily, so keep your carbide lamp away from them. Also, bat guano is both flammable and explosive (it was extensively mined for gun powder in the 19th century). And your nice friendly bonfire might be just the thing to ignite it.

If you're wondering how to have a hot meal during a cave trip (believe me, in a cold wet one, nothing picks you up like hot soup or boned turkey), you could bring a heat tab stove or sterno kit. Some cavers even seem successful at heating canned food with their carbide lamps. If you want hot food, try to enjoy your meal in a fair sized room or a passage that's blowing air so the fumes from the spent fuel will be easily dispersed.

Decaying Ropes and Ladders. Once in a while, you'll find an old ladder made of two by fours (or worse) or an old hemp rope with knots. These were put in to help would-be explorers on short drops. You'd be well advised to treat these with great caution. It is a fact that I (and I'm not alone in this) have used an old ladder or two in my day. But only with the greatest of care, such as a proper belay (safety line). Falling accidents continue to be reported each year from the failure of old ladders.

Frayed and frazzled old ropes are another matter. Few experienced cavers would trust their lives on an old decrepit rope. In any case, the practice in recent years has been to remove these old artifacts before someone really gets hurt on them. If you find any that are still in place, be careful.

In project caves, where continuing studies or surveys are going on, it used to be common to install semi-permanent ladders for unavoidable drops. This is still done to some extent, but the threat of liability in case of an accident has caused some rethinking about this practice.

Disease Hazards

Bats and Rabies. Cavers have a special affection for bats. I suppose it's because we both share a love for those dark, forbidding holes in the ground that other people love to hate. But even discounting our prejudice in favor of bats, there really is little to account for the superstitious fear that so much of the general population feels towards these harmless little mammals.

Bats are truly beneficial to humans. This is so well accepted in some cultures that bats are positively revered for the jobs they do in catching insects and pollinating plants, among other things.

Part of the fear of bats undoubtedly derives from sensationalized reports about rabid bats that rise to the surface from time to time and float about mindlessly in the ether of the media like an oil spill defiling a pristine beach. Yes it's true, some bats get rabid. But the number of rabid bats is tiny. In California, for example, it's about one in a thousand with normal appearing bats. (Although it's five times higher in some southwestern states and Mexico). And if they are rabid, insect eating bats, the kind most people are going to have contact with, rarely attack people. Bats are thus far less likely to bite someone than rabid dogs, foxes, or skunks. So it would seem that the general public hasn't much to fear from bats.

They don't bite people or—another baseless superstition—

Fig. 4.7. Bat flying in the dark (at least until the flash went off), easily misses caver in a narrow cave passage.

get in your hair, or your Aunt Fanny's hair, either.

Cavers and Bats. Cavers encounter bats much more often than the general public. Earlier I warned you about not handling a bat that has fallen to the cave floor. It's obvious that something must be wrong with a bat if it's lying on the floor, so leave it alone. About one in ten bats found sick or dead proves to have rabies.

Bats live on the ceiling or on high ledges in caves. They fly with great skill in complete darkness using a form of sonar to navigate. After a time, they memorize the passages and tend to ignore their sonar somewhat. Rarely, if a whole squadron of them is flying past you in a small narrow passage, one may accidentally brush against you.

This occurs because the passage is now somehow different

from their memory of it and they may get mixed up. In a small passage, it's best to hold quite still. This makes it easier for them to sight on you with their beeps to be sure of missing you. Not to worry, however. There is little danger to you from these rare brushes with nature's smallest mammals.

Nursery Colonies. If you find yourself in a cave with a huge colony of bats, your best course would be to leave right away. It's likely that this is a nursery cave and you could upset the delicate balance of nature. Many nursery caves have been identified and are protected by the government with posting and gates to help develop the bat colonies. So if you happen on one, there's a good chance it may be unknown. As a responsible caver, you should make an effort to report it to your state or federal wildlife conservation or similar authority for proper inventory and registration.

There also can be a danger from airborne rabies viruses. These have been reported in a few caves containing a million or more bats, high temperatures, poor air circulation, and an atmosphere heavily saturated with ammonia. This is another excellent reason to keep out of caves that rightfully belong to our cave dwelling friends, the bats and their offspring.

Preexposure Rabies Immunization: If you think you may be exposed to rabies from regular visits to caves with large bat colonies, you may want to consider inoculations for preexposure immunization. This is a simple procedure that many veterinary and animal shelter personnel use regularly. My family and I, along with a number of other cavers, have also taken it with good results.

Officially known as Rabies Vaccine or HDCV (human diploid cell vaccine), it is currently (1986) available from a French company, called Merieux Institutes. Under a doctor's supervision, you take a series of three shots, the second one week after the first, and the third three weeks after the second. Side effects are minimal. After the inoculations, it is recommended that you have a blood titer test to confirm the presence of virus-neutralizing antibodies.

The protection usually lasts at least two years. It can be confirmed at the end of that period by another antibody test, and if necessary a booster shot can be taken.

Postexposure Treatment. If exposed to rabies, a vital first step is to thoroughly wash the wound with soap and water. Then, if you have taken the preexposure inoculations, two boosters are required. Without this protection, a confirmed exposure calls for immediate treatment with a serum and five shots of vaccine. This has to be begun before any symptoms begin (normally five days to a year after exposure). If the symptoms have begun, the disease is nearly always fatal.

The postexposure treatment is expensive and never convenient. The moral is get the preexposure shots if you're going to be dealing with a lot of bats.

Hypothermia

Killer of the Unprepared. Hypothermia occurs when your body's temperature regulating mechanism fails. Your body begins to lose heat faster than it can replace it. This begins a downward spiral where your core temperature gets lower and lower until you fall into a coma and die. You can avoid hypothermia by being prepared for it.

Hypothermia comes from prolonged activity and exhaustion, plus constant cold and water against the skin. As you may have guessed, these conditions are found on many hard-core and even border-line hard-core cave trips. And for any totally unprepared souls, it can even happen on a Sunday afternoon flashlight excursion. If the cave is cold and wet and if someone wearing a T-shirt and blue jeans gets soaked to the skin from falling into 30 to 50 degree (F) water, they could die.

You don't have to have freezing temperatures for you to start shivering and freeze to death. And the cause of death would be what used to be called exposure and now is more

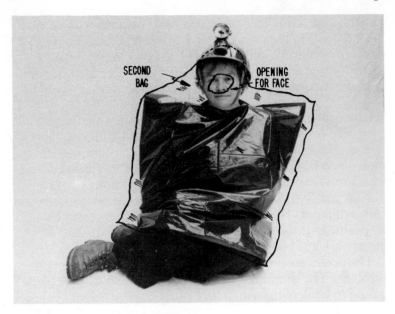

Fig.4.8. Doubled garbage bags for hypothermia defense.

properly called hypothermia. (Although as recently as 1976, some coroners still did not list it as a cause of death.)

Be Prepared. Not all caves are cold and wet, but a lot are. Especially in the northern latitudes and at high elevations. These caves are perfect breeding grounds for hypothermia. So what do you do about it? Be prepared. It's not all that difficult. The first step is to recognize that it's a problem. From there, it's all common sense and doing what your mother has been telling you for years: Dress warmly!

If you're going on a slow trip (translated, that's usually a survey or photographic trip), wear several layers of clothing and socks. Begin with woolen or polypropylene underwear. Tops and bottoms. Cover these with a wool or flannel shirt and wool or synthetic pants. Avoid cotton. It actually chills you when it gets wet rather than keeping you warm like wool or polypropylene will. These latter fabrics can absorb a whole lot of water and still keep you warm.

Finish off with coveralls over the whole shebang and you're ready for just about anything except a wet suit cave. That, by definition, is when you know you'll be swimming or crawling or lying (surveying those nasty low passages) in a lot of really cold water. In those caves, wet suits are what they're all wearing these days.

Finally, every caver needs to carry a garbage bag in the helmet or pack for an emergency heat tent or poncho (see Fig. 4.8, for a doubled version).

Other Factors. Clothing is the most important part of being prepared, but there are other factors too. Don't get overly fatigued. Rest often and well. Remember that you need food to stay warm. Eat a good meal before the trip and bring nourishing food with you. This is one time that a hot meal can not only pick up your sagging spirits, it may help keep you alive. Hot chocolate or tea are great too.

Avoid alcohol and never give alcohol to a chilled victim. It does just the opposite of what you want and actually will make them colder

Speaking of spirits, keep them up too. A positive mental outlook is an asset under these conditions. In fact if any of your companions gets droopy or seems to lack the will to go on, stop and look for other symptoms. Low spirits is one of the classic giveaways for the onset of hypothermia. Here are some others:

Symptoms of Hypothermia

- **Uncontrolled shivering**
- **Lack of coordination**
- **Weak or irregular pulse**
- **Feeling of numbness**
- **Stumbling**
- **Slurred Speech**
- **Lack of will**

Treatment of Hypothermia

- **Start treatment immediately.**
- **Position victim out of water, drafts.**
- **Move gently (as if neck broken).**
- **Replace wet clothes with dry clothes.**
- **Insulate from floor (ropes, packs, jackets).**
- **Keep awake if possible, gently.**
- **Raise body temperarure gradually with:**
  - **Down clothing.**
  - **Skin to skin contact (forget modesty)**
  - **Keep warming for an hour or more.**
  - **Cover head and shoulders.**
  - **Don't give hot liquids by mouth.**
  - **Never give injured person alcohol.**
- **Don't leave the victim alone.**
- **Send for help if not better after warming 30 minutes. Time is against you now.**

Alcohol and Caving. Alcohol and caving don't mix. Fortunately, there seems to general agreement on this point among experienced cavers. Around the campfire, beer or wine are enjoyed with gusto (as they say in the beer commercials)—after the trip is over. But underground (with but two exceptions in my 30 years of experience), cavers act like they have taken the pledge—the collective pledge of temperance, that is.However, hangovers are something else. I've seen plenty of hangovers from the campfire conviviialities the night before. Hangovers yes, but drunk in a cave, no.

This is fortunate, because alcohol is really bad news in any high risk, strenuous sport. Alcohol makes you dull, slows your reflexes, and cuts your concentration. It also opens peripheral blood vessels and draws heat from the body core by making the blood circulate closer to the skin. This is why you must never give alcohol to an injury victim. It will cool them down and could throw them into shock or lower the temperature of a hypothermia victim even further.

First Aid and Shock. As you may know, shock is the first step of the downward spiral called hypothermia. You can be thrown into shock not just by being chilled. Any injury, even a cut finger, will cause some shock. Basic first aid counsels us to stabilize the patient's condition first. That is, stop the bleeding, clear the air passages, and check for broken bones.

  And what's next? That's right. Treat for shock by making the victim warm and comfortable. This is the way to keep shock from escalating into hypothermia. In a cave where it's usually cold, wet, and drafty, these lessons apply even more.

First Aid Kit. At least one member of any cave trip needs to carry a minimum first aid kit. More elaborate items such as tourniquets, splints, and the like are better left to rescue teams. Incidentally, a good source for field first aid items is Indiana Camp Supply (see Appendix for the address). Here is what the minimum first aid kit could contain:

Minimum In-Cave First Aid Kit

- **In a small plastic or metal box:**
    - **Band aids, several sizes.**
    - **Two butterfly bandages**
    - **Two or three guaze pads.**
    - **Roll of adhesive tape.**
    - **Disinfectant or first aid cream.**
    - **Aspirin or stronger pain killer.**
    - **Water purification tablets.**
- **Everyone should carry a garbage bag.**

Cave Rescue

Cave rescue is well beyond the scope of this book but I'd like to make a few comments from personal experience.

If you are ever involved in a rescue, the first thing you must do is to follow the directions of the person in charge. Cavers pride themselves on their independence. To them, the spirit of anarchy remains alive and well in caving .

But the last thing anyone needs in a life and death situation is a chorus of second guessers. I mention this for both seasoned veterans and new cavers alike. When you've seen the fantastic amount of effort it takes to get an injured person out of a cave in one piece, you'll appreciate the need for an almost military like chain of command. Your best contribution will be to apply your expertise, whether mental or menial, as directed by the rescue coordinators.

If you're serious about rescue, or setting up a cave rescue team, the first thing you need to do is to establish your credentials with the professionals in the business, your local sheriff, civil defense, or emergency agency.

You can learn how to do this and just about everything else you'll need to know about cave rescue by attending one of the week long seminars given each Summer by the National Cave Rescue Commission of the National Speleological Society (NCRC/NSS). You'll work hard and learn a lot.

But most of all you'll come away believing me when I say "Don't Hurt Yourself" in a cave. You'll find out how hard it **really** is to get someone out of there.

———————

5

Getting Started

The best way to get started in caving is to join a club. Clubs have five things you can't get anywhere else, as this chapter will show you.

Assuming we haven't lost you so far, let's get specific about how you actually get started in the business of caving. If you've been paying any attention at all, I'm sure you know that my recommendation is to join an organized club.

What Clubs Offer. Organized caving clubs offer five things you can't provide for yourself—and for the most part you won't be able to find any other place. These five items are summarized in the box on the next page. Taking them one at a time, the first is:

1. They know how to cave and can show you how. Experienced cavers by definition know how to cave. Just as vital, they know the caves in their area and know what's needed to explore those caves. Whether they have a formal

training program or just take you out to some easy caves on
your first trip, this is the way to learn. You're with other
cavers, so that meets the proviso about not caving alone.
And by following what they do and asking questions you
can learn the basics much more safely than you can alone or
with some other inexperienced recruits.

WHAT ORGANIZED CAVING CLUBS OFFER

1.They know how to cave and they can show
   you how.
2.They know where the caves are.
3.They have ropes and other specialized gear.
4.They go caving.

And in most cases–unless you're a complete klutz,

5.They will welcome you, whether you're a
   beginner or an experienced caver.

---

2. They know where the caves are. It doesn't matter
what part of the country you live in, this is worth the price of
admission all by itself. Every new caver soon finds out that
the best way (sometimes the only way) to find a cave is to go
there with some one who's been there before. Clubs have
been there before. More on this later.

3. They have the specialized gear. This is why some
groups got together in the first place. They wanted to share
the cost of an expensive piece of equipment like a long rope,
or some surveying equipment. One club I know passes the
hard hat at every meeting to save up for new equipment.

4.They go caving. What this actually means is that they
have regularly scheduled trips, probably once a month or
more in good weather. Trips are often varied, some to easy
horizontal caves, some to vertical caves, some for beginners,
some more advanced.
  Many clubs lay out the schedule in January for the whole

Fig 5.1.Double skylight in a California lava tube with seasonal ice stalagmites in foreground.

year. This lets them make the most of holidays or three day
weekends. Also, members can plan their time off to go on
a Christmas trip to Mexico or a June excursion to the annual
caving convention.

So strongly do cavers prize their three day weekends, that
when my youngest daughter got married (you'll see her
picture several times later in this book), she felt compelled to
apologize to local cavers on two counts. Not only was she
marrying a non-caver, she was getting married on Memorial
Day Weekend. (It was the only time the college chapel was
free.) Many of them came anyway, three day weekend or
not. It only proves that all cavers worth their weight in
carbide would never turn down free food and beverage!

5. They will welcome you (usually). As I said,
unless you're a complete klutz, most caving groups will
welcome anyone with a real interest in the sport. Now, I
know of some exceptions that prove the rule, but by and
large it's true.

However, I'll give you this warning gratis— if you're
shy, you may be completely overlooked at your first
meeting. Don't be afraid to speak up. Tell the group who
you are and why you've come to *their* meeting instead of
staying home to watch your favorite TV show.

Some clubs have an official meeter and greeter who looks
for new people and hands out membership applications or
new caver info sheets. If you're lucky, you may locate this
kind of group. If not, don't be put off at first by the inside
jokes and comments about activities that seem completely
foreign. Stick with it for a meeting or two even if it seems
like you're being treated like an outsider.

Whatever you do, don't start out by asking for a complete
list of local caves with detailed directions on how to find
them. This will not endear you to the group, because many
of us are super sensitive about conservation.

If you've been caving elsewhere but are a newcomer to
the area, you can usually expect to be welcomed too. By
the way (if you'll pardon the commercial), this is one of the
hidden benefits of being a member of a national caving

Fig. 5.2. The Whale's Mouth, a particularly beautiful translucent drapery in Carlsbad Caverns, New Mexico.

organization, like the National Speleological Society. With an NSS membership list in hand you can chart your course to locate kindred caving spirits all over the country. Most will invite you to their meetings or on a cave trip. If you're on the road, you might get lucky and even be asked into their homes (if you don't mind camping on the floor!).

To sum it up, cave clubs offer fellowship and a framework for cave exploration. So the next question is how do you find a club?

The National Speleological Society. A good bit of the action in caving takes place in and around the chapters and individual members of the National Speleological Society. As of 1986, the Society has about 6,500 members

and more than 100 local chapters or grottos. Most are in the
United States, but Canada has a number of members too, as
well as a few grottos.

To find out if there is one near you, contact the:

> **National Speleological Society**
> **Cave Avenue**
> **Huntsville, AL 35810**
> **Phone: 205/852-1300**

Since they get a whole bunch of inquiries every month,
a self addressed stamped envelope would be appreciated,
even though it's not required. The Society has a few paid
professionals in its Huntsville office, but the administration,
committees, and local clubs are all run by volunteers. Be
patient if things seem a little slow.

It's worth noting that new members are now being
assigned numbers over 25,000. Numbers have been given
to members consecutively since the society was set up in the
early 1940's. That means that for every one current member,
there are three former members, most of whom are now
only armchair cavers.

Besides the 6,500 cavers who are active Society members,
it is variously estimated that there are three to six times as
many other cavers who regularly go caving.

NSS Convention. One of the most rewarding Society
events is its annual convention held usually in the last week
of June. It rotates around the country, and is a tribute to the
hard work and stamina of the local volunteers who put it on
in their area.

The annual NSS convention is the one time of the year
when the Society really comes together—cave trips,
meetings, fellowship, technical sessions, papers, more
fellowship, slide shows, seminars, workshops, banquet,
and even more fellowship. I think it's the best thing the
Society does. You meet friends old and new, and swap
caving stories (some of them even true), during a week so
full of activities you just can't do everything you'd like to.

Other Caving Clubs. In case you can't locate a chapter
of the National Speleological Society in your area (or the
local chapter doesn't turn out to be your style), where else
can you find this all–essential experienced group? A good
place to look is outing groups at local colleges, universities,
athletic clubs, hiking clubs, sporting associations, back-
packing groups, biking clubs, and the like.

If there are caves in the area, the chances are some outing
group or another will have a few active cavers, whether they
function as a formal club or not. Local commercial caves and
owners of wild caves often have had some experience with a
local group (we hope an agreeable experience for your sake).

They can often put you onto some cavers who have been to
their cave. Check with commercial cave guides too. Chances
are they may be cavers in their spare time.

Sierra Club Chapters. Similarly, local chapters of the
Sierra Club often have some caver members. A lot of cavers
are into mountaineering, so the rock climbing or peak
climbing sections of a local chapter are a good place to start.
Information about Sierra Club membership and chapters can
be had from its headquarters, at P.O. Box 7959, San
Francisco, Calif. 94120 Again, a stamped self addressed
envelope would be appreciated.

Getting Underground

Finding a Cave. As I said earlier, the best way to find a
cave is to go with a congenial group that's been there before.
I know it sounds   simple minded, but what it reflects is:

  1. How small a lot of cave entrances are, and
  2. How hard it is to find them.

It also touches on something a little more subtle. A lot of
groups have become very reluctant to give cave locations to
people they don't know. Both conservation and safety
considerations are tied up in this decision to be secretive.

However, groups are usually willing to take newcomers
to a well known cave. This may be a cave that's already
vandalized or one that's essentially bombproof. The idea is

Fig. 5.3. When getting permission to visit a cave, spend
a few minutes in friendly conversation with the owner.

to see how well you get along and to be sure you're not a mineral collector in disguise. So don't be surprised if your innocent question about how to find the best and most beautiful caves in their area meets with a cold stare or worse.

Your First Club Trip. But let's pretend you're not an apparent klutz or a dissembled vandal and you're all set for your first trip with this wonderful group of friendly cavers. Here are some suggestions that will make it more rewarding.

As part of your pre-trip prepartions, be sure to query the others ahead of time about what clothes to wear, any special gear required, and generally what to expect. If the cave has been mapped, you might check the map before the trip. Someone who knows the cave can point out the main sections, the different levels, and any special features or hazards. However, in my experience, cave maps make a lot more sense after a trip than before, at least until you get used to studying them.

Good Cave Owner Relations and Permits. Keeping good relations with cave owners is vital if you expect to keep visiting their caves. This isn't hard to do if you combine common courtesy with common sense. Just don't forget that entering any cave requires permission of some kind, whether it's gated or not. If the land owners live nearby, your job is to find them and seek permission. Usually, you won't have any problems. However, if they should say no, apart from your politely trying to find out why, don't press the point.

If the owners are not home, it may be ok to leave a note, but only if this had been done before and the owners are comfortable with it. If not, seek out another cave.

Sometimes, you can change an owner's mind by offering to prepare and sign a liability release. However, I don't recommend raising the specter of personal injury and liability unless it's clear that the owners are already knowledgeable about such legal niceties. If they already are, a waiver may actually be the next logical step. However, proceed with caution in this litigious land of ours. You could end up getting the cave closed permanently because of newly awakened concerns about insurance and liability.

Caves on land without resident owners or caretakers present a different set of problems. Permission is still needed, but may be made by phone or letter instead of personal contact. The principal is the same, only the mechanics differ.

Common Courtesies. But let's say you've found the owner, exchanged pleasantries, and gotten permission to enter the cave. What's next?

Park where they want you to, even if it means a longer hike to the entrance. Leave gates already open *open* and gates already closed *closed*. They've been left that way for a reason. Carry away all trash, yours and other people's too, particularly carbide. It's poisonous to man and beast. And

Fig. 5.4. Surveying in a high elevation alpine cave at about 10,000 feet in the Sierra Nevada, California

don't bury it. It could contaminate the water supply.

It's a good idea to make a potty stop before going into the cave. If it's inconvenient to use the owner's facilities, try the great out of doors, but be considerate and bury solid waste. The rule is always leave the cave—and the owner's property—cleaner than you found it.

Be sure to tell the owners when you expect to come out of the cave. As mentioned earlier, it's best to add a couple of hours to the estimate to allow for contingencies. When you leave, stop to let them know you're out or leave a note. Tell them how much you enjoyed the trip and what a wonderful cave they have.

You can make points with any cave owner by keeping them posted about their cave. Give them copies of maps and photos. Offer to have a clean up trip to carry out trash inside and outside the cave.   Send them Christmas cards thanking them for letting you visit their caves. Treat them with courtesy and you'll get the same in return.

Caves on Public Land. Some western states have a large percentage of their land held in public trust and administered by an alphabet-soup list of federal agencies. These include the Bureau of Land Management, the Forest Service, the Park Service, the Bureau of Reclamation, and the Army Corps of Engineers. For example, over 85% of the land in Nevada belongs to the federal government.

In many states, state governments also have large holdings for recreation, conservation, resource development, or wildlife management. The state agencies you need to deal with often have one or more of those words in their title.

Usually, with a little persistence and queries to local caving groups, you can figure out which of these agencies you're supposed to get permission from. That's right, you still need permission for caves on government land just as you do for privately owned caves. Once you find the right agency, you need to follow what ever procedures they have set up.

Just bear in mind that every agency plays the game a little differently. Be ready for different shades of red tape in case you have more than one governmental entity managing the

Fig. 5.5. Single file movement is best both for conserva-
ton and safety, as in this extensive Yugoslavian cave.

caves you want to visit.

Often, you need to give these folks two or three weeks notice before you can get a permit. Nearly always, you'll have to sign a waiver absolving the United States government of any blame if you injure or kill yourself.

Some caves require vertical work or wetsuits. If so, the cognizant agency (that's government talk) may make an equipment check or ask questions to confirm your earlier experience and qualifications.

Whatever the rules, be sure to follow them carefully. And don't forget to return the keys to the right place and let the agency know that you're safely out of the cave.

Trip Leadership. On any caving trip, someone needs to be in charge. On occasion, this is carefully spelled out beforehand. Other times it may be implicit. For instance, on a trip with experienced cavers, you may not have so much a trip leader as a trip coordinator.

This is the trip organizer, who does things like establish the size of the group, pass out a sign up sheet, arrange for car pools, and get the owner's permission. Once in the cave, no formal trip leader may be needed. Everyone helps out by performing their own specialty, like rigging, mapping, climbing, or photography. But if an accident or emergency occurs, a leader almost always seems to emerge, as if by unspoken agreement, based on the needs of the emergency situation.

This pro-tem leader could be the person most familiar with the cave. Or it could be the one most expert in the technique needed for the emergency, such as climbing, first aid, flooded passages, or vertical work. It could be the original trip coordinator, but it doesn't have to be and often isn't.

Beginners Trips. For all beginners trips (and for some difficult caves), a formal trip leader is almost always a good idea. If the trip is made up mostly of beginners or younger people, we have found that a ratio of one experienced caver to every four or five neophytes seems to work out well. Two experienced people is the absolute minimum, one to lead the way, the other to bring up the rear. You'll see this technique in many commercial caves—one guide up front, a second one at the rear rounding up the stragglers.

Size of Group. This brings us to the question of how many people you should have on a cave trip. Earlier, I said that four is the minimum number for safety, but that three (or rarely two) might be safe under some conditions. Four is safer because if one gets hurt, someone must stay with the victim and it's always best if two go for help (remember, never go caving alone).

As for the maximum, it really depends on the cave. But more and more, current cave management practices call for no more than six to ten at any one time in a wild cave. Some government agencies have even set up annual carrying capacities for certain caves. This limits the total number for a given cave or section of a cave during that time period.

In extremely delicate caves or sections of a cave, this might mean only one trip per month with no more than six or eight participants on each trip. Admitedly, some caves can handle a lot more than that. However, the trend seems to be toward smaller, less frequent trips, at least in government managed caves, to minimize the impact of traffic.

How about heavily vandalized or essentially damage proof caves, how big can trips be? The absolute max, except for maybe a clean up trip in the entrance rooms, is probably 12 to 18 in any one section at a time. This assumes you have enough experienced cavers if there are plenty of beginners.

But maybe the cave has some bottlenecks that could slow things down. Like a drop where only one rope can be set up, or a squeeze that everyone needs at least five minutes to negotiate and is the only way out. In that case, the size of the group might be cut back to six or eight as a practical matter.

It's clear that these are only guidelines, and local conditions and common sense must always prevail in real life.

Trip Length. It seems as if many weekend cave trips devolve into long one day affairs on Saturday or Sunday. Depending on the distance to the caving area, the journey

by car can start the night before or at the crack of dawn on
the day itself. In either case, a lot of groups try to get into
the cave (or on the trail to the cave) fairly early. Translated,
early often means before 9:00 am, although it can vary from
as early as 7:30 to as late as noon.

So how long is the cave trip itself? In any kind of decent
cave system (or a group of nearby caves), a one day trip
frequently becomes your standard eight to ten hour trip.
Allowing for the usual in-cave delays (surveyors and
photographers), this often as not turns into your basic 12
to 14 hour excursion.

That's why weekend trips are often concentrated into one
day and it's usually Saturday. You need all day Sunday or a
very compassionate employer if it's Monday, to make it
home and recover after that basic eight hour trip became a
14 to 16 hour epic.

Shorter trips to smaller caves (or closer ones), may be the
four to six hour type. These are either on Saturday or Sunday, and are often timed to get to a friendly cafe or pizza
parlor before closing time in the evening.

Beginner trips are usually cast into this shorter-duration
mold for the first few outings. After that, they may be
extended to the basic eight to ten hour variety.

6

Personal Gear

*Choosing the right clothing, boots,
and other personal gear is important
not just for comfort, but safety too.*

You might think there isn't too much to say about what you
should wear in a cave—certainly not enough to fill up a
whole chapter. After all, you only have to grab some old
clothes, probably the ones you use for painting or working
on the car, and go for it. Well that's at least half true, but the
other half is that what you wear under or over those clothes
can be vital to your comfort and your safety

First off you should understand that caving doesn't have
any sort of standard uniform. And if it did, you probably
wouldn't recognize it anyway underneath the usual layer of
mud. Most of what cavers wear won't be found in the fancy
outdoor stores or catalogs. Rather, exploring caves is truly
a come-as-you-are affair. The only common thread is that
most caving outfits look old, tattered, and stained.

Speaking generally, cave clothes need to keep you warm

Fig. 6.1. The Compleat Caver. Taking it from the top: hard hat with chin strap, plastic garbage bag inside hard hat, carbide lamp, coveralls over woolen shirt and pants (plus, if a cold cave, an under layer of polypropylene or wool), caver's sling with locking carabiner, cave pack with two other light sources, lamp spares, and snack food, boots with lug soles.

for those times when you're sitting and waiting, yet not confine you when you need to climb and crawl. They should
also be free of protruding loops or belts. After you've had to
back out of one or two snug crawlways to free a snagged
strap, you'll see the wisdom of this warning. Be prepared.
Cut off all straps and loops before they hang you up.

To select the right garb for the caves in a particular area,
the two most important things you need to know are:
1. The temperature of the cave.
2. The amount and depth of the water.

Cave conditions range from warm enough for only a
T shirt and jeans, to cold or wet enough for a full wetsuit.
Except for some entrance areas, cave temperatures normally
remain pretty constant at the average yearly temperature for
the region. Thus many caves seem cool in the Summer and
warm in the Winter. Alpine caves are almost all cold or
wet, even during the short Summer season, which is
usually the only time they're accessible.

Warm Caves. For warm caves, the prescription is quite
simple. Usually, it calls for a T shirt and jeans, or in the
tropics, even short pants. In the south, southwest, and
Mexico, year around cave temperatures in the 60's and even
the 70's (°F) are not uncommon. This is T shirt caving with
a vengeance (assuming it's not a river cave or a high
elevation cave that demands a wetsuit). In addition lava tubes
and gypsum caves, which often are relatively close to the
surface and have multiple entrances, may be good
candidates for your T shirt wardrobe during the Summer
months (see Fig. 6.2).

However, during the Winter in states like Arizona and
New Mexico, the caves may stay on the warm side, but
outside temperatures may be as much as 50 or 60° lower.

Wintertime Striptease. As an illustration, one frigid day
during a Christmas trip, we were hunting for an elusive
entrance in the Guadalupe Mountains of New Mexico. The
outside temperature stood at 5°F above zero . It was also a
little windy in the steep sided canyon, which lowered the

Fig. 6.2. T-shirted Molly McClurg traverses a convenient ledge above a breakdown strewn floor on a Summer
trip to a lava tube.

temperature even more due to chill factor. Eventually, one
of the party who had hung back to do some bird watching
spotted the entrance, a small fissure, with her birding
binoculars and waved us over to it. It's a short (30 foot)
drop into the cave, so people entered one at a time by
climbing down a cable ladder.

After belaying the last one down, I descended with a self
belay (see Chapter 14). Almost immediately, I was amazed
to find the floor of the passage temporarily decorated with
hastily discarded down jackets, hats, mufflers, and
sweaters, the pile getting higher and higher the deeper I
went into the cave. Temperature inside, to the delight of the
assembled group, was nearly 70°. That's fully 65° warmer
than the outside canyon, not even allowing for wind chill
factor. You might well ask why anyone would go caving in
5° weather. The fact is we were on a tight schedule on that
trip and couldn't waste one whole day out of our six total
cave days just because of a little brisk weather.

Cold Caves. For caves below 55° to 60° F, you need to
dress warmly to guard against hypothermia. If you're not
sure about the dangers of this Killer-of-the-Unprepared,
see Chapter 4 for the lurid details. Cold/wet caves are an
almost perfect breeding ground for hypothermia.

To keep warm, by far the best approach is layering. This
is now so well accepted, that one prominent outdoor supplier
actually divided its Winter catalog into under-layer, middle-
layer, and outer–layer attire. For those of you not familiar
with this terminology, it simply means that several thin
layers keep you warmer than one bulky layer. Cavers and
skiers, among others, have known this for years.

Each layer provides an insulating air barrier that reflects
back natural body warmth to keep you warm Also important
for an active sport like caving—multiple layers don't tend to
restrict your movements as much as one thick layer does.

A good beginning in layering is tops and bottoms of
polypropylene or wool over your regular underwear. Both
can absorb several times their weight in water without
making you cold. Polyprop is especially good at wicking

perspiration away from the skin, although wool does this
well too. Avoid the so-called thermal underwear. Most of it
is pure cotton, and cotton can chill you to the bone if it gets
soaked and you have to be inactive for any length of time.

A wool shirt and wool pants make a good middle layer.
(Orlon or acrylic materials would be an acceptable option.)
Many cavers tend to rely on tried and true blue jeans, but
they're somewhat less than ideal for caving. Compared to
woolen or acrylic pants, they aren't as warm, they're more
confining for climbing, and their denim fabric is a bit too
thin to offer the knees much protection for crawling.

For the outer layer, coveralls seem a universal favorite.
Fig. 1.1 shows my daughter Rachel's outfit when she was
an active caver. (You'll note that all the coveralls in this book
are remarkably mud free. They were especially laundered for
the pictures. We didn't want to shock the publisher.)

Coveralls cover everything up, as the name says, and have
the major advantage of not pulling apart as separate jacket
and pants so often do in tight places. Coveralls should be the
heavy duty rather than the light duty type with a stout zipper
or snaps. They're going to take quite a beating from the
mud, water, and sharp rocks underground. The seat seems
to come in for a good deal of the punishment. Eloquent
proof of this can be found in the wide assortment of rear end
patches adorning caving coveralls. (See Fig. 14.5 for the
oversized patch on an earlier incarnation of my daughter
Molly's caving suit).

Sitting Solutions. If you're going to be sitting a lot, two
tips about ensolite pads covered in my earlier books are
worth repeating. The first is from my wife Janet. She
always carries a small ten by ten inch ensolite pad in cold
caves. Many times this has kept her from getting chilled
while waiting for the more macho elements to finish their
vertical or whatever derring-do. An ensolite pad is also
highly recommended to insulate an injured caver from the
cold cave floor.

The other tip comes from Luther Perry who has survived
many long push and surveying trips in California's Lilburn

Cave. His solution is to build a large open-topped pocket
inside your coveralls to slide the pad into. That way it goes
right along with you and is always precisely there where you
need it the most. Cut the pocket material about an inch larger
than the pad. Slot both the material and the ensolite so it
extends down several inches into the legs of the coveralls for
a more comfortable fit.

Short Water Hazards. Some caves have a single short-
distance water hazard like a nearly sumped (flooded) passage
or a small lake. This is the only water hazard in the cave and
it isn't worth wearing a wet suit for five minutes or less in
the water. What to do?

Remember what the Cincinnati cavers did in the 130 foot
low-ceiling passage in Precinct No.11 cave? They took off
nearly all their clothes, pushed on through the water using
the three inch to two foot air space. Once on the other side,
they donned dry clothes brought through the water in
waterproof containers. This is clearly preferable to getting
your whole outfit totally soaked and suffering the con-
sequences all day long. The Gomex Latex suit described
below may also be an alternative for this duty.

Getting Soaked. If you do happen to fall in the water
and get soaked to the skin, here's a reminder of what you
should do. First, take off all your clothes. Then, with the
help of another person, carefully wring them out as dry as
possible and put them back on. They'll be clammy at first,
but you'll survive the discomfort, and within a few hours,
your body heat will dry them out.

Incidentally, it's a good idea to have a change of clothes
back in the car. You'll appreciate this especially if you ever
get soaked through.

Sumps. Should you push a totally sumped passage (often
called a siphon)? I certainly wouldn't if I didn't know
anything about it. Experienced cavers sometimes push well
known short siphons (short to me means less than five or six
feet), when they're with a group of strong cavers and are

properly dressed. But my advice to you is leave sumps
alone. Several inexperienced cavers have drowned in sumps.
They got into something they couldn't get out of until it was
too late and paid with their lives.

French Coveralls. For regular visits to medium-grade
wet caves where you will get wet but not totally immersed,
some American and Canadian cavers swear by the French
caving coveralls made by Petzl and others. Specifically designed for underground use, they are made of nylon with an
outer coating of heavy duty PVC. They are essentially water
proof and are more abrasion resistant than cotton coveralls.
However, they can be torn or punctured. Fortunately, like
wetsuits, they can be repaired fairly easily with patches and
glue. Also like wetsuits, they're great for cold wet caves,
but tend to be too warm for caves above 55 to 60° F.

The Gomex Garment. Another medium-grade wet cave
conqueror is the Gomex suit made by a French company
called Latex Gomex. This suit seems to fall about midway
between a regular coverall outfit and the wetsuit. As the
company name says, the suit is made from sheet latex
fashioned into a Farmer John overall. It comes up over the
chest and stays put with the aid of over the shoulder
suspenders.

These suits are reported (NSS NEWS July 1985) to be
regularly used by Canadian cavers in the wet/cold caves of
Victoria Island (British Columbia). They prefer it as a more
flexible, lighter weight alternative to a bulky wet suit. You
wear the Gomex suit over regular polypropylene or wool
long johns, and cover it with coveralls to protect its delicate
outer surface from abrasion. It essentially waterproofs you
from toes to armpits. Like wet suits, they can be on the
warm side, but according to the reports, they work very
well as a substitute for a wetsuit for chest deep water,
short wet crawlways, or rappelling in a waterfall.

You can order these suits by mail from Latex Gomex,
64560 Liq-Atherey, France. Telephone, from the United
States, (011) (33) (59) 28.61.20.

Fig. 6.3. Wetsuit of 3/16 inch foam rubber, lined inside with nylon. Hard hat replaces wetsuit hood. Coveralls protect unlined surface. Knee pads protect caver's and wet suit's knees. Unsoled wetsuit booties serve as socks inside jungle boots. For vertical work, Kathy Williams wears seat harness inside of coveralls.

Wetsuit Caving

Water Hazards. So what happens when you want to explore an industrial grade cold/wet cave. This is one where you have to walk forever in chest deep water, slosh through nasty water filled crawls with only inches of air space, swim innumerable lakes, or do drop after drop in waterfalls or into deep pools?

Congratulations, you've just graduated into wetsuit caving.

Remember what I said in Chapter 4 about being prepared so you don't become a hypothermia victim? Getting totally soaked in 40 to 50°F cave water (or colder) calls for the comfort of a wetsuit, like our brethren in rafting, scuba diving, and surfing demonstrated many years ago.

According to a leading wetsuit manufacturer, water draws heat from the body twenty-five times faster than air. This makes a dunking in cold water comparable to standing naked in a cold, brisk wind. So what does a wetsuit do? It keeps you warm in cold water. It's made from Neoprene foam rubber with thousands of tiny closed air cells which create a network of insulating barriers. Any water that seeps inside the suit through body openings or a tear is quickly warmed by body heat.

Wetsuits are indispensable to advanced cavers all over the world for pushing river systems, stream passages, waterfalls, and underground lakes. Many caves could not be explored at all without the protection of a wetsuit. And the wetter the better, as far as wetsuits are concerned. While you're immersed, a wetsuit is warm and toasty However, you get overheated very rapidly when you leave the water and have to trek for any distance in dry cave.

Selecting a Wetsuit. Cavers usually choose wetsuits made of 3/16-inch or 1/4-inch foam with a nylon inner lining, and sometimes, a nylon exterior too. A wetsuit is best if it fits tight like a glove. So tight that you may have to dust the inside with talcum powder to get into the thing. The interior nylon lining helps a lot in this regard.

If you can afford it, a wetsuit with a nylon exterior costing

10 to 20% more resists cuts and tears. But for cost reasons, many cavers opt for the inside lining only, choosing to protect the uncoated outside with coveralls (see Fig. 6.3). Regardless of type, try to find a suit with stitched as well as glued seams.

For caving, wetsuits should be a little looser than for diving. An ideal fit is when the suit just touches the body at all points when you lift your arms over your head. Zippers make the suit easier to put on, but colder. Look for a suit with zippers backed with a layer of rubber. Some cavers prefer the 3/16 inch thickness as the best compromise be-tween warmth and flexibility. If you expect to spend long periods of time in icy water, the 1/4 -inch material is probably better. Thinner (1/8-inch) suits designed for rafters and surfers give somewhat better freedom of movement. But these are less popular because they tend to be too fragile and cold for cave use (excepting of course, for sea caves).

Two Piece Suits. A wetsuit is often worn for longer periods in caving than in scuba diving. For this reason, the two piece suit with overlapping top and bottom is more comfortable as well as easier to put on, especially if it has a nylon lining. The top is a long sleeved jacket with a beaver tail that wraps between the legs and attaches back up on the jacket. The bottom is pants that come up above the stomach.

An alternate "Farmer John" bottom comes right up to the armpits and has suspenders. Except for caves where you expect to be in the water almost constantly, the standard belly-height version is less bulky and will probably be more comfortable. Avoid suits with an attached hood. You probably won't use the hood anyway, and if it's hanging outside, it's bound to get caught on something.

Occasionally, cavers will wear only the top or bottom half in partially wet caves where the conditions are simply grim but not devastatingly cold.

Wetsuit socks or soleless booties of 1/8 or 3/16 inch thickness complete the outfit. The 1/8 inch size will neatly replace the two regular pairs of caving socks and can usually be slipped into boots fairly easily if first inserted into small

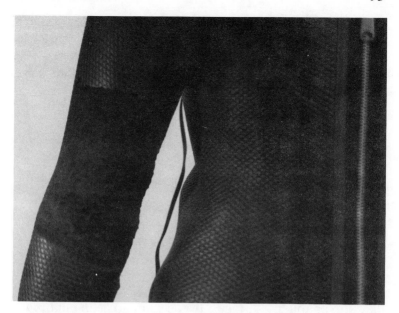

Fig. 6.4. To reduce chafing and allow for more freedom of movement, outer layer of rubber at inside of elbow has been purposely snipped away. Similar treatment can be applied to back of knee and front of ankle.

plastic bags. The 3/16 inch size may require boots a size or two larger. The versatile Vietnam jungle boots have water drainage holes and make a good wetsuit caving boot. Incidentally, this combination of wetsuit socks and Vietnam boots also works well (without the rest of the wetsuit) if a lot of wading is to be done in stream cave.

A big plus for wetsuits is their ease of repair when torn or ripped. Just cut a patch from a scrap, apply Neoprene cement, and stitch around the edges to complete the job. This technique is also good for adding extra layers of padding at the knees, elbows, seat, or wherever extra comfort or wear protection is desired. Pieces of old inner tubes glued and stitched in place are also good for repair or reinforcement of wetsuits.

Dry Suits. Compared to the wetsuit, the dry suit popular
in Britain some twenty plus years ago is made of thin rubber
construction, not of cellular rubber like a wetsuit. It is designed to be sealed at the ankles, wrists, and neck to keep
water out. Although new versions of these suits are beginning to be seen again, they have failed so far to attain
the popularity of Neoprene foam wetsuits.

Other Clothing Items

Boots. Light weight leather or synthetic material boots with
lug-soles seem to be the most popular footware for caving.
Today, these are available nearly everywhere at very agreeable prices compared to 10 years ago. The new lighter
weight boots have benefited greatly from running shoe
technology and offer good value. Lug soled surplus jungle
boots (Vietnam boots) are also an excellent choice.

   Lug soles grip well on both wet and dry limestone, but
may slip on muddy surfaces. If you run into deep mud,
stomp the foot sharply (but don't damage the cave doing it)
to remove the mud between the lugs before trying to climb
or traverse on small footholds.

   Boots come in two heights, ankle high and over the ankle.
I prefer the more popular ankle-high type (five to six inches
high), because they're a little more flexible for climbing.
The over-the-ankle style includes fabric-topped jungle boots
and leather work boots. Work boots are usually very well
made and offer excellent ankle support. However, you may
find them too confining. The choice is yours.

   With either style, the toe should be hard enough to protect
the toes and allow pushing off in tight crawls. Some light
weight boots don't have a heel. These are OK for general
caving, but for vertical work, particularly climbing a cable
ladder, you'll want heels. Another no-no for ladders is boots
with speed lacing clips. They catch on the cable with
remarkable ease and really hang you up.

   Avoid tennis shoes, soft shoes, or smooth soled shoes.
Tennis shoes are often left behind in the mud accompanied
by a strange sucking sound as you try to step forward. They

also don't support or protect the ankles very well. Don't try to prusik with them either. By the time you've gone much over 30 feet, if you have thin Perlon slings, they'll have made painful grooves in the side of your feet.

Socks and Gloves. For the feet, two pairs of socks are recommended, one light and one heavy. The lighter inner socks can be cotton, wool, or polypropylene. For the outer sock, wool is preferable because it will keep you warm even when wet. To help keep your feet dry in shallow stream sloshing, small plastic bags worn inside your boots will help. Be sure they're big enough to extend up above the top of the boot. Outside the water, however, these will make your feet sweat too much. For serious stream sloshing, wetsuit socks or booties worn inside Vietnam jungle boots are very effective.

It's next to impossible to go caving without gloves. Your hands either get torn up or get muddy or both. The gloves I like the best are leather faced cloth gloves. I get the ones with gauntlets that cover the gap between hand and wrist to keep out water and mud. Many prefer plain cotton gloves. They're cheap and can be easily discarded if they don't recover after washing. Another widely used style are the rubberized plastic gloves with a knobby surface. They are a bit clumsy, but they will outwear cotton or leather.

A note about nails–finger and toe, that is. Be sure finger and toenails are clipped on the short side before caving. Your hands get so muddy that long fingernails either break or become reservoirs for what seems like acres of dirt. Long toenails are also a bother since they can be forced against the toe of your boot, causing irritation and pain.

Garbage Bag. A plastic garbage bag is another indispensable item that every caver should carry (see Fig. 6.5). It takes up almost zero room inside your helmet or in the bottom of your pack. But it could save your life in a cold miserable cave.

A good size for the average dimensioned person is the Glad Disposer bag. This version is 1 1/2 mils thick and

Fig. 6.5 Garbage Bag, shown here on Janet McClurg, should be carried by all cavers. It keeps you warm in a cold/wet cave and could save your life.

measures about   2 1/2 by 3 feet. Cut a hole in the center of the top for your head. If you need to have your arms free, cut two additional holes at the two top corners. This bag will warm you up very fast just by capturing your own body heat. From time to time, you may want to turn the bag inside out to let trapped moisture evaporate. Outside the cave, these bags also make a tolerable poncho if you get caught in a storm on the hike back to the car.

If you or someone else is at the shivering stage of hypo-thermia, sit down with the bag on and place a carbide lamp between your legs. This converts the bag into an effective warming tent. Further warming can be had by putting a second garbage bag over the first to gain another air barrier (Fig. 4.8 shows this diagramatically). For this usage, cut only a face hole in the second bag so the helmet rests directly on the bag. This will protect the head and neck from drafts.

Packs

Cave Packs. In addition to muddy clothes and a hard hat, another vital item in every caver's kit is the cave pack. Although they're getting scarcer all the time, surplus stores still have some sturdy canvas types like navy gas mask bags or marine fanny packs. Fig. 6.6 shows a Navy gas mask pack and its complete contents.

Besides surplus packs, several caving suppliers now offer good packs specifically designed for caving made of cordura or or other synthetic fabrics with Fastex plastic fasteners.

A good cave pack has these general characteristics. It needs a wide two inch or so shoulder strap, long enough to go over your head and across your chest. In this configuration, the strap won't slip off your shoulder, and you have both hands free for crawling or climbing. Besides a strap, the pack should have a handle or another short strap so it can be carried by hand or tossed forward in a tight spot. Some cavers also like a waist strap to keep the pack close to the body when leaning forward to climb or crawl.

A cave pack should open and close easily yet securely. Cave mud and grit can cause problems with certain kinds of fasteners, but the Fastex type and the heavy duty snaps or buckles found on surplus packs hold up pretty well. By the way, the snap type military fasteners can be opened easier if you rotate them while pulling upward at the same time. When you hit the right position, the upward pressure will pop them open easily.

The standard rucksack or smaller backpack is also popular for carrying gear and ropes to the entrance. However, unless you're blessed with a lot of large walking passages in your caves, you may find a rucksack too bulky. For most caves, the single over-the-shoulder strap seems to work better. Rucksacks are also good for storing caving gear at home—helmet, coveralls, and cave pack—so that everything is ready to throw in the car when the call comes.

Besides a pack for cave gear, you often see cavers with a separate vertical pack or camera pack. Separate small packs are often better than one large one because small packs fit through tight spots easier. In really wet conditions, waterproof containers like surplus ammo cans or sealable plastic bags designed for boating and rafting are also used.

Camera Packs. Minimal protection for a camera in easy horizontal caves can be provided by putting the camera in its

Fig. 6.6. The well equipped cave pack. *Bottom Row:* spare batteries, flashlight, matches in water proof case, candles, carbide lamp spares, lamp bottoms with carbide. *Middle Row:* emergency space blanket, first aid kit, baby bottle with carbide, water bottle. *Top Row:* caver's sling and locking carabiner, Tenstron Prusik slings, surplus Navy gas mask bag.

own leather case inside a plastic bag, and in turn putting this combination in a regular caving pack. But for tougher caves, high impact plastic cases or ammo cans padded with foam rubber are widely used. Some photographers even make up fitted wooden or aluminum cases for their cameras.

I have had good luck with rectangular refrigerator boxes (like Tupperware). These come in a multitude of sizes and have lids that are nearly water and dust proof. Select a size that will accommodate camera or flash and wrap each of the heavier pieces in 1/4 or 3/8 inch foam rubber. Put film in a sealable plastic bag in the main box or in a smaller one like the size for sandwiches. To keep the top of the box in tow, a hinge of two-inch plastic tape (boiler or gaffer tape) is helpful. Finally, a canvas cave pack of appropriate size encloses the plastic boxes.

Other Useful Items

Caver's Sling. A valuable addition to your personal equipment is a caver's sling. I recommend that all cavers carry this sling and a locking carabiner in their cave packs on every cave trip.

The caver's sling is simply a 12 foot length of one-inch tubular webbing (see Fig 6.1 and 6.6). It can also be a doubled 24-foot length. The caver's sling has many uses: a waist loop, chest sling, rigging sling (runner), diaper sling, tie-in line, or hauling line. To make it into a loop, it is first tied with a water knot (see Chapter 9). For a chest sling, the same loop can be worn over the shoulders in a crossed loop configuration (see Chapter 10). Tying several together makes a very respectable emergency handline.

Hand Line and Prusik Slings. In addition to a caver's sling, I always carry 50 feet of 8mm Perlon rope in my cave pack as a handline. I can't tell you how many times this and its predecessors have proved essential in so-called easy horizontal caves. See Chapter 8 for handline techniques. I also frequently carry Prusik slings (as shown in Fig. 6.6) for the unexpected pit or emergency use.

Knee Pads. Knee pads are essentially indispensable in caves where any amount of crawling is to be done (see Fig. 6.3 for knee pads on a wet suit). After thirty years of living with caver's knees, I have concluded that the best knee pads for me are wrestler's knee pads. They are sold in sporting goods stores. Of tubular construction, they contain an Ensolite pad which gives excellent comfort and insulation from cold/wet cave floors. The pad is enclosed inside a strong knit fabric which seems to be remarkably immune to cave damage.

Probably their best feature is the wide elastic band in the back. Look for the type with a large cutout in the middle. This keeps the band from bunching up or pinching the inside of your knee when you walk or move about. Recently, some excellent roller skating knee pads with high-impact plastic inserts in front have also come on the market. These may be a little more expensive, but they are easy to walk upright in and appear to be very durable.

To reduce chafing on the back of the knees, I wear knee pads over my pants. But to keep them from snagging or sliding around, I put them under my coveralls. For hiking to the cave or in big walking sections, I pull them down over the shins into a kind of parade rest position. Then for crawling or chimneying (they're great for friction in narrow chimneys), I pull them back up into the operating mode.

Industrial knee pads of thick rubber with straps in the back are worn by many cavers outside the pants or coveralls. If you get this type, try crossing the straps in back to help keep them in place and reduce chaffing. Unfortunately, you can't easily slide them down if walking is required, so they may have to come off if you run into much walking passage.

First Aid Kit. A minimum first-aid kit should be carried by at least one member on each caving trip. For suggested contents, see Chapter 4. A more complete first aid kit back in one of the cars is also a worthwhile precaution.

Other Essentials. Every caver should carry water in a canteen or plastic water bottle for drinking (and a carbide lamp, if used). Don't skimp on water. It's essential for your well being and health on a cave trip. Many also carry a pocketknife, can opener, paper and pencil, and a watch to keep track of time. If you wear glasses outside, you'd better plan to wear them inside, too.

Cave Food. You should eat a good well balanced meal before a cave trip. Also, carry high-energy food with you to snack on during the trip. Energy-giving foods keep you going and help keep the body temperature up. On a long trip, bring enough food for one or more full meals.

Cold/wet caves put more demands on your system both for energy and for heat restoration. Plan to bring extra food on trips to these caves.

Generally, everybody has a favorite variety of cave food. But it all has two common characteristics: high energy and imperviousness to the rigors of the wet, muddy cave environment. Sugary foods give quick energy. Proteins and fats stick to the ribs more and give longer lasting energy. Bring some of each type for balance.

Here are some of the foods you often see emerging from cave packs when cavers stop to rest and regroup:

- Granola bars
- M&M candies
- Beef jerky or meat sticks
- Raisins, or nuts.
- Dried apricots or figs
- Trail mixes of granola, nuts, and coconut
- Canned tuna, Vienna sausage, or boned chicken
- Snack packs–pudding or fruit (beware of sharp edges)

Equipment Repair

Except for vertical gear, caving equipment is relatively inexpensive. But it tends to disintegrate almost before your very eyes in the harsh cave environment. To counter this problem, long time caver Bob Ehr has come up with some remarkably versatile repair techniques to keep you engaged in your favorite sport (caving).

Bob's secret is a combination of fasteners and adhesives
that can transform what looks like the most devastated piece
of cave gear into a useful article again. At one of the NSS
Caver Short Courses I organized, he took a pair of blue
jeans that were separated into two completely independent
parts. Before the very eyes of the eager neophytes, Bob
glued and pop-riveted the jeans back together. To cap it off,
at the end of the class, he invited all concerned to render
them asunder again, if they were able. None could. We
were all believers after that.

Bob's repair kit consists of:

The Official Bob Ehr
Cave Gear Repair Kit
(None genuine without these contents)

- **Canvas Grip fabric cement**
- **Super glue**
- **Barge cement (for leather)**
- **Pop-Rivet gun and rivets**
- **"0" size grommet set**

Dealing with the Damage. Here in quick reference form
are some specifics on dealing with damaged goods.

- **Pants, jackets, and coveralls.**
    - Rips and holes—Glue on patch with Canvas Grip.
    - Seam ruptures—Glue seams with Canvas Grip then
      Pop-Rivet at stress points.
    - Blown belt loops—Pop-Rivet.

- **Kneepads and gloves**
    - Holes and torn seams—patch with Canvas Grip.

- **Shoes**
    - Holes—Glue on a leather patch with Barge Cement then Pop-Rivet around edge of patch.
    - Seam failures—Reglue seam with Barge Cement then Pop-Rivet at stress points.
    - Sole delamination—Reattach vibram soles with Super Glue
    - Torn eyelets or speedlaces—Replace by setting a size "0" grommet.

- **Packs**
    - Seams and holes—Patch with Canvas Grip patches and Pop-Rivets at stress points.
    - Torn-out attachment points—Regrommet.

7

Helmets and Lighting

Climbing vs construction helmets, carbide vs electric. This chapter presents the pros and cons of each to help you decide.

A hard hat is one item of equipment that all cavers must wear. There was a time in the early days when a few thick skulled souls favored the soft cap or no cap at all. But today it's safe to say that all cavers wear hard hats (the only possible exception is the Saturday afternoon flashlight crowd). The word helmet, by the way, seems to be used interchangeably with hard hat.

A caving helmet protects you in three ways.

- **It keeps you from banging your head on rocks and overhangs.**
- **It protects you in case of a fall (that's why you need a chin strap).**
- **It helps fend off falling rocks.**

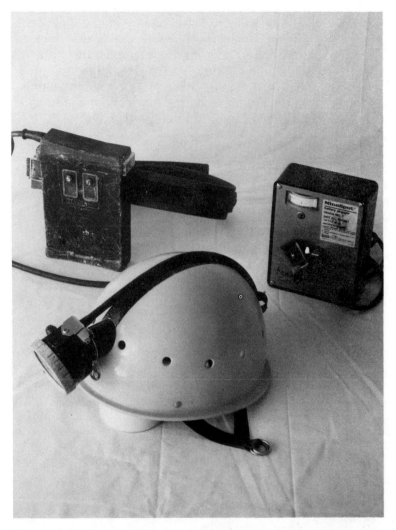

Fig. 7.1 MSR climbing helmet made of Lexan polycarbonate has all ideal characteristics listed below. Lamp is an MSA miner's light, shown with battery case and AC charger unit

Types of Hard Hats. The newer (and more costly) helmets designed for rock climbing are to my way of thinking clearly superior to the bump helmet borrowed from the mining and construction industries. The irony is that although climbers clearly have the best helmets, almost none of them wear helmets at all, good ones or otherwise. In caving, bump helmets continue to outnumber the more expensive climbing style. But if you're just at the point of purchasing a new one, you really ought to consider the pros and cons carefully. Climbing helmets cost about $35 to $50.

Here's what an ideal caving helmet should have:

Characteristics of Ideal Caving Helmet

- **High-impact outer shell of Lexan, polycarbonate, or fiberglass.**
- **Rounded top to deflect overhangs and falling rocks**
- **No brim or a narrow one (to see better in crawlways).**
- **Crushable liner on top and sides.**
- **Good side to side rigidity.**
- **Approved safety suspension of nylon or plastic.**
  - **Solidly attached to outer shell.**
  - **No protruding screws or rivets.**
- **Chin strap to keep helmet on during a fall .**
  - **Adjustable.**
  - **Four-point attachment to outer shell.**
  - **Non-stretching.**
  - **Quick release velcro or Fastex.**
- **Lamp bracket with no protruding bolt or screw heads.**

Helmets that have many or most of these ideal characteristics are:

- Joe Brown
- MSR (Mountain Safety Research, Seattle. Fig 7.1)
- Petzl (UIAA approved; less side-to-side rigidity)
- Speleoshoppe Deluxe (Fig 7.5)
- Ultimate
- Wild Country (UIAA approved)

Construction helmets usually have safety approved suspensions and may be made of fiberglass. But on the minus side—compared to climbing hard hats—most have flatter tops, front brims, no crushable liner, two point elastic chin straps, and less side to side rigidity.

Construction helmets sell for about $10 to $15. Two widely available construction type helmets are:

- FibreMetal
- MSA (Mine Safety Appliance)

A final point: MSR also warns against painting their helmets because it might weaken the shell material. This precaution is probably best heeded with all helmets.

Helmet Lamps

Carbide versus Electric. Helmet mounted carbide and electric lamps are the two most popular types of cave lights on this side of the Atlantic. Although carbide lamps used to be cheaper than electric, either can be had now for about $15 to $20. Although electric seems to be gaining, carbide continues to be more widely used.

Some feel that electric lamps are more reliable and less finicky than carbide lamps. While this is probably true, carbide clearly has the edge for long trips or expedition use. Spare carbide is lighter and less bulky than spare batteries for the same duration of light. The table on the next page shows these compaarisons.

Spares for 20 to 24 Hour Trip

• **Carbide Lamp**
    Carbide.............13 oz in a large (8 oz) baby bottle
    Water............... 20 oz including weight of bottle.
    Total.............About 2 pounds.

• **Alkaline Batteries**
    3 sets of four...... 3 1/2 pounds, and bulkier.

• **Miner's Lamp Batteries**
    2 battery cases......7 pounds, and even bulkier

Carbide/Electric Cohabitation. There are some places, of course, where both light sources are used at the same time. In the big river systems in Mexico, for example, and in many Alpine caves, you need a cap mounted electric along side your carbide for waterfalls and swims. This is handled by having a second lamp bracket on your helmet for the electric. Carbide is the prefered main light source because as indicated, carbide spares provisioning is superior.

Other Pro and Cons. A good news/bad news feature of carbide lamps is the open flame. On the one hand, it's useful for providing heat or cooking. But the flame blows out easily in windy passages and is next to useless in a waterfall or swim. It can also damage ropes, though experienced cavers don't have too much problem with this.

  Biggest hassle with electric lamps is the cord. The batteries are in a belt mounted case, and the cord can and will get caught (or get in the way) at every possible opportunity. On the plus side, the weight of the lamp head on your helmet is far less than a carbide lamp . This fact alone endears electric to many cavers and makes them choose it despite the cord hang up problem. The beam of many electric systems can also be focussed from broad to narrow. This is a valuable feature, the broad beam is good for walking and general illumination, the narrow beam for spotting formations or passages off in the distance. It's nice to have at least one caver in the party with a bright focussed beam like a miner's lamp to penetrate the blackness.

So you pays your money and takes your choice. Carbide for long trips, electric for convenience and lighter helmet weight. Most serious cavers I know have both kinds.

I use a carbide lamp most of the time, probably because I'm old fashioned and the carbide lamp is so deliciously low tech. But I also have a miners lamp, an MSA brand that I bought used at an NSS convention for $50. Its bright spot beam is a pleasure to use in big passages or dark lava tubes.

Carbide Lamps

Premier. This excellent British lamp, is now the most widely sold carbide lamp in the U.S. Several of its parts are interchangeable with the discontinued American lamp, the Justrite—except for the tip, and occasionally a bottom. A worthwhile modification to a Premier is to replace the stock aluminum reflector with a parabolic reflector (unless you are a surveyer, in which case the aluminum is necessary). Its concentrated beam increases light output and extends carbide life. A less expensive carbide lamp is the Butterfly. I have not been impressed by its quality, but I hear it's been im-proved, so you might want to check it out.

Petzl. Petzl (the French caving equipment giant) makes a carbide lamp with a separate cap mounted reflector and a large-capacity belt-mounted canister for carbide. A rubber hose runs from belt to hat and delivers the acetylene gas to the nozzle.Capacity of the cylinder shaped canisters is either seven or ten and a half ounces of carbide, enough for some eight plus hours. These lamps are very popular in Europe.

Unfortunately, they seem to me to be saddled with the worst features of both carbide and electric lamps. You have the open flame of the carbide lamp and the always-get-snagged-on-everything cable (hose) of the electric.

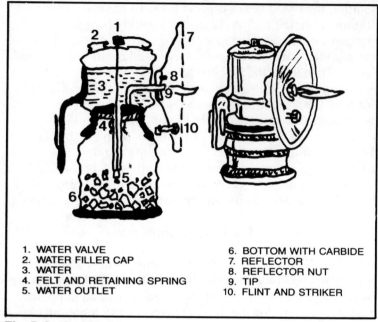

1. WATER VALVE
2. WATER FILLER CAP
3. WATER
4. FELT AND RETAINING SPRING
5. WATER OUTLET
6. BOTTOM WITH CARBIDE
7. REFLECTOR
8. REFLECTOR NUT
9. TIP
10. FLINT AND STRIKER

Fig. 7–2. Carbide lamp.

Petzl also sells a combination acetylene/electric lamp head. The carbide department gets its gas from a standard belt mounted canister. It is ignited by an ingenious piezo-electric sparker. The electric side of the house is actually a back up lamp. It runs off a flat four and a half volt battery or three AA batteries mounted at the rear of the helmet. I haven't seen this used by many American cavers. However, it might have possible application in river caves where you need both types of light.

How to Use a Carbide Lamp. Carbide lamps use small chunks of calcium carbide onto which water drips from the water compartment to produce acetylene gas. The gas comes out the tip where it is lit with a spark, lighter, or another carbide lamp. A circular piece of felt or foam plastic acts as a filter for small particles of carbide.

To charge a carbide lamp, you fill the bottom about one-half to two-thirds full (about one and a half ounces) of carbide. Then you fill the top with water (typical capacity is one and a half fluid ounces) and adjust the flow by moving the water lever on the top one or two clicks. It takes several seconds for the effect of water level changes to take place. To check for proper water flow, watch for a steady stream of droplets before reassembling the lamp.

After screwing the parts back together snugly, gas should be coming from the tip. You can tell by holding the lamp close to your face so you can feel or smell the flow. Next, place your hand over the entire reflector assembly to trap a quantity of gas. Count slowly to six, then draw the heel of your hand sharply across the striker wheel on the reflector. This move takes a little practice but it's fairly easy once you get the hang of it. If you can't seem to get it, try carrying a throw-away cigarette lighter and use that. When the gas ignites, you'll hear a loud pop. This can be deafening in small rooms or passages. An economical flame size is one half inch to one and a half inches long. Some prefer the greater light output at the expense of less time per charge.

A charge usually lasts two to three hours. As it runs down, the flame will get lower and lower. Be sure to blow it out before it goes so low that it clogs the tip with carbon. If this happens, remove the carbon with a wire tip cleaner.

Spares. A plastic baby bottle makes a good nonbreakable, waterproof container for extra carbide. The larger plastic bottle (eight fluid ounces) holds about 11 ounces of carbide, enough for about eight typical one-and-a-half ounce charges or 20 to 24 hours of light. The smaller bottle (four fluid ounces) cuts these figures in half and would be suitable for a smaller cave. Don't try to use the two pound cans that carbide comes in. The lid pops off easily.

A pint or quart sized plastic bottle is good for water. One with a squirt-top, like those for dishwashing detergent, is handy. Be sure to clean it thoroughly to get rid of all traces of the detergent. Otherwise, your lamp may turn into a bubble machine. The water will taste terrible too!

Used Carbide. For spent carbide, a plastic bag or another baby bottle are good. If you use a container with a top, don't seal it too tightly. When tapping the lamp bottom to loosen the carbide, be careful not to damage the threads. Bent threads will cause the bottom to leak and force it into early retirement. If the carbide is really packed solid in the bottom, use a blunt tool like a stick and tap on the bottom.

Be especially careful when blowing away spent carbide from lamp parts or bottoms. Chemically, it's no longer calcium carbide, but has changed to calcium hydroxide. This is very harmful to the eyes, particularly if it's rubbed in. Those who get a good eyeful of used carbide should see a doctor immediately.

Don't scatter or bury used carbide in the cave. Carry it out along with your other trash. And don't dump it around the cave entrance or anywhere on the owner's property. It's very messy and can be dangerous to plants, animals, and people, particularly if dumped into a stream.

Spare Bottoms. Instead of the baby bottle and plastic bag routine, an easy way to handle recharging is to use spare bottoms. Besides a small baby bottle, I often carry two or three filled bottoms, each complete with a gasket and top. These weigh about four ounces each, including carbide. Simply exchange the old one with a new one. Don't tighten the top on the old bottom too snugly. There is usually a little life left in spent carbide and acetylene generation may still be going on. Admittedly, spare bottoms aren't a viable solution for really long trips or expeditions, but for your basic eight to ten hour trip, they're tidier and sure speed things up.

Cleaning. Clean out lamp bottoms after each trip, scrubbing them with water and a toothbrush if necessary. Be sure they're dry before reassembling or filling with carbide. Usually felts will dry out and become brittle after several hours of use and can be tossed out. If you're using the one-quarter inch foam plastic filter, they can be rinsed out and reused for a while.

A more thorough cleaning is a good idea after every eight or ten trips. Take the lamp completely apart and carefully remove accumulated carbide with water and a small brush. Polish the reflector with soap and water or a mild abrasive like toothpaste. Lime-Away, available in many grocery and hardware stores, is a whiz for carbide encrusted bottoms, felts, and gas tubes. It's potent though, so be careful with counter tops or car finishes. Vinegar in a weak solution with water is also used by some cavers to clean off old carbide.

Carbide Lamp Troubleshooting

- **No Flame:**
  - Clogged tip—clean with tip cleaner.
  - Out of carbide or water—refill.
  - Flooded bottom—time to recharge.
  - Loose bottom—tighten bottom, wet or reverse gasket
- Leaking Gas (you'll be able to smell it):
  - Check bottom with flame from lighter or another lamp.
  - Tighten bottom, wet or reverse gasket
  - Try another bottom.
    - Clean threads of offending bottom later.
- Flame around gasket (one of life's exciting moments).
  - Tighten bottom, wet or reverse gasket.
  - Replace bottom.
- Flame around tip.
  - Bad or loose tip.
  - Dirty tip seat.
- Balky or Uneven Flame:
  - Wet or clogged felt filter.
- Water Spurting from Filler Top or Flame too Long
  - Water too high.
  - Wet felt.

Electric Lamps

Electric helmet lamps have been getting more and more
popular in recent years. In addition to the ubiquitous Justrite
you see quite a few Koehler and MSA miner's lamps now.
   Electric rigs offer reliability, simple operation, and lighter
weight on the helmet. An electric lamp head only weighs
about four and a half ounces. A fully charged carbide lamp
weighs about 11 ounces, some two and a half times more.
The Justrite lamp head can also be swiveled downward to
light up the area directly in front of your feet. This handy
feature plus the light weight are enough to drive a lot of
cavers into the electric camp.

Head and Cord. An electric lamp consists of a head
assembly and a separate battery pack connected to the head
with a cord. The battery pack is usually hooked or threaded
on the belt, but can be carried in a separate shoulder or waist
pack. It's the interconnecting cable that's the biggest
drawback of electric rigs. A hung-up cable is a real bear in a
tight cave when you have to wiggle out backwards to free it
from a protuberance. Modifying the cord so it's detachable
at both ends is a help in these situations, but is more
complex and potentially less reliable. Some cavers run the
cord inside the coveralls to avoid snagging.

Variety of Bulbs. A big plus with electric lamps is that
you can operate them with bulbs of different light outputs:
average, bright, or dim. Besides the bright death ray for big
passages, you can switch to a lower output bulb and extend
battery life. See Fig. 7.3 for a comprehensive listing of bulb
characteristics.
   Incidentally, when resting, most electric cavers switch off
their lamps to get a free ride off the carbide cavers and
conserve batteries. Typically, the life of a set of alkaline
batteries can be increased about 50 percent (from eight to
twelve hours) by turning off your lamp whenever safe.

ELECTRIC LAMP DATA

Number	Volts	Amps	Candlepower	Avg. Lamp Life	Base	Remarks
PR-2	2.38	.50	0.80	15 hr	flange	2 D cells
PR-3	3.6	.50	1.5	NA	flange	3C or 3D cells
PR-4	2.33	.27	0.40	10 hr	flange	2AA or 2C cells
PR-6	2.47	.30	0.45	30 hr	flange	2AA or 2D cells
PR-9	2.7	.15	0.25	45 hr	flange	emergency use
PR-12	5.95	.50	2.9	NA	flange	lantern battery
PR-13	4.75	.50	2.0	NA	flange	lantern battery
PR-17	5.0	0.3	NA	NA	flange	lantern battery
395X	2.0	.06	NA	1000 hr	flange	emergency use
425	5.0	.50	2.3	15 hr	screw	for 5-volt
27	4.9	.30	1.4	30 hr	screw	system or
502	5.1	.15	0.6	100 hr	screw	4 cells
1913	4.0	.06	0.06	1000 hr	screw	emergency use
605	6.15	.50	3.4	15 hr	screw	for 6-volt
31	6.15	.30	2.0	15 hr	screw	system or
40	6.3	.15	0.52	3000 hr	screw	5 cells

Fig. 7-3. Electric lamp data (adapted from R. Strudwick, 1972 NSS Convention presentation).

Justrite. The most widely used brands of electric lamps are the Justrite and the miner's lamps made by Koehler and MSA. Some gell cell systems and replacement batteries are available from caving suppliers too. A clear choice among the lower cost models is the Justrite. It has an excellent lamp head, with an integral swivel bracket. It is supplied with a utilitarian plastic battery case that can be modified rather easily to improve its reliability. It takes four D cells. Alkaline or nickel cadmium are best. Out of the box, it comes with an elastic head band. For cave use, this needs to be replaced with a hard hat bracket. If you buy from one of the caving supply shops, the bracket may already be mounted or will be available from them.

Justrite Modifications. A standard Justrite lamp isn't perfect but it's easy to make improvements. To see better and keep from blinding your carbide friends, try replacing the standard clear glass with a honeycomb lens. This diffuses the beam and makes it better for general illumination, besides keeping peace in the family.

A second modification is to wedge long strips of cardboard between the batteries to hold them tightly together. Otherwise they tend to wiggle around a lot and lose contact with the terminals. An immediate action remedy for this malady is to pound the case smartly on the closest available rock (Don't damage the cave!). After you're been around electric cavers for a while you get used to these loud smashing sounds as they try to destroy their battery cases. (They claim they're only trying to get the damn thing to work. But if so, why do they curse so much when they're pounding the poor case senseless.)

Smaller pieces of cardboard behind the spring contacts will also help keep them pressed tighter against the battery. RTV potting compound (silicone sealant by GE) can also be used for this duty and makes a more permanent fix. If you fill the entire area behind the contacts, it cuts down the stress where the cables twist around and connect to the terminals, another

Fig. 7.4 Justrite elecrtric lamp on Janet McClurg's red helmet. This is a nearly inacessible area of a California Cave, completely unvandalized and still as beautiful as when it was created.

common failure point. While you're at it, clean the contacts with an eraser.This removes a film that inhibits current. Finally, if you're really ambitious, you might want to install mud-proof, screw-on connectors either at the lamp end or the battery pack end (or both), to relieve the problem of snagged cables. Quarter-turn BNC electronic signal connectors are good for this purpose.

Miner's Lamps. If you don't mind the extra weight and bulk, the miner's lamps—also called Wheat lamps—made

by Koehler and MSA (Mine Safety Appliance) are really
nice. An MSA lamp is shown in Fig.7.1 (mine as a matter of
fact on my wife Janet's MSR helmet).

These rigs are extremely rugged, having been developed
for continuous-duty operation in mines and other dis-
agreeable places. They use lead-acid cells that can be recharged hundreds of times (500 times or 6,000 hours
according to Koehler). Lead acid cells don't have a memory
like nickel cadmium. You can recharge them at any time
without problems, not just after a full discharge.

Caution!: Battery electrolyte (potassium hydroxide) used
in vented lead-acid and nickel-cadmium batteries will damage
nylon ropes and slings. You must be very careful to keep
vented-type batteries away from ropes in caves or in storage.
Be especially careful not to throw your lamp and batteries
into the trunk of a car with your ropes. Sealed lamp batteries
can leak too, so make it a practice to keep all batteries away
from climbing gear.

Automatic chargers (meaning they won't over charge) for
AC or car battery are available. Charging time is overnight
or about eight hours. A charge gives about 12 to 15 hours
of light. Koehler lamps have a dual-filament bulb: each filament with a 1.0 or 1.2 amp rating and a life of 275 hours
each. This compares to only about 15 hours life for the
typical bulb used in a Justrite. The MSA bulb has two
filaments, one broad, the other narrow. A switch on the
lamp housing selects between the beams. Koehler also has
an optional Hi-Lo bulb with normal and bright filaments.
Bulb life is about 335 hours: 275 hours for the normal
filament, 60 hours for the bright. None of the Wheat and
MSA bulbs are interchangeable.

Battery Vents. Miner's lamp lead acid batteries have to be
vented during recharging. This is done via two vent holes
which are designed to be spill proof in normal (presumably
mining) usage. However, since spill proof is not 100 %
leakproof, it is best to cover these holes with rubber

Fig. 7.5   Ni-Cad batteries in a canvas belt pack. In foreground, a spare Ni-Cad cell. Lamp head is standard Justrite. Caving helmet, Speleoshoppe Deluxe, is made of fiberglass with a four point non-elastic chin strap, very narrow brim and crushable foam liner.

or plastic electrical tape when caving (they come this way from the manufacturer). During recharging this tape should be removed, but in case you forget, the battery will still vent itself and won't explode.

To make my MSA battery vents 100 percent leakproof for vertical caving, I went a step further and screwed two sheet metal screws with rubber washers into the vent holes. If you choose this option, be aware of the danger from explosion if you forget to take out the screws when charging. It would be prudent to put a red sign on your charger as I did stating: Danger: Remove screws before recharging.

Gell Cells. As a replacement for a miner's lamp lead acid cell, some of the caving suppliers offer gell cell batteries.

These are sealed units that fit into the the Koehler or MSA
battery case and can be recharged with the original
equipment battery charger. Their main advantage is that
they are sealed to prevent battery acid damage and are a
little cheaper.

Gell cell batteries in their own cave-ready cases are also
offered by speleo suppliers. By combining one of these
batteries with a Justrite lamp head, you can have quite a
respectable rechargeable system at lower cost than a miner's
lamp. These cells are sealed, as indicated, an advantage of
some importance to vertical cavers.

Typicaly, a gell cell will give about ten hours of light and
can be recharged overnight hundreds of times.

Alkaline Batteries. Alkalines are easily the best type of
dry cells for use in caves. They're more expensive and a
little heavier than standard zinc carbon cells. But they last
anywhere from five to ten times longer and have a three year
instead of a one year shelf life. Shelf life can be extended
by freezing or refrigerating them.

Alkaline batteries provide a very usable but gradually
diminishing light for eight to 16 hours depending on bulb.
Remember, you can also extend battery life as much as 50
percent by turni ιg your lamp off whenever possible.

Alkaline cells in the D size are rated at 10 ampere/hours.
However it's smart to derate them about 20 % to account foɪ
shelf-life and aging losses. That means that four alkaline D
cells matched up with a no. 425 bulb (0.5 ampere), should
deliver about 16 hours of light. To be safe, we recommend
you plan on eight to 12 hours maximum in calculating the
spares to carry.

Mercury cells, widely used for transistor and other low
current applications, are not practical for caving use. They're
too sensitive to cold and lose their voltage when the
temperature drops.

Nickel-Cadmium Cells. Some cavers like to make their
own electric systems with the gell cells mentioned earlier or
nickel-cadmium cells. One of the simplest ways to begin in

the do-it-yourself electric lighting world is to put four D size Ni-Cads in a Justrite case. For this application, it's probably best to use the ones with solder tabs rated at four ampere hours. This will give eight hours of light with a half-ampere 425 bulb. These cells cost about $15 each. Avoid the low capacity 1.2 amp hour versions from Eveready or GE. They're cheaper but too short lived.

With proper recharging, Ni-Cads can be used indefinitely. It's better to discharge them completely before recharging. This defeats their tendency to remember shorter duty cycles. Storing them when completely discharged apparently doesn't damage them.

Ni-Cads maintain almost their full rated output until they are just about ready to quit. This also means they give you little warning that they're about to poop out You can count that as a blessing or not depending on your situation. This is not true of alkaline or lead-acid cells, by the way, where the light gets dimmer and dimmer until it's gone.

Surplus Ni-Cads are sometimes still available in a bewildering array of types and sizes. Most common are usually a four or six ampere-hour capacity. Using these requires a lot of dedication and specialized knowledge, beyond the scope of this book. If you're interested, you might want to contact the Underground Lighting Section of the National Speleological Society. Write the NSS office in Huntsville (Alabama) for the current address.

Back-up Lights

How many sources of light do cavers need? If you didn't answer three without hesitation, you haven't been paying attention. This translates into a main helmet-mounted lamp plus at least two back-up sources. We recommend three back-ups: a flashlight, a candle with matches in a waterproof container, and a chemical light stick.

The Second Source. An almost instant success as the most popular around-the-neck flashlight seems to be the compact Mini-Mag Lite. It hit the caving scene in1983 and 1984 and sells for about $14 or less on specials. It takes two AA cells and has a life of about three hours. The bulb is a tiny high efficiency type. A spare is tucked away in the battery cap—very handy for caving purposes.

Prior to the meteoric ascendency of the Mini-Mag, the Tekna II used to hang around a lot of caver's necks. It sells for about $11. However, the Tekna II always did suffer from some severe reliability problems that seem to be missing in the equally compact Mini-Mag Lite.

I also continue to use the Tekna IV, which runs on four AA cells. Price is around $22. It puts out a sensational beam, not as good as a miner's lamp, but in the same ball park. Life is about one and a half to two hours. Reliability has been excellent except that I have scratched the lens pretty badly, which dims the output somewhat.

Popular among more conventional flashlights is the Eveready Skipper model. Available in both C and D sizes, it's cheap, reliable, waterproof, shockproof, and floats in water. Again, alkaline batteries are mandatory. C cells have less life than the D's, but the smaller size and weight are convenient since this isn't going to be your main source of light anyway. But if you're using D cells in your main light (as in a Justrite), you may prefer to carry a D size flashlight to simplify the spares problem.

An advantage of the Skipper light is its recessed push-button type switch. Not only has this proven reliable for us, but it is nearly impossible to switch on accidentally. If you use a flashlight with a conventional surface-mounted switch, we suggest you reverse one of the batteries when it's in your pack.

The Third Source. Candles are the odds-on favorite for the third source of light. Common types are four and five inch long plumber's candles, one by two inch food warming candles, and votive or religious candles about one and a half by two inches. These are available in hardware stores and some supermarkets. With the longer candles, some people like to cut them to an inch or an inch-and-a-half long. If you do this, don't forget to dig the wick out carefully so it can be easily lit even in their shortened condition.

You'll want to carry candles in 35mm film cans or a plastic bag to keep everything else in your pack from getting all waxed up. Store the accompanying matches in a waterproof container. These can also be handy for starting a carbide lamp if your flint or striker fails due to mud or disagreeableness.

The Fourth Source. As a light source to mark a trail or a waiting area, the Cyalume chemical light is a good choice. To use it, just remove the wrapper, bend it till the inner cylinder breaks, and shake vigorously. It gives a surprising amount of light and it keeps glowing for at least sixteen hours. However, it's not really a good light source for moving about in a cave. But in a real emergency, you can get back to the entrance in a fairly easy cave with one of these things if you move slowly and carefully.

A problem with light sticks is that there's no way to test them to be sure they'll work. And since they lose some light output as they age, it's best to put a fresh one in your pack every caving season just to be safe.

———————————

8

Horizontal Techniques

*Here are the techniques you need for beginner
and intermediate caves—walking, crawling,
scrambling, hand lines, and hasty rappel.*

About This and Later Chapters. Up until now, this
book has dealt mostly with the equipment (and attitudes)
needed for cave exploration. The following chapters deal
primarily with techniques, beginner, intermediate, and
advanced. Here's how they're set up.

This chapter deals mainly with the skills needed to explore
beginner and intermediate level horizontal caves. These
skills include walking, crawling, squeezing through tight
spots, and scrambling down slopes and breakdown piles.
But I've also included handlines and arm rappels, because
both are often needed in many of these so called easy caves.

More advanced techniques like chimneying, free climbing,
rappelling, and prusiking are covered in Chapters 12, 13,
and 14. As a preliminary to those techniques, knots, ropes,
and rigging are presented in Chapters 9, 10, and 11.

Beginner Caves: Before getting down to specifics, let me give my definition of a beginner cave. I know that all caves are unique and the ones I have in mind are certain to be different from yours. But I hope you'll bear with my generalizations for purposes of discussion and instruction.

A typical beginner cave (see Fig. 8.1) is made up mainly of horizontal passages. There may be more than one level, but to change levels doesn't require vertical techniques Getting from one level to the next is done by walking or scrambling down slopes, boulders, or breakdown blocks. No handlines or ropes are needed. The floor is often rough and filled with rubble or breakdown. Though essentially horizontal, many passages incline up or down like the ramps in a sports stadium and have broad steps two to four feet high. Crawling on knees and belly may be required. These and other characteristics are summarized below.

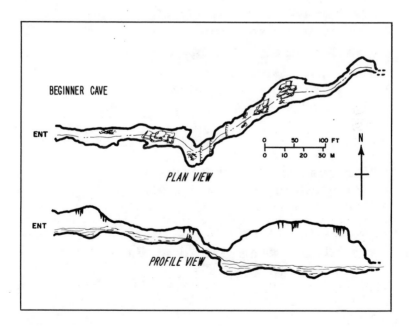

Fig. 8.1 Beginner cave with climbable drops in one main passage.

Beginner Cave Characteristics

- Mostly walking passages, some crawling.
- Short climbable drops (less than 10 feet).
- Length: Few 100's to few 1000's feet.
- Trip Duration: 2 to 3 hours (5 to 6 max).
- Hazards:
    - Streams and lakes.
    - In Lava: Jagged breakdown, ice.
- Equipment needed:
    - Helmet with light, two other light sources.
    - Lug soled boots.
    - If a cold cave layered clothing.
    - If wet, woollen clothes.
    - Knee pads if many crawls.
- Pack with lamp spares, plus:
    - High energy snack food.
    - Caver's sling with locking carabiner.
    - Garbage bag.
    - Water (1 quart).
- Plus, group should have:
    - A minimum first aid kit and space blanket.
    - Extra warm sweater or jacket.
    - 50 foot hand line (8 or 9mm static).
    - Watch to keep time.

Figure 8.2. Big walking passage in a gypsum cave near Carlsbad New Mexico.

Horizontal Techniques

Horizontal passages can be classified according to their
height, but the problem with that is they don't stay at the
same height for very long. And, as the height changes,
so do the techniques you need

Four to Six Feet: Walking. Passages from 4 to 6 feet
high can usually be walked with some stooping (Fig 8.3).
Walking in a cave is a lot like cross-country hiking away
from established trails. You scamper over boulders and
outcroppings, climb small hills and rock faces, ford streams,
and even walk right down the stream bed itself for fairly long
distances--this sometimes being the only available trail
    Just like on rough terrain above ground, always try to
look before you step. By lighting the way in front, you can
plan two or three steps ahead and let your feet follow. If
you have to do a lot of stooping (like in the infamous Back-
breaker Passage in Indiana's Sullivan Cave), it may help to
place your hands on your knees to rest and maintain balance.
    On really rough floors, you may have to move from rock to
rock, testing each before applying weight, just like crossing a
stream. In fact, you can expect to do quite a lot of actual
stream crossing in your typical cave. If there's a wall
nearby, you may want to brace yourself with a hand on it
(but be careful not to damage formations) to keep good
balance. If you want to study something, stop and look.
You can't sightsee and walk at the same time over rough or
slippery floors.

Two to Four Feet: Crawling. In passages two to four
feet high, try to alternate methods to avoid getting tired
(Fig. 8.4). The most obvious one is on all fours, but this
puts your weight on your knees which should be avoided if
you can. Kneecaps are so delicate that a damaged one can be
painful enough to cause complete blackout. If a lot of crawling is expected, don't forget your kneepads. Your knees
will thank you for that consideration in your waning years.

Fig 8.3 Four to six foot passages, stoop walk or crouch walk.

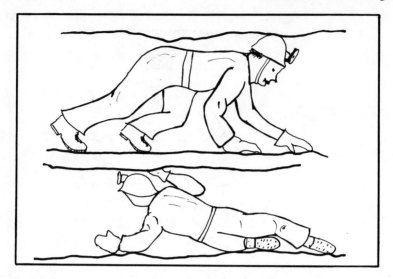

Two to four feet: Move on all fours (avoiding knees), or lie on side.

Ten inches to two feet: Flat out belly crawl.

Fig. 8.4A Crawling movements.

Under two Feet: Belly Crawl. Crawling isn't the only thing that cavers do. It just seems that way! In passages from 10 inches to two feet high, the best method is the flat-out belly crawl. Just lie down on your stomach and go for it.

In case you've gotten a little out of practice since age one, here are some hints. For a serious belly crawl, the elbows go flat out to the side of the body. Your pack and sometimes your helmet gets pushed in front. By the way, it's considered caving courtesy in tight crawls for the person ahead to reach back and give the caver behind an assist with the pack.

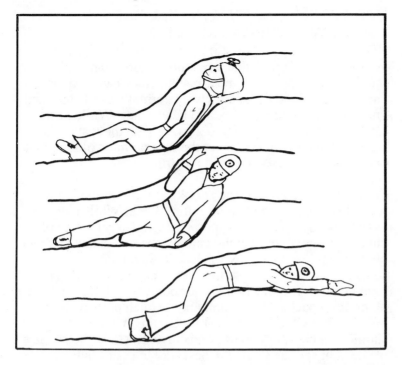

Fig. 8.4.B   Crawling Movements. Study the passage, then pour yourself into it. In a tight, twisting passage, turning over half way through often helps adapt your body to the passage shape.

Another way to move a pack is to hook it on the boot and drag it along. Few crawlways are so tight that a dragging pack will get stuck, though it may slip off once or twice. (Don't try this if you're last.)

Once you get used to the idea of lying down on the ground to get going, crawling is surprisingly easy. It also helps if the floor is relatively smooth and you don't have to go more than 20 or 30 feet. It's when the floor is rough or the ceiling drops down below 12 inches that things get interesting.

A word of caution about crawlways that go down. Never go headfirst down into a steep unknown crawlway. It's much too hard to back out if you go in headfirst. Also, the passage will sometimes bell out suddenly, leaving you with no support. So, unless you know that a downward crawl ends in a flat area, don't go in headfirst!

For really snug passages, it's usually better to start on your stomach. Turned that way, most people can get better purchase with their toes and arms than they can on their backs. Even the tightest crawlway normally has ledges and knobs that can serve as foot and hand holds. While pushing off with the toes, wriggle like a snake with the rest of the body. Whenever possible, let the legs do most of the work, since they're far stronger than the arms.

Getting Stuck. One of the spookiest parts of caving to many beginners is the fear of getting stuck. While many of us have been caught by temporary (fortunately) bouts of claustrophobia in our caving careers, the fact is that you can get through just about any squeeze with practice.

Here are some secrets of the trade. Before negotiating a tight crawl or fissure, empty your pockets and take off your helmet and pack. Then, think about which parts of your body are the widest. On most folks, this will be the shoulders, chest, hips, or pelvis. Next, study the shape of the tight spot and plan the best way to pour yourself through. Be as relaxed as possible. Then, as you ease yourself in, adjust your body to fit the passage. The process is very analogous to the way you wiggle and stretch your hand when you put on a tight glove. Experienced cavers do that with the whole body to get through the really tight ones.

If the crawl is really tight, you often have to narrow your shoulders by putting one arm ahead and dragging the other at your side (Fig. 8.5). You will lose some of your pulling power when you do this, but quite often it's the only way.

If there are turns to be negotiated (see Fig. 8.4B), lie on the side facing the direction of the turn. Once your hips are past the turn, you may have to turn over on the other side to get your knees to bend the right way. Remember that they bend opposite to the waist.

Learning Your Size Limit. Early in the game, it's prudent to find out just how a small a hole you can get through. You'll probably be surprised at how small it is.

Fig. 8.5 Putting one shoulder in front of the other is a valuable technique for very snug squeezes.

Your shoulders, rib cage, pelvis, or hips are usually the limiting dimensions. Try measuring the thickness or width of these anatomical protruberances. This way you can get an idea as to which particular part is going to give you a problem. Typical vital statistics are nine inches for an average caver, about 7 1/2 inches for really small cavers, and 11 1/2 to 12 inches for large cavers. Mostly it's bone structure that holds you up. Most everything else will compress. However, the bones don't give--without breaking.

With me, it's my chest. Once I get my shoulders and rib cage through a squeeze, I stop worrying and just squirm on through. Others can seem to get the upper body through, but panic when they have to force the pelvis or hips past a constriction.

Once you learn your limiting dimension, getting through a squeeze is often a matter of getting the right foot hold. You may have great pressure on your chest or pelvis, but if you can get the right purchase on a foothold, your leg strength can usually propel you on through unaided. If not, you may need someone to give you a foothold by wedging in a boot or helmet or a webbing loop technique described below.

Exhaling Makes You Thinner. A trick that many of us chest limited types use is the letting-out-the-breath ploy. You can reduce your chest thickness by 1/2 to 1 inch by this means. When trying to inch through a really tight spot, you let out all your breath, shove forward with everything you've got, and take a small breath. Then let it out, and shove again. Needless to say, this is not the moment to panic. Also, be sure before you employ this technique, that the constriction is not going to be more than a few feet.

Freeing a Stuck Caver. So what do you do if you really get stuck? First, be sure you really are hung up. Sometimes simply unhooking your pack or clothes will free you.

If you really are stuck, the most obvious remedy is for the other cavers to grab you and pull. Or, someone behind you can jam your foot against the wall to give you a solid foot-hold to push off from. These techniques work almost all the time.

If they don't, another successful technique is to run a length of rope or webbing through the passageway with a figure-of-eight loop tied into the line so the poor soul can get a good hold on the rope and the others can pull.

If this is to no avail, you or a caver on the other side can place the loop around one of your feet. This allows you to use the line as a foothold. Push hard with your foot until you move forward 2 or 3 feet. Then raise your knee again, have the others take up the slack, and repeat the process.

Surprisingly enough, this will usually free the stuck caver in the worst situations. In fact, in any crawlway known to give cavers a problem, a line with or without loops can be carried through by the first caver for the others to use for hand or foot holds.

Intermediate Caves

This category of cave is still loosely called horizontal, but now the levels are connected by steeper and deeper slopes, pits, and breakdown blocks. They're still climbable (no vertical rope techniques required).

But they require skills that while not quite classifiable as advanced, are certainly not for neophytes. These include handlines and hasty rappels. In the water hazard category, intermediate caves often have water deep enough for the unwary to get really soaked and hypothermic.

So they're called intermediate caves and the skills used in them are intermediate skills. Many caves and lava tubes fall into this intermediate category.

Hazards include active streams, lakes, climbable pitches, and long low crawls (under 12 inches) with some tight S's requiring twisting and turning over. Lava tubes can have ice hazards instead of water. Cave length averages from under a mile to five miles or more. A typical trip is eight to ten hours, with 12 to 16 plus not uncommon.

Fig 8.6 shows a map of such a cave, the accompanying table summarizes its characteristics.

If the cave had a sizeable number of intermediate hazards, the chances are it would be called advanced even though it could be explored completely without vertical techniques.

Two classic caves that bridge the gap between intermediate and advanced are Church Cave in California and Onyx Cave in Arizona. Both are usually explored without vertical rope techniques, even though each has considerable vertical extent and a lot of climbing and chinneying are required.

Intermediate Cave Characteristics

- Mix of walking, stooping, crawling, scrambling.
- Many steep but climbable drops.
- Length: under a mile to several miles.
- Trip duration: eight to ten hours (12 to 16 max).
- Hazards:
  - Active streams and lakes.
  - Steep slopes, boulders, blocks, pits.
  - 12 in. twisting, turning crawls.
- Equipment needed:
  - Full caving gear.
  - Proper clothing or wet suit.
  - Garbage bag.
- Pack with lamp spares, plus:
  - Back up light sources.
  - Food for snacks and 1-2 meals.
  - Basic sling, locking carabiner.
  - Water (1 1/2 quarts).
- Plus, group should have:
  - First aid kit and two space blankets.
  - Extra warm sweater or jacket.
  - 50 foot hand line (8 or 9m static).
  - Map of cave.
  - Watch to keep time.
  - Heat tab or sterno stove.

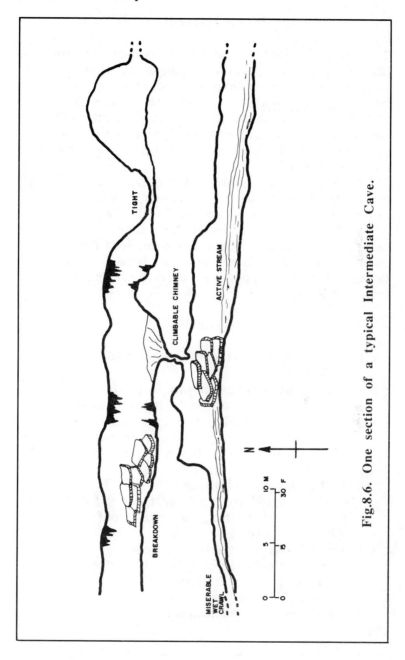

Fig.8.6. One section of a typical Intermediate Cave.

Water Hazards

The difficulties that water can add to caves are more subtle than vertical hazards, but no less dangerous. If you were writing a set of specifications for conditions to produce hypothermia, the wet, cold environment of many caves would be ideal. Flooding, too, is an ever present danger in caves with active streams or a steeply sloping sinkhole entrance. In threatening weather, it's best to stay out of such caves (see Chapter 4).

For a discussion of sumps–do you or don't you–and short water hazards, see Chapter 6. As a reminder here, it's no on sumps and take your clothes off for short wet hazards.

Don't forget too that streams do flood caves and can also wash out underpinings from breakdown. See Chapter 4 for some advice on going over not under breakdown or boulders.The map and table below categorize water hazards into three levels of danger and show the characteristics.

Water Hazards

- **Level 1: Shallow streams, 2 to 8 in. deep:**
  - **Woolen socks**
  - **Wet suit booties in jungle boots**
  - **Woolen/polyprop underlayer if also cold.**
- **Level 2: Accidentally getting soaked**
  - **Deep enough to get soaked through**
  - **If soaked through, begin hypothermia treatment immediately**
  - **Multilayered clothing**
  - **PVC coated coveralls or Gomex Latex**
  - **Change of clothing in waterproof bag**
  - **Full wet suit if really bad**
- **Level 3: Getting wet on purpose**
  - **Wading or swimming in chest deep water**
  - **Pushing low wet crawls**
  - **Rappelling in waterfalls**
  - **Full wet suit mandatory**

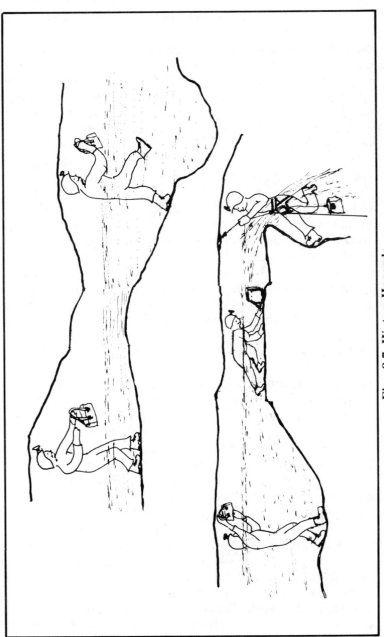

Fig. 8.7 Water Hazards

Scrambling

Scrambling is an intermediate technique that you use when a passage is too steep to walk up, yet isn't steep enough to call for classic rock climbing skills. It combines several types of movements, including walking, climbing, sliding, bridging (applying pressure to two points with extended limbs or back), and jamming (inserting hand, knee, or foot into a crack or slot).

Generally speaking, any cave passage of less than 45 or 50 degrees can be negotiated by scrambling. If it's steeper than that, the chances are it will have to be climbed using rock climbing or vertical rope techniques. But a surprising number of slopes that seem very steep at first glance can be scrambled using a combination of three-point climbing and the seat of your pants.

Another word about conservation at this point. I don't like to keep bringing it up, but you should avoid scrambling (or exploring) in formation areas where delicate speleothems could be destroyed by a careless movement. Use an alternate technique like rigging a free hanging rope for rappelling and prusiking or seek another route.

How to Scramble. When scrambling down, gravity and friction are on your side. Use the entire body, arms, legs, feet, back, shoulders, seat, and even your helmeted head once in a while. The trick is to stretch out an arm or a leg down to the next handhold or flat area, keeping the other three in close contact until the new hold is secured. (Fig. 8.8). This is a first cousin to the three-point climbing technique used by rock climbers. Going back up is more strenuous because gravity fights you, but in some ways it is easier because you can see the holds better.

As in climbing, the arms are used primarily for balance. A hold offered by a hand line is always a little shaky and a natural hold is to be preferred if available.

Don't confuse hand line climbing when your feet are against the wall with climbing a free hanging rope. Climbing a free rope hand over hand is nearly impossible

Fig. 8.8. Caver keeps at least two secure points of contact while extending a foot to locate the next. This pit connects the top two levels in Three-Level Ice Cave, a California lava tube.

and very dangerous. Only well conditioned athletes can climb a free hanging rope for more than 10 or 15 feet without a lot of practice (especially a thin line like 8 mm.) .

A hand line is usually a regular caving rope. But it can be tubular webbing, like several caver's slings tied together. Typically, the length is 30 to 50 feet. This will handle the common 10 to 20 foot pitches nicely and leave enough extra to tie off to a secure anchor. A 50 foot length can also be doubled around an anchor and pulled down after use.

After years of using 9mm, I now prefer 8mm (5/16 in.).

It's smaller and lighter then 9mm. Fifty feet fits into my cave
pack very neatly. Eight mm tests at over 3300 lbs, strong
enough for use as a handline In an emergency, it's also OK
for careful use as a rappel line (Chapter 13), or a tight static
belay line (Chapter 12). Nine mm is admittedly easier to get
a grip on, but loops can be tied in 8mm if that's a problem.
Nine mm tests at over 4600 lbs

Using A Handline. To use a hand line, first tie it off to
a suitable anchor (Chapter 11). Then wrap the line two or
three times around the forearm and wrist of one hand to
increase friction. Start pulling your self up by placing the
other hand on the rope above this hand or use it on a natural
hold.
   Stand out from the wall with your knees bent and use what
ever foot holds you can locate. On especially tricky or
muddy slopes, tie a series of Figure 8 loops (Chapter 9)
about 3 feet apart or less to provide extra handholds and
footholds. Remember to keep moving your hands along the
line as you proceed.
   A hand line can only give you a hold at one point. Often it
will shift on you unexpectedly and throw you off balance.
 So, before putting your weight on the line, be sure you have
some other footholds or handholds within reach.

 Safety Ascender. You can increase the safety of a hand
line immeasurably, by tying yourself to the line using an
ascender connected to your seat harness (see Chapter 10).
A Jumar or Gibbs ascender (see Chapter 14) or a Prusik
knot (Chapter 9) can be used. A Jumar or Prusik knot must
be moved by hand, but the Gibbs will trail along without an
assist.(see Fig 8.9). However, I usually prefer a Jumar
since its handle makes a very convenient hand hold. .
   A note of caution: this technique assumes that you are up
against the wall and won't be hanging free on the rope. If
you were hanging free, loosening a Prusik knot or ascender
would be next to impossible with your full weight on it.

Generally, hand lines are best on moderate slopes of up to about 50 degrees. You can hand line up a steeper slope of 60 degrees or use the hand line for a hasty rappel (see next section) to go down such a slope. However, it can be dangerous for much more than ten or 15 feet without an ascender attached to your seat harness.

Fig. 8.9. A safety acscender attached to your seat harness adds a great measure of safety to conventional hand line techniques.

Hasty Rappel

A hand line is usually used for going up (not always but usually). So how do you go down 10 to 15 foot slopes of less than 50 or 60 degree steepness. Answer— the hasty or French arm rappel is useful (Fig. 8.10). For longer pitches, the regular rappel is safer (Chapter 13).

   To do a hasty rappel, run the rope across your shoulders and extend your arms as far as possible. Grasp the rope in each hand, taking one or more turns around the forearm and wrist. Gloves must be worn. Take care that the rope runs on your sleeves and that the sleeves don't ride up exposing your skin to painful rope burns.

   You can face either left or right depending on which way the slope runs. Then, just walk down sideways tilting the head away from the body to see where you're going. To stop, bring the lower hand up to the chest. It's easy, if the slope isn't too steep.

_____

Fig. 8.10. Hasty or French arm rappel, useful for moderate slopes. Run the rope across the back and wrap it around wrists and forearms. Gloves prevent rope burn.

9

Knots

*Knots are vital for all cavers. Advanced
caver and beginner alike should master
five basic knots before going underground.*

Archaeologists tell us that the knots we use today are direct
descendants of the ones invented by primitive peoples at the
dawn of civilization. Life itself depended on knots—they
attached spear head to shaft, bow string to bow, and hook
to fishing line.

Today, knots continue to perform life saving functions for
cavers. These functions and the five basic knots needed for
them are shown below. Learning these knots isn't very hard.
Anyone can learn them with practice.

Basic Caving Knots

Water Knot	**Ties webbing together**
Grapevine	**Ties Perlon sling together**
Bowline	**Multipurpose non-slipping loop**
Fig.8 Loop	**Multipurpose non-slipping loop**
Prusik	**Ties you to a fixed line**

Fig. 9.1 Me come out this entrance? NO WAY!

Getting Started. To get started with knots, go to an outdoor, mountaineering, or caving supplier and get:

• Six feet of 7mm Perlon cord.
• 12 feet of one inch tubular nylon webbing.

Ropes come in bright colors these days. Pick your favorite hues and use these short lengths to practice your basic caving knots. Later, you can turn them into two very useful slings:

The Perlon cord becomes your safety loop (Chapter 10). Use it as a Prusik sling, back-up waist loop for the diaper sling, or a rigging runner.

The one-inch webbing becomes your caver's sling (Chapter 10). It makes into a diaper sling, a runner (loop) for rigging, and several other things too.

You may also want to get a five feet of five mm Perlon. Use this at school or work to practice your knots when you have a spare moment. You'll get some blank stares, but it sure breaks the ice with strangers. (It's also handy for tying off rope pads.)

I should add that some people can learn knots from drawings and self practice. Others do better with a live instructor (like an experienced caver). Try whichever is best for you. The drawings here are good for either initial practice or later review.

General Considerations. Traditionally, a piece of rope has several parts (Fig 9.2):

The ends
A loop (a closed loop, that crosses itself).
The middle (anywhere except at the ends)
The standing or load-bearing part
A bight (an open loop)

Forming the Knot: When tying a knot, form it carefully and be sure it keeps its shape as you tighten it up. Study the drawings for each knot, so you know exactly what it looks like when it's finished. If it doesn't look right, untie it and do it again. Your life may depend on it.

Don't forget to leave a big enough loop in the middle if you're tying a bowline or Figure 8 Loop. Also, leave some extra at the end for back-up knots. Caving ropes are made of nylon which is famous for trying to untie knots. So these knots and others must have back-up or keeper knots to prevent them from working loose on their own..

After snugging a knot up, set it with a really hard pull. With loops put your foot inside and apply as much force as you can. With in-line knots, have two people pull hard from opposite sides of the knot. Later, while the knot is being used, and before its next use, check to be sure it's still tight.

Weakening Effect of Knots. All knots weaken the rope because of their sharp bends and curves. As a rule of thumb, knots reduce rope strength by 25 to 50 %. Modern caving ropes are designed to compensate for this loss of strength.

Tying any knot uses six to 18 inches of rope. Keep this in mind when taking up slack to tie a knot.

Finally, knots should not only be easy to tie, but also easy to untie. After loading a knot with your full body weight, you'll appreciate the ease of untying one knot over another (e.g. a Bowline, instead of a Figure 8 Loop).

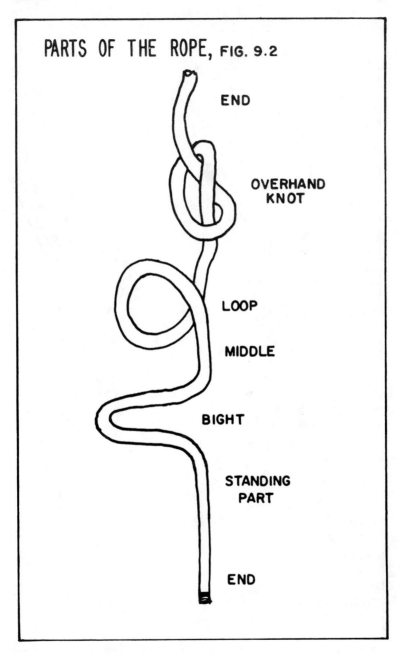

PARTS OF THE ROPE, FIG. 9.2

END

OVERHAND
KNOT

LOOP

MIDDLE

BIGHT

STANDING
PART

END

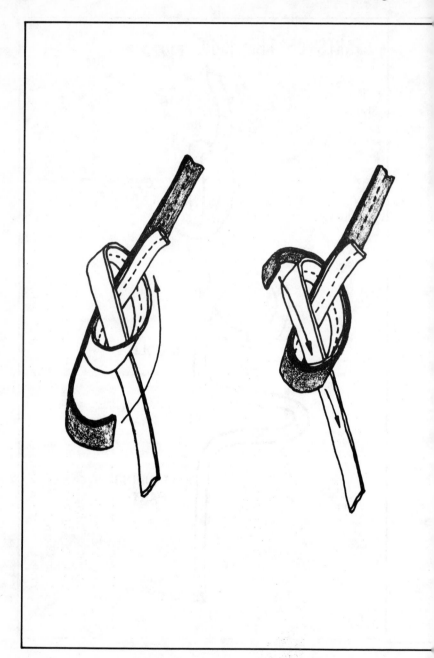

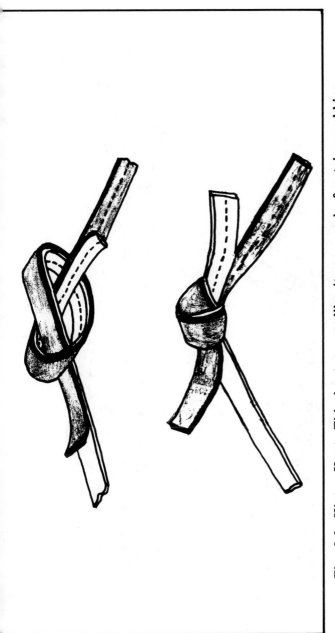

Fig. 9.3. Water Knot. This knot seems like it was made for tying webbing together. Simply tie an overhand knot in one end. Then take the other end and thread it back through the first knot the opposite way. Snug up tightly and check it occasionally, because it can work its way loose. Leave two inches or more outside the finished knot for safety.

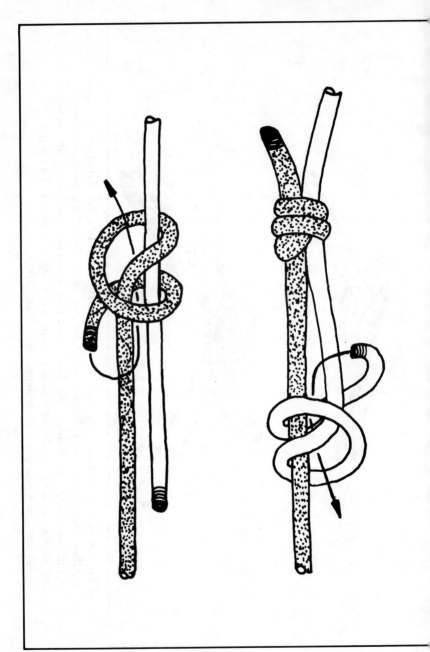

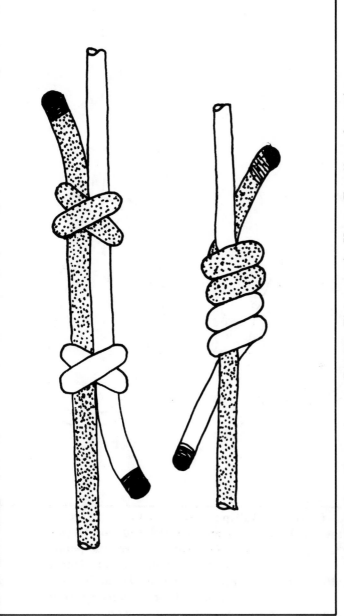

Fig. 9.4. Grapevine or Double Fisherman's Knot. Excellent for tying Perlon sling together. Grapevine is self locking and doesn't need back up knots. A little harder to tie than single Fisherman's, but single Fisherman's needs backup knots for safety.

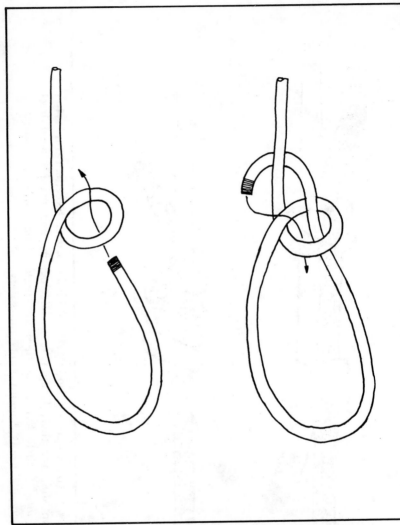

Fig. 9.5A. Bowline. Multipurpose non-slipping loop.
To form the small central loop that the end goes through,
grasp the upright line in right hand with thumb pointing
down. Invert right hand so thumb is up and the loop is
automatically correct. Proceed as shown. To untie, turn
knot over and pull down on loop. Ease of untying after
heavy loading is a major advantage of Bowline.

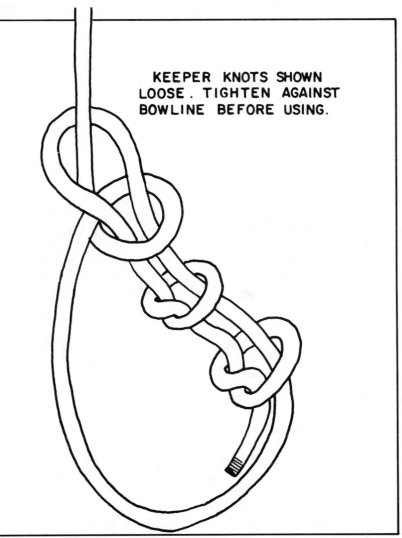

KEEPER KNOTS SHOWN
LOOSE. TIGHTEN AGAINST
BOWLINE BEFORE USING.

Fig. 9.5B. Finished form of Bowline. Study carefully and imprint in your brain. Keeper overhand knots are shown loose for clarity. Snug them tightly up against Bowline.

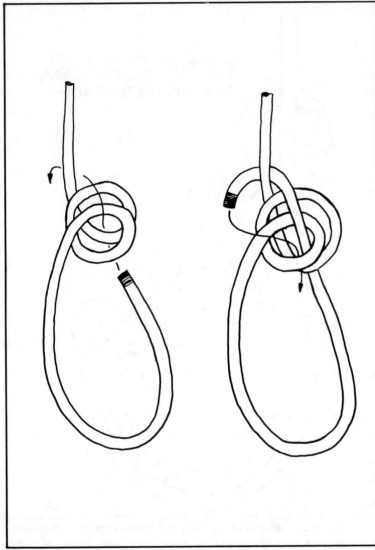

**Fig. 9.6A. Mountaineering Bowline. Good for rigging
main line. Simply form two loops to thread the end
through instead of one, and tie same way as bowline.
Very easy to untie by pulling down the loops even after
heavy loading.**

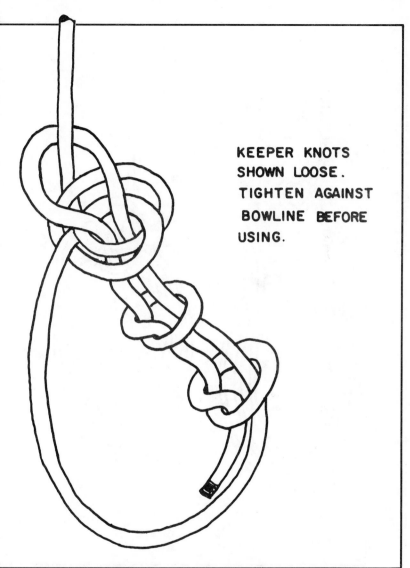

KEEPER KNOTS
SHOWN LOOSE.
TIGHTEN AGAINST
BOWLINE BEFORE
USING.

Fig. 9.6B. Finished Mountaineering Bowline. Keeper knots are shown loose for clarity. Be sure to snug up tightly against the Bowline.

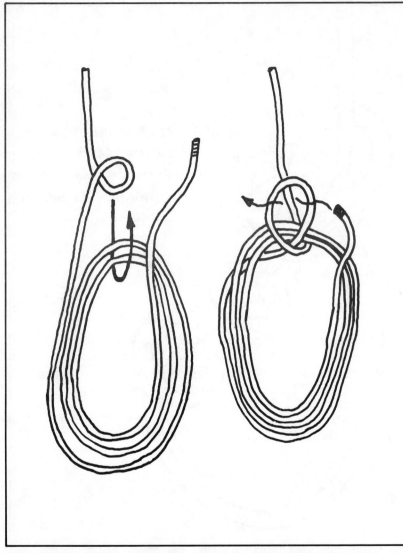

Fig. 9.7. Bowline on a Coil. Used to tie yourself in to be belayed. Wrap coils tightly around your midsection. Knot and keeper knots are shown loose. Snug up tightly before loading. Caution: OK if climbing against wall. Not safe if hanging free on line.

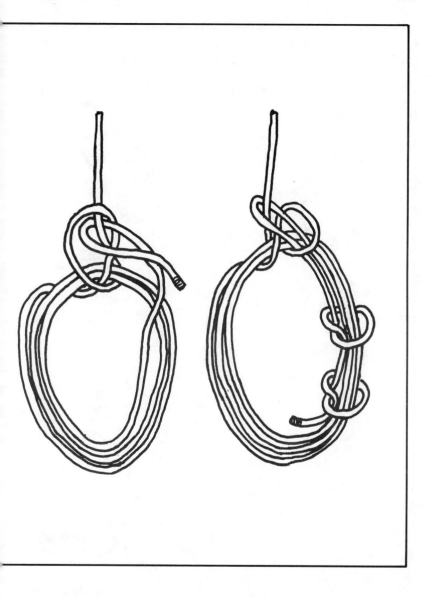

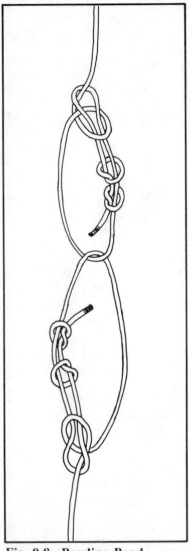

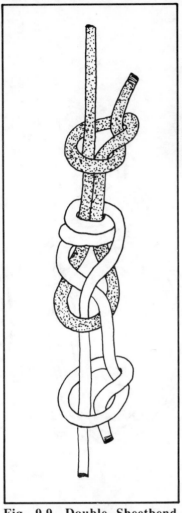

Fig. 9.8. Bowline Bend.
Used to tie two main ropes
together, even two of different
diameters. Looks a bit odd,
but a very effective way to
join two main ropes.

Fig. 9.9. Double Sheetbend.
Excellent for tying two main
ropes together. Part of the
Bowline family, so it's easy
to untie by pulling down on
loop. Shorter overall than two
bowlines, so easier to cross
when rappelling or prusiking
on knoted main rope.

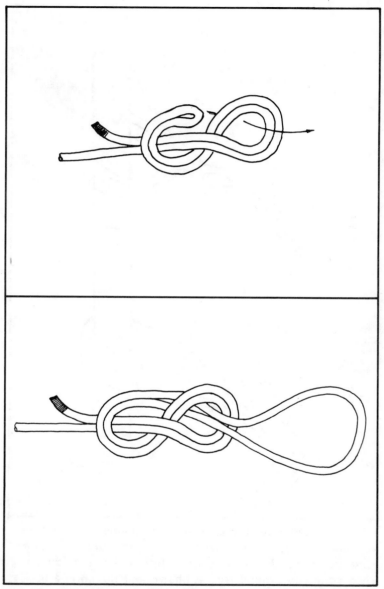

Fig. 9.10. Figure 8 Loop. Figure 8 is another multi-purpose knot like Bowline. Fig. 8 Loop is most used version. Easy to tie, harder to untie.

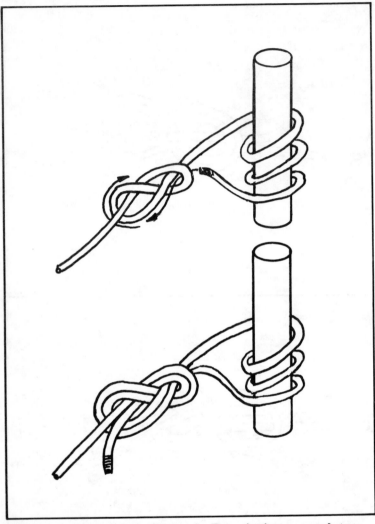

Fig. 9.11. Rethreaded Figure 8. For rigging around tree or column. Best with two or three wraps around tree. First tie simple Figure 8 several feet in front of anchor. Then wrap end around tree as shown and thread end back through knot. Good knot, but hard to untie after loading. See Chapter 12 for simpler wrap-around rigging with Figure 8 Loop or Bowline around main line.

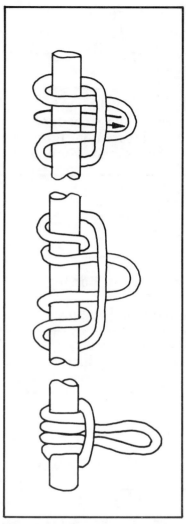

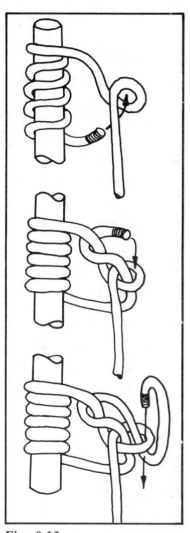

Fig. 9.12. Prusik knot. Grips rope when weight applied, slides up relatively easily when weight released. Four-loop version shown. For muddy or icy ropes, another loop around line in six loop version adds friction.

Fig. 9.13.
Ascender Knot, popular alternative for knot Prusik systems. Easier to slide up rope.

Summary of Functions
and Recommended Knots

Function:	Knot:
Tying ends together	Water Knot–Webbing: Grapevine– Sling cord: Two Bowlines–Main line Double Sheetbend–Main line
Loop to tie to seat harness or haul gear	Bowline Figure 8 Loop
Rigging	Mountaineering Bowline Figure 8 Loop. Wrap Around Rigging
Loop to be Belayed	Bowline-on-a-coil Bowline to seat harness Figure 8 Loop to seat harness
Tying to fixed Line	Prusik Knot

10

Ropes and Slings

Parallel to the growth of vertical caving has been the developoment of high quality ropes, slings and harnesses that provide safety and comfort to the caver.

Ropes are tools—like wetsuits—that have allowed cavers to penetrate into a type of cave that couldn't be explored with conventional methods.

Today we are very fortunate to have two domestic rope manufacturers—Blue Water Ltd. and PMI (Pigeon Mountain Industries, Inc.)—that produce ropes of superb quality, well matched to the harsh conditions encountered in underground use.

The development of caving ropes has played an important role in the growth of American vertical techniques. These techniques have opened up the deep pits of TAG Country (Fig. 13.1) and Mexico, and the big river systems of Mexico, Central America, and North America that continue to be pushed today by American and international teams.

American caving ropes have these vital characteristics:

- **Low stretch.**
- **High breaking strength.**
- **High resistance to abrasion.**
- **Minimum spin.**
- **Good handling characteristics.**

Both the Blue Water and PMI companies were originally set up by cavers to produce ropes for long free drops. Their success in doing this is well known and their products are accepted worldwide. Fortunately, many of the qualities needed in caving ropes are similar to those needed for rescue, fire department, emergency, and mountaineering use. This has enabled Blue Water and PMI to broaden their base into these much larger markets, a fact that benefits the caving fraternity both directly and indirectly.

Low Stretch Static Ropes. Caving and rock climbing ropes have several similarities, but diverge on the important question of how much they stretch. Caving ropes are static or low stretch. Climbing ropes are dynamic or high stretch.

Climbing ropes need more stretch to serve as a shock absorber when protecting a falling lead climber. Lead climbing—where the climber is some distance above the last rope anchor—is not that common in caving. Besides, when prusiking, a highly elastic rope makes taking the stretch out to get started much harder than with a low stretch static rope.

Static caving ropes, like Blue Water and PMI, stretch less than 2% at low loads (200 lbs). At their breaking points, they stretch 15 to 20%. Dynamic climbing ropes have pretty much the same low-load stretch, typically 3%. But before breaking they elongate as much as 80% to cushion the shock when catching a fall.

Caution: Never use static caving ropes for dynamic belaying in leader climbing. With care, however, caving ropes can be used for static belaying on short caving pitches using a tight sitting hip belay (Chapter 12).

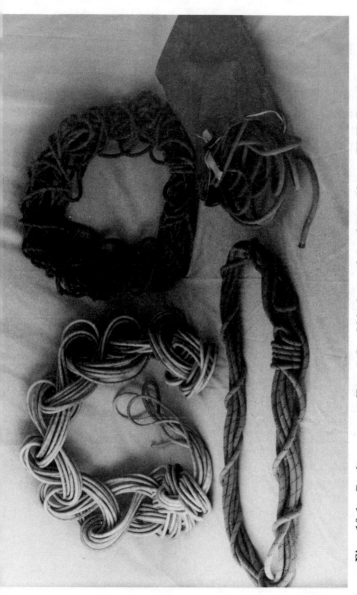

Fig. 10.1. Caving ropes. Top left: 300 feet of braided 10mm PMI Regular. Top right: 200 feet of Blue Water II in a snake wind or snake fight. Bottom left: 100 feet of Blue Water II coiled with a outer spiral winding. Bottom right: PVC rope bag with 200 feet of loosely stuffed PMI Regular. Tie end inside bag for stopper. (Thanks to Phil Whitfield for snake fight data.)

BW II, PMI Regular, and Flex. Current products
from these two manufacturers are Blue Water II and PMI
Regular and Flex. PMI Regular has better abrasion resistance than Flex. Flex is more flexible and therefore easier
to handle and tie knots in. PMI Regular is somewhat stiffer
than Blue Water II, and both seem to get stiffer with use.
Even so, both can be very effectively knotted. And if the
knots are properly backed up—which they should be in any
event—the stiffness is only a bother, not a real problem.

Blue Water and PMI ropes have excellent abrasion resistance. Just which is better in this category is open to some
debate. Both companies have set up their own abrasion
tests. I'm sure you won't be surprised to learn which rope
comes out on top in its own test. I'm not a materials
engineer and am not qualified to critique the fine points
of one test vs another.

However, without taking sides, I can say that for years I
have used both Blue Water II and PMI Regular extensively
in the field under all kinds of conditions. I have never
experienced any abrasion damage of any kind with these
ropes. In contrast, I have seen considerable abrasion
damage to other ropes, particularly non-caving ropes. I'm
not saying Blue Water and PMI are made of iron. But if
rigged and padded properly, they are exceptionally resistant
to abrasion.

Breaking Strength. Static caving ropes are generally
rated by average breaking strength. Climbing ropes use an
entirely different rating system called breaking elongation
or the ability to sustain a certain number of leader falls.

Typically, caving ropes have an average breaking strength
in laboratory tests of 5500 to 6500 lbs. This strength is
reduced in the cave environment by water, mud, and
abrasion. Water reduces rope strength by about 15%, knots
by 25 to 50%.

800/900 lbs Safe Working Loads. Taking all these
factors into account, safe working loads for caving ropes
are usually specified at 12 to 15% or about 800 to 900 lbs.

CAVING ROPES AND SLINGS

Rope	Diameter or Size Inches	Millimeters	Construction	Pounds per 100 feet	Breaking Strength Pounds	Stretch with 200 pound (90 Kilogram) load	Maximum Elongation at B/S†	Price per Foot	Remarks
Skyline II	7/16	11	Mtn. Laid [Three strand twisted]	6	6200	7%	50%	.40	General caving and climbing use, incl. dynamic belaying.
Blue Water II	7/16	11	Core and Sheath	6	Approx. 5800 to 6500	2%	21%	.45	Rappelling and prusiking in caving and Rescue
PMI	7/16	11		6½		2%	17%	.45	
Kernmantel [Mammut, Edelrid]	—	11	Core and Sheath	5	5000	3%	55%	.70	Climbing, incl. dynamic belaying.
	—	9		3½	3500	3%	55%	.60	
One inch Nylon Webbing	1	25	Tubular	—	4000	—	—	.18	Rappel, waist, chest, seat, and tie-off slings. All purpose sling material.
Two inch Nylon Webbing	2	50	Flat	—	6000	—	—	.35	Rappel and various body slings.
Perlon	—	6 to 8	Core and Sheath	—	2000	—	—	.40	Safety loops
Perlon	—	9		—	3500	—	—	.65	Hand lines
Blue Water II & PMI	5/16	—	Core and Sheath	—	4900	—	—	.38	Prusik slings.

* Estimated. European ropes are not rated in total breaking strength, but in resistance to breakage when holding a fall. NA: Not Available. — Not applicable.
† (% of original length)
Source: Manufacturer's catalogs.

Fig. 10–2. Caving ropes and slings (from manufacturer's specifications).

Assuming an average caver weight of 125 to 200 lbs, you can see that there is some margin of safety. However, it's a bit sobering to think that a rope testing at 6000 lbs in the laboratory is only safe for 800/900 lbs in the field. Rescue teams, by the way, often use 1/2 or 5/8 inch ropes to increase this safety margin.

Concerning sizes, 7/16 inch (11 millimeter) is the most popular size in regular use by American cavers. As far as length goes, 200, 300, and 600 are popular lengths. For Mexican pits, 1200 feet is often chosen, but may need to be ordered in advance. As indicated below, 10mm is big in Britain, and apparently has a few proponents here too for expedition use.

Hand lines are commonly 8 or 9mm (5/16 or 3/8 inch) and 30 to 50 feet in length. The larger diameter is easier to hold on to, but takes up more room in a pack. I carry 50 feet of 8mm (5/16) static line in my cave pack at all times. Both Bluewater and PMI make 5/16 inch line.

Other Static Ropes. Recently, British suppliers have been listing in their catalogs some low stretch static ropes from Edelrid (an Austrian climbing rope manufacturer) and others. Edelrid Super Static10 mm is described as their most popular rope for SRT (single rope technique or what we call vertical caving). Stretch is specified as 2.2% at 175 lbs, and breaking strength at 5800 lbs. So far this rope hasn't appeared on this side of the Atlantic.

However, as to the 10mm size (11mm is considered standard here), I understand PMI has supplied 10mm to several customers for applications where lighter weight and less bulk are important.

Skyline. Skyline from New England Rope (successor to Plymouth Cordage) is a dynamic rope of three-strand laid construction with about a 11% elongation at 500 lbs and about 50% at breaking. Skyline is a new version of Goldline, a rope that was very popular with cavers in the pre Blue Water/PMI era.

I used Goldline for years because it was readily available

and cheaper than European climbing ropes. It could also be used for both climbing (belaying, that is) and caving, a plus for those with both persuasions.

In recent caving, I haven't seen Goldline used too much either underground or at practice climbs except as a back up brought along by some old timers. It and its successor Skyline are still excellent dual purpose ropes. But I feel they've been eclipsed by the outstanding ropes specifically designed for caving.

Natural Fibre Ropes. Natural fiber ropes such as manila, sisal, or hemp are totally unsuitable for caving. Manila used

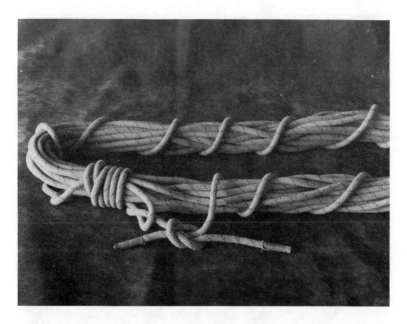

Fig. 10.3. Coiling is OK for ropes under 200 feet. Wrap around both knees and both feet for about a 36 inch diameter coil. When done, collapse knees, and pull free about 6 feet from beginning and about 3 feet at end. With 3 foot length, lay 12 inch bight on top and finish off as shown. Then, spiral the six foot length around coils, tying off to end of 3 foot length as shown.

to be used for prusik slings, but even this usage has largely been discontinued. Nylon fiber ropes are superior in every way for the wet, muddy conditions of caving, and have made natural fiber ropes obsolete.

Core and Sheath. Modern caving and climbing ropes are of core and sheath construction. They gain their tremendous strength because each of the 18 to 20 bundles of strands in the core is made up of continuous nylon filaments running the entire length of the rope. Surrounding this core is a sheath of tightly braided nylon, sewn at regular intervals into the core to prevent slippage when used with mechanical

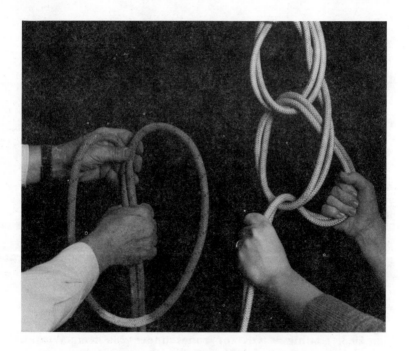

Fig. 10.4. Braiding is better than coiling for ropes 200 to 600 feet. Double entire length twice into four equal lengths. Make beginning loop as shown and then feed reasonably tight loops though each succeeding loop. If washing, tie tightly at end to prevent unraveling.

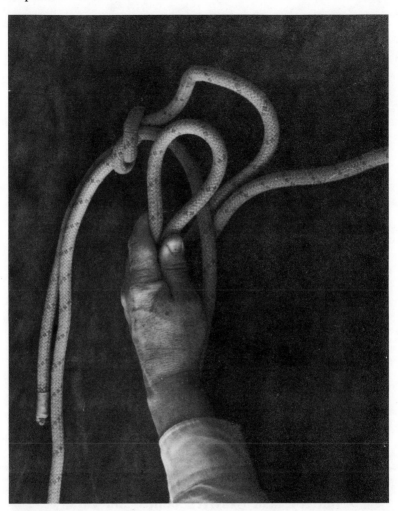

Fig. 10.5. Snake wrap or snake fight looks a mess, but can be unraveled effortlessly without snagging. Much harder to describe than do. It's like braiding a single strand on alternate sides of coil. Begin with 36 inch coil tied at top with square knot. Form loose bight and position it outside of coil. Pull a new bight through first bight, but position second bight inside coil. Pull third bight through second bight, but now position this third bight outside coil. And so on. Slower than coiling or braiding, but worth it.

ascenders. In English this is called core and sheath rope. In German it's kern (core) and mantle (sheath) or kernmantle, a term now used interchangeably with core and sheath.

About two thirds of a rope's strength is in the core, the other third in the sheath. That means that if the sheath is completely cut through, the rope still has the majority of its strength left. Nevertheless, watch carefully for sheath damage such as abraded braiding or white core showing through. At the first sign of damage, cut the rope at that point. You'll end up with two good—albeit shorter— ropes instead of one questionable one.

Inspection. Inspect ropes inch-by-inch at least every few trips or any time they experience abrasion, stress, or severe elongation. To be safe, ropes should be retired after three or four caving seasons, whether used heavily or not. There is some evidence now being accumulated that nylon deteriorates with age. Play it safe and buy yourself a new lifeline every so often.

Nylon yarn used for ropes is Dupont 707, Type 66. Perlon, a European term for nylon, was at one time, loosely applied to all core and sheath ropes. But now the word is more often applied to 4 to 8mm accessory cords

Chemicals and Nylon. Although nylon is unaffected by many chemicals, there are a few that can cause fatal damage. Therefore, we believe the best policy is not to mess around and just consider them all dangerous. Among these, the ones you're most likely to run into are:

- **Battery acid (NaOH), lamps and cars.**
- **Phenols (carbolic acid C6H5OH).**
- **Cresols (C2H8O).**
- **Household bleaches and paints.**

Nylon on Nylon Fusing. At about 500°F (260°C), nylon will melt and fuse. Temperatures that high can be reached if nylon rubs against nylon, and will cause weld abrasion. This can occur in an out-of-control rappel where the main climbing rope is pressed against a nylon seat harness in order to brake. The main rope isn't usually damaged because the heat is spread over a wider area.

But on the harness, the heat is concentrated at one spot, and the temperature can quickly rise to the melting point. Even under control, fast rappels of more than 40 feet per minute generate excessive heat and can cause damage.

You can learn about weld abrasion quite easily. Tie a one inch sling to a tree or rock just over your head. Take an old or retired rope about 12 feet long and make foot loops in the ends. Put your feet into the loops and saw back and forth with as much weight and force as possible. After a few dozen strokes, the rope will cut right through the webbing.

Transporting Rope. For transporting rope, it should be coiled, braided, snake wound (also called snake fight), or packed loosely into a rope bag or sack. If it's important that it pay out smoothly with no kinks or stoppages—as when belaying—use the snake wind or loosely stuffed bag. Unless you get lucky, coiled or braided rope will not pay out freely. It must first be undone and put in a scrambled, untidy pile on the ground in order for it to pull away freely. I know this sounds strange, but try it for yourself.

Coiling, braiding, and snake winding are shown in Figs. 10.3, 10.4, and 10.5.

Cutting Rope. A loaded rope can be cut through like butter with a knife. Keep knives away from caving rope, especially ropes rigged and under stress. If ropes and slings get tangled, untangle them with extreme caution by untying if any of them is still loaded. Don't start playing surgeon with a sharp knife.

Washing and Fabric Softeners. As far as cave ropes are concerned, cleanliness is next to godliness. A dirty caving rope is unsafe. Besides needing washing when dirty, it's also a smart idea to wash a rope when it's new before taking it on its first underground journey. Washing removes the oil and lubricants left over from manufacturing and

Rope Care Check List

- **Never step on ropes.**
- **Don't drag ropes across the ground.**
- **Pad all rough spots and sharp edges.**
- **Keep knives away from ropes.**
- **Store rope inside, out of direct sun light.**
- **Coil, braid, snake wind, or put unwound in bag.**
- **Untie knots before coiling and storing.**
- **Don't mark with tape, paint, or ink.**
- **Don't store in a car trunk—too hot, too many chemicals.**
- **Wash after every muddy trip.**
- **Inspect regularly for damage.**

tightens the fibres of the core and sheath to keep out dirt.

Here are two good ways to wash a rope—in a washing machine or with a PMI rope washer. For a machine wash, first locate one of those large front loaders intended for big families. Avoid machines with plastic windows in the front door. In the spin cycle, the rope can contact the plastic and may melt or fuse.

Next, braid the rope so it won't become impossibly tangled by the rotating action. (Braiding is better than coiling for this.) Use a regular detergent with a cold or warm water setting. Don't use a chlorine bleach.

While you're at it, you can get rid of some of the stiffness due to use and aging with a commercial fabric softener such as Downey. This will also help reduce wear by forming a barrier between the rope fibers and dirt particles. After washing, unbraid the rope and stretch it out in the shade to dry, clear of the sun's ultraviolet radiation.

A second method of washing is with the compact rope washer from PMI. See Fig.10.6 for details on use.

Before using your brand spanking clean rope, be sure it's completely dry. This can take overnight or a couple of days depending on the weather. As mentioned earlier a wet rope is about 15 % weaker.

Fig 10.6. PMI rope washer. Feed rope into end where water streams out. With one hand, pull about two feet through. At same time, grasp rope tightly in other hand between index finger and thumb (as shown) and alternately with all fingers, to loosen dirt. Pass each two foot section back and forth at least twice. Color of water indicates cleaning action.

Seat Harnesses

If you're going to get into vertical caving, the first thing you
need is a good seat harness. It must be comfortable and
support your entire body weight without damaging internal
organs. That translates into a sewn (fail safe) harness made
of two or three inch webbing.

Sewn Seat Harnesses. Several excellent commercial
harnesses are available now from REI, Forrest, Troll,
Eastern Mountain Sports, Petzl, and others. Or you can use
one of these for a pattern and make one yourself to your
exact measurements or needs. Each brand is made a little
differently and will have a different balance point and
positioning of the straps and belts across and under the
sensitive parts of your anatomy.

   Here's the way to find out which harness is best for you.
After installing yourself in the harness, hang on a rope using
an ascender or Prusik knot for least five minutes with your
full weight in the harness . You'll be spending a good bit of
time hanging off the cave floor in one of these things—
resting, adjusting your gear, or waiting for some damn
photographer to get one more shot. So it needs to fit your
form and keep you balanced comfortably in an upright
position. The more upright you are the better, both for
comfort and efficient movement.

Texas Seat Sling. An inexpensive seat sling—it's not
sewn, so it's not a harness—is the Texas seat. It comes
with two rings for carabiner attachment and a buckle to
tighten it. It's infinitely adjustable, so it's great for practice
sessions since several people can use it.

   However, it has the same fatal failing as a diaper sling.
It's not sewn and could unravel if it breaks. If you find the
Texas seat to your liking, you can stitch the leg loops to the
waistband and turn it into a very respectable and inexpensive
custom harness--tailored to your own measurements. Many
people find the balance a little low, so be sure it's OK.

Fig. 10.7. Commercial Seat Harnesses. At right, REI made from two inch webbing, has sewn leg and seat loops. At left, Forrest has similar construction.

Chest Harnesses. A good chest harness is a valuable addition for ascending with a chest box or chest ascender. Many chest harnesses are simply a band of two inch webbing with a buckle. Shoulder loops of one inch webbing are added to keep it from riding down. For added safety, a strap should be run down to the seat sling to give redundancy to both slings. Some commercial chest slings, such as the Petzl are also available. An emergency crossed-loop chest sling can be made from the basic caver's sling (Fig 10.10).

Warning. Any time you're away from the wall and your full weight must be supported on a free hanging line, never use a chest harness alone. Either have a back up connecting loop between chest and seat harness to transfer the load to your seat, or always make your primary tie in to your seat harness. If you need balance, go ahead and connect to your chest harness, but not to the chest alone.

  If you were to hang free with your full weight supported only by your chest, you would be dead in less than 30 minutes. Cause of death would be asphyxiation. Or if the sling were loose and slipped over your head, death or injury would come from falling. Almost as dangerous as a solo chest loop, is a sling tied only around your waist (instead of encircling your legs and derriere too). Almost invariably, a waist loop will ride up and put the same killing pressure on your chest as a chest loop if you have to hang free.

Fig.10.8 Slings. From left to right. 1) Safety loop—five feet of 7 or 8mm Perlon—with   Figure 8 Loops in ends. 2) Safety loop tied into single 20 inch diameter loop with Grapevine Knot. 3) Safety loop shortened by tying Figure 8 Loop in middle. 4) Caver's sling—12 feet of one inch webbing—tied into loop with Water Knot.

Slings

Slings are used to attach ropes to anchors to save rope or to position them better, or attach vertical gear to you. They are made of short lengths of one inch webbing or 7 to 8mm Perlon accessory cord (Fig.10.8). Typical lengths before tying knots are 5 to 12 feet Usually, they are tied or sewn into a single loop, but they can also be tied with a loop in the ends.

Webbing for slings is usually one inch tubular. Flat webbing is also available but is stiffer and harder to knot. Webbing has a greater surface area than rope and its edges are easier to damage. Inspect webbing edges regularly. Even the smallest cut or edge unraveling is reason to toss the sling out.

Sewing Webbing. Sewing the ends of one-inch webbing together, if done correctly, makes a much stronger joint and uses less material than a knot (Fig10.9). You can sew webbing on a home sewing machine or have it done at an awning-maker, cobbler, or parachute harness shop. Nylon or polyester thread is best, but is sometimes hard to locate. One source is Paragear Equipment Company, 3839 West Oakton Street, Skokie, IL 60076.   Another option is 100% nylon thread (CONSO #16 Nylon), available at some leather and craft shops.

Fig.10.9. Sewing webbing. Make a three inch overlap and sew a two inch splice with ten or more rows of longitudinal stitches. Make first pass in center to keep splice aligned. Run several stitches full three inches as stress indicators.

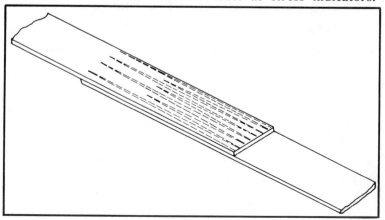

Basic Caver's Sling. One of the most versatile slings is
nothing more than 12 feet of one inch tubular webbing.
Every caver should carry this sling plus a locking carabiner.

Caver Sling Uses

- **Tie in sling to rope or anchor.**
- **Hauling line, several for more length.**
- **Hand line or traversing line.**
- **Rigging runner.**
- **Diaper emergency seat sling (Fig 10.12)**
- **Emergency chest sling for Prusik or Gibbs (Figs. 10.10, 10.11).**

Safety Loop. Another versatile sling is the safety loop
made from a five foot piece of 7 or 8 millimeter Perlon
(Fig.10.8) It can be made up into a single 20 inch loop
with a Grapevine knot, or with two small loops in each
end tied with Figure 8 Loops.

Safety Loop Uses

- **Prusik sling for ascending or tie in.**
- **Loop for spelean shunt (Chapter 13).**
- **With two loops—tie in to line or anchor**

Fig. 10.10. Emergency Chest Harness. Tie caver's sling
into loop to fit chest size.   Cross loop and insert arms
into loops.   Lift crossed strands in front of chest over
head. Pull resulting vertical chest strands together and
link with locking carabiner.   Attach chest prusik sling
or ascender to carabiner. Note how tie-in sling continues
down to main carabiner on seat harness to transfer weight
from chest to seat and provide redundancy for both slings.

Fig. 10.11.   Emergency Gibbs Chest Sling. Tie sling to chest size. Pull sling through hole in cam to middle of sling. Put left half over left arm and head, then right half over right arm and head. Won't keep you as close to line as chest box, but can help get you out in emergency.

Diaper Emergency Seat Sling. A diaper sling is a quick and dirty emergency seat sling. It is not 100% safe by itself without a waist loop backup. See Fig 10.12 for directions on how to tie it.

A lot of vertical cavers started out with the diaper sling. I did, and I lived to tell about it. But I haven't recommended a diaper for years for anything but emergency use. As I said at the beginning, the first thing you need for vertical caving is a comfortable, sewn fail-safe seat harness, not a fail-unsafe diaper sling.

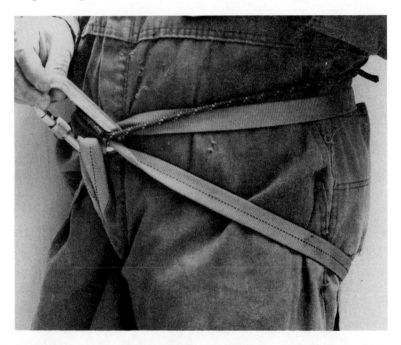

Fig 10.12. Diaper Emergency Seat Sling. Make 7 to 8 foot loop with water knot. Pull ends of loop around waist and snap into locking carabiner. Pull one strand of loop tight around waist allowing other strand to hang down loosely in back. Reach between legs, pull slack strand up in front, and clip it into locking carabiner too. For safety, back up diaper with waist band of webbing or sling (as shown), also clipped through locking carabiner

Mini Etriers. These hero loops are compact two or three step etriers. They take up practically no room in pocket or pack and are most useful for adding a step-up at anchors, lips, or knots (mid-rope knots that you have to cross). Half inch or 9/16 inch webbing, either tubular or flat, is used to make these guys. I usually carry one in my vertical pack or two if it's a tough cave where I expect problems. Standard six or seven step etriiers are usually made from one inch webbing. They're useful too, but bulkier.

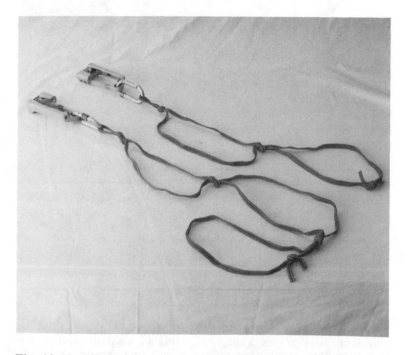

Fig 10.13. Mini Three Step Etrier. Make these from 15 or 20 feet of 1/2 or 9/16 inch webbing. First double, then tie Figure 8 Loop in top for carabiner. Make three slightly offset steps with Figure 8 Loops 12 to 14 inches apart in one leg, 10 inches apart in other.

11

Anchors and Rigging

Familiarity with proper rigging techniques is vital not only for those doing the rigging, but for all cavers who put their lives on the line.

Rigging is the process of attaching ropes, ladders, and cavers to secure anchors. Rigging a cave properly can be complex and time consuming. It requires experience, judgement, and help from other members of the group.

Every caver should know about rigging for these reasons:

Why You Should Know How to Rig

- To serve as the primary rigger.
- To help the rigger.
- To double check the rigging.
- To give you peace of mind.

Point number three is especially important since all rigging should be routinely checked by at least one other practiced rigger. Anyone can make a mistake. The time to find out is when you're alive and well at the top of the drop, not when

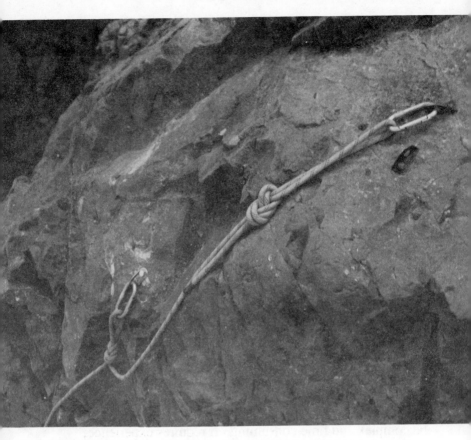

Fig. 11.1. Primary anchor (lower bolt) and backup (upper bolt) placed in line vertically as much as possible. Lower anchor takes main load. Knots and carabiners face downward in line with main load. Minimum slack between primary and backup prevents sudden shock load on backup if primary goes. Bolts are in different sections of rock for added safety. Hangers are flat-lying type so as not to lever the bolt loose.

you're half dead at the bottom.

Rigging requires team work. Unless the rigging points are well established, the rigger and backup rigger should normally discuss the pros and cons of available anchors and play the "what if" game. If this anchor goes, what would happen to the backup? How much would the rope be stressed if this backup rather than that one is chosen? How easy is it to get over the lip or off the rope if this anchor is

used? These and other questions should be part of the
routine of rigging every time decisions need to be made.

Anchors and Backups. An anchor is a secure point for
attaching rigging. For safety, I strongly urge you to put in
one or more backup anchors (Fig. 11.1). In case it's not
already obvious, a backup goes above or higher than the
main anchor. As much as posssible, it should be placed in
line vertically with the main anchor to reduce the shock load
on the backup in case the main anchor goes. Anchors and
backups that are not in line can sometimes be improved by
backing up to the second rope (if one is being rigged), as
shown in Fig. 11.2.

Backups may be able to turn a marginal anchor into a
reasonably safe one if the load is distributed evenly between
them, so that neither will receive a sudden load if one fails.
Really marginal main anchors should have two or more
backups with careful analysis of the what-if factors. With
artificial anchors, a backup is even more necessary. When
using bolts, try to place the primary and secondary bolts in
different bedding planes (sections of rock), if possible. This
will lessen the chance of simultaneous failures.

Natural anchors are preferred to artificial ones both for
conservation and aesthetic reasons. Put simply, artificial
anchors damage the cave. To rig an entrance drop, suitable
natural anchors can often be found on the large rocks or trees
near the entrance. Avoid small or precariously balanced
rocks or shallow-rooted trees.

Inside a cave, natural anchors include breakdown
boulders, limestone knobs, flakes, and certain massive
formations. However, be aware that formations sometimes
have an irregular concealed structure that makes them
susceptible to breaking. Tie around the bottom or maximum
cross section of a formation. Run your hand over the entire
surface checking for sharp edges or prickly knobs. Pad if
necessary to protect the rope or webbing runner. And, it
goes without saying, that you must never tie off on a
formation if it would damage its beauty or break part of it.

If no suitable natural anchor can be found, an artificial

anchor such as a bolt is usually installed. However, putting
in a lot of unnecessary bolts is definitely not recommended.
Check existing bolts by loading them to see if they are loose
or move. If OK, use them with a suitable backup before
you start hammering away to place a new one.

Second Rope as Backup. Sometimes a secondary
anchor is not readily at hand. Dante's Descent in Arizona is
a case in point (see Fig. 11.2). This classic free fall pit is
about 300 feet deep with an giant entrance about 80 to 100
feet across. A big sink with moderately steep sides
surrounds the pit and leads down to the lip. At the lip, a
rope-eating basalt (lava) layer extends down about 35 to 50
feet. Trees are usually used for anchors at Dante's, but since
it's out in the middle of nowhere, there aren't many trees.

 Below the perimeter, the pit bells out so that the drop is
free except for about the first 20 feet—if you rig at the right
place. To get a free drop all the way from the top to a
breakdown pile 248 feet down, you rig at a spot on the lip
marked by some white rocks that clearly stand out among the
nearly black basalt cap rock. We usually rig two ropes about
two to three feet apart. This speeds up the exit and gives
redundancy if anyone gets tired coming up or has equipment
problems and wants a nearby companion for moral or
physical support.

 To get independent primary rigging points for both ropes,
there are two trees of suitable thickness more or less in line
with the right spot on the lip. But backing up is a problem
because there aren't any other suitable trees behind these
either in line or close enough. You could backup the ropes
by tying each to both of the primary trees. Unfortunately,
the trees in question are offset from each other and if one
pulled out, it would subject the other tree to a sudden stress
that might pull it out too. Besides, that takes up a lot of rope,
and we normally only bring two 300 footers for Dante's.
Two slings of 30 feet or so could be used but still wouldn't
solve the not-in-line problem.

 What's the solution? Simply tie a Figure 8 Loop in each
rope at some convenient point out in front of the trees and

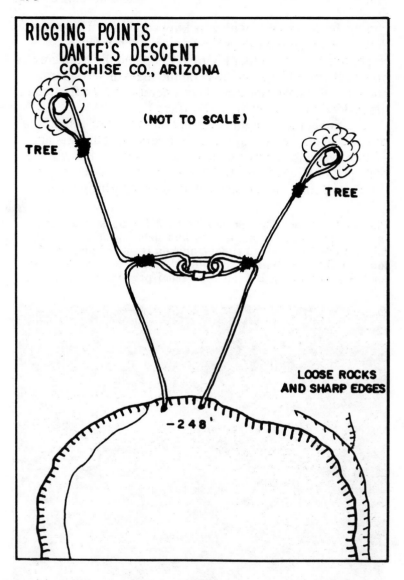

**RIGGING POINTS
DANTE'S DESCENT**
COCHISE CO., ARIZONA

(NOT TO SCALE)

TREE

TREE

LOOSE ROCKS
AND SHARP EDGES

-248'

Fig. 11.2. Backing up one rope on the other at Dante's Descent to rig the free drop of 248 feet (see text). A 20 foot long rope pad of double thickness denim at lip protects the line from rope-eating basalt cap.

clip the loops together with a locking carabiner. This makes each of the Figure 8 Loops the primary anchor for its respective line. The other Figure 8 Loop and the trees are now backups. (The actual load on the main or secondary anchor in this case is lessened considerably by the friction of the padded lip and the ground surface.)

As a final note, I might comment on the use of vehicles to provide an anchor at Dante's. I have used the bumpers and axles of vehicles many times for tie off points. However, I don't personally recommend it at Dante's because it requires driving off road and outside the established parking area.

Fig. 11.3 Six foot rigging runner used for backup around large knob conserves main rope and helps position line at better rappel location. Primary anchor is out of picture at lower point. Carabiner is positioned to put load on long or load bearing axis and keep rope from pressing on gate.

This leaves tire tracks and ruts that could seriously damage the easily eroded soil at the top of the sink if it became a regular practice.

Runners. Short six or 12 foot lengths of sling called runners are a great help when rigging (Fig 11.3). Single runners are made from 6 feet of one inch webbing tied with a water knot. Double runners are made from 10 to 12 feet. Two or three of each are very handy for rigging.

Purposes of Runners

- **Conserve main rope.**
- **Position the rope:**
  - **Away from a lip.**
  - **Out of a waterfall.**
  - **Away from a sharp edge.**
  - **Better spot to get on or off rope.**

When connecting the rope to a carabiner on a runner, be sure the direction of the load is across the carabiner's long axis and won't force against the gate. Also, resist the temptation to make a chain of three or more nonlocking carabiners to add length to a sling. If twisted, the gates can quite easily open up. This is easily demonstrated. Try it—you'll be surprised how easy is to pop open one of the carabiners.

Finally, always attach the main rope to the runner with a carabiner, not directly. This is especially true if you use a doubled rope for rappelling.

Wrap Around High Rigging. One of the best ways to rig a pit is off a tree near the entrance or a large column near the lip. This is shown in Fig. 11.4. The secret here is to wrap the three to five coils upward on the tree or column, so that the rope into the pit (the load bearing part of the rope) comes off the top of the wrap.

This wrap around rigging is considered safer because the weakening effect of the wraps—which are taking the

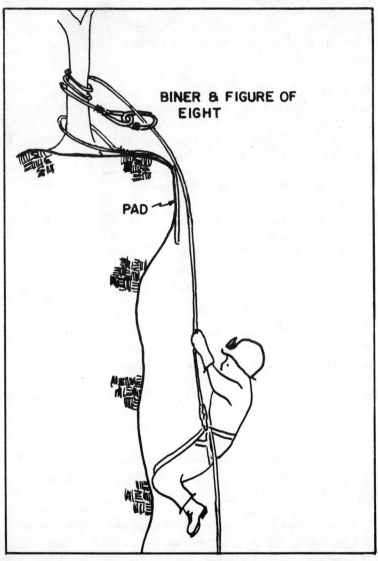

BINER & FIGURE OF EIGHT

PAD →

Fig. 11.4. Wrap Around Rigging. Take several upward wraps around tree so rope comes off top wrap. Secure with knot or carabiner on main line. Preferred because rope is weakened less than with knot. High rigging on tree makes it easier to start rappel and come over lip. Rope pad tied to tree with separate cord protects rope.

load—is less than than the weakening effect of a knot.
Instead of bearing the load, the knot simply keeps the wraps
from unraveling, which is only a remote possibility anyway,
considering the friction around the tree. The knot is tied
either directly or with a carabiner around the main line.

Positioning the rope up high on the tree, makes it easier to
start your rappel because the angle of the rope lets you step
back more comfortably. When coming up it's easier too.
Instead of the rope pressing tightly against the ground, the
high angle lets you fit your hand under the rope. This way
you can haul youself up by hand or put on a safety Jumar
(Chapter 14) to assist in getting over the lip.

In-Cave High Rigging. Rigging high inside a cave is also
to your advantage and can be done more often than you think,
if you'll study the possibilities instead of just tying off to the
most obvious anchor. Fig. 11.5 shows this in a 60 foot pit in
Virgin of the Guadalupes Cave (New Mexico). Traditional
rigging routes the rope flat dab on an overhanging slab that
makes coming over the lip a real bear. When you get up
there, your feet flail around under the over hang trying
fruitlessly to find a foot hold and your chest is jammed
against the slab. Instead, the high rigging is a dream. It lets
you come right up alongside the slab and literally step off
onto it, almost like you were getting off an elevator.

Safety is also a consideration here in addition to comfort
and convenience. A 1984 fatality in Cass Cave (Virginia)
points this up. A safe dry rigging is located high up in the
Belay Loft reached from an upper passage. This rigging
keeps you from getting soaked by a waterfall with a
temperature in the 30's°F. Two relatively inexperienced
young cavers who didn't know about the high rigging point,
rigged lower down. One got trapped in the water and died of
hypothermia. Seven years earlier, another caver died in the
same waterfall in the same way.

Gardening, Stopper Knots, and Lowering. Before
actually putting your anchor to the test, there are a
few preliminaries. The first is to garden loose rocks and
debris from around the entrance. Many injuries, most of them

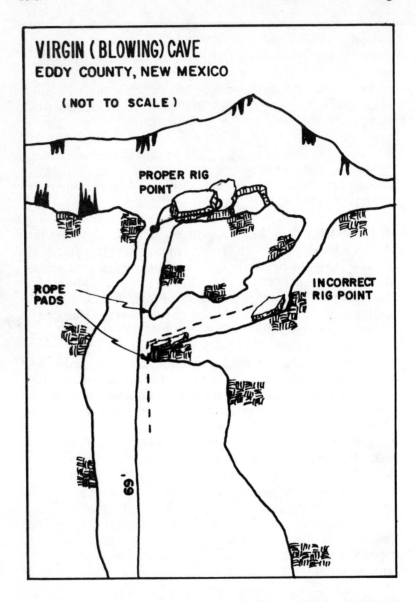

Fig. 11.5. Virgin Cave (New Mexico). High rigging point lets you step off onto overhang that otherwise requires brute force and much foul language to manage.

Fig. 11.6. Gardening loose rocks and debris at original discovery entrance to what became multi-mile Gaping Holes lava tube system. Note smooth log protecting rope from jagged lava lip.

fortunately minor, are caused by rocks falling into the pit. Gardening is a necessary step that shouldn't be overlooked in your haste to get underground.

That accomplished, the next step is to tie a Figure 8 Loop in the end of the rope. In case the rope doesn't reach the floor, this keeps you from rappellling right off the end. Being a loop, it gives you something to stand up in if you need to don ascending gear to go back up.

Finally, just before lowering the rope, yell down and ask if the drop is clear. Then, yell "ROPE" very loudly and lower away slowly rather than rapidly to keep from snagging on projections. Even so, the first person down must be alert for snags and be ready to free or reroute the rope.

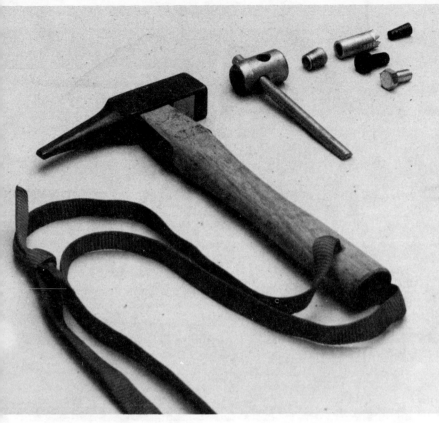

Fig. 11.7. Bolt Kit. From left to right: • Piton hammer with five feet of 1/2 inch tie-off webbing • Shield driver with handle for rotating • Tapered collar shown broken off • Drill shield with teeth at right end • Conical shaped expansion plug at far right locks shield in hole • Beneath shield—case hardened Allen head bolt and standard hex head bolt, both 3/8 inch.

Bolts

When an artificial anchor is called for, most cavers on this side of the Atlantic (and the other side too, apparently), dive into their packs and pull out their Jim Dandy bolt kits, complete with hammer, driver, and self drilling expansion bolts (Fig. 11.7). An expansion bolt has a housing or shield complete with teeth to drill its own hole. After drilling, the shield is pounded into the hole with a conical plug that expands it to lock it in place.

Bolts are great in that they can let you place a rope in just the right place for a drop. Usually that means out of the water, free of sharp edges, or where it's easy to get on and off the rope. Sometimes you just can't find a natural anchor in the right place. That's why the two types of anchors often team up to solve a particular rigging problem. A stout natural anchor becomes the backup because it isn't right for the drop. Then a bolt is installed to serve both as primary anchor and to route the rope into the right position.

Bolts are preferred to pitons (flat, blade-like metal wedges). It's not too often that a suitable crack for piton driving can be found in cave limestone. Rock climbing's current "clean climbing" trend has brought forth a wealth of camming devices for cracks and holes—eccentrics, wedges, cams, chocks, nuts, and friends among others.

They're apparently very successful as temporary anchors for lead climbers. So far, they haven't really found much application in caves. Pure rock climbing isn't required much in caving. And, what artificial anchors we do need are usually of the permanent variety like a bolt rather than the temporary variety like an eccentric piece of metal.

Self Drilling Concrete Anchors. Made by several different companies, self drilling expansion bolts are designed as concrete anchors, and this is the name most hardware or building supply people know them by. One fairly common brand is Phillips Red Head Concrete Anchors. Other brands are: Rawl Products Sabre-Tooth, Star Concrete Anchors, and VSI Fasteners Corporation Concrete Anchors. Petzl also makes excellent bolts and a bolt kit (which several caving suppliers stock), as does Troll in England, among others.

You should be aware that there are several other types of screw and bolt anchors. Just remember, the one you want is the self drilling type with chisel like teeth on the biting end. Avoid the lead lag-screw shield, plastic screw inserts, fibre screw anchors, or the Star Dryvin (a nail driven into a soft metal shield).

Expansion bolts are available in both 1/4 and 3/8 inch sizes. I prefer the 3/8 inch size. The Petzl bolts and drivers are apparently available in either 8mm (5/16 inch) or 10mm

(3/8 inch) size.

Two slightly different types of drivers and bolts are available. One type of holder (the one shown in Fig. 11.7 and 11.8) fits over a tapered collar at one end of the shield. The other holder screws directly into the shield, so it doesn't need the tapered collar. The Petzl is of this latter type. In other respects, the shields are the same.

An expansion bolt gains its strength from the rear of the hole by means of a conical wedge that expands as the shield is driven home into the hole. Because the strength comes from deep inside the hole, this type is advantageous where the outer layer of rock may be weathered or soft.

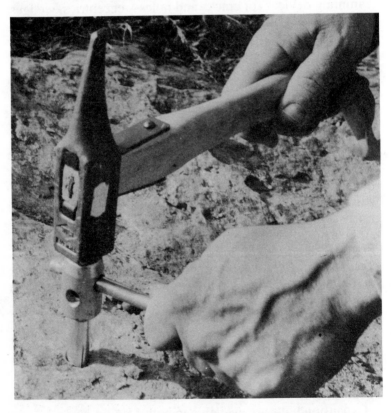

Fig. 11.8. Drilling a bolt hole calls for solid but not too heavy hammering and rotation of driver about 120° after each blow. Blow out dust regularly. Drill until break off groove or shield top is flush with surface.

Recommended safe working load is 1544 pounds in "normal" concrete (3500 pounds per square inch) according to Phillips, manufacturer of the Red Head brand. (They define working load as 25 percent of their test results.)

Caution. The actual strength of an installed bolt depends heavily on proper drilling, the depth of the hole, use of the proper length bolt, and proper installation of the hanger. With all those variables, you know why I say you should always have a backup for a bolt, preferably a bomb proof natural anchor.

Setting a Bolt. When setting a bolt, try to confine cave wall damage to as small an area as possible. Before beginning to drill, study the limestone bedrock carefully for cracks and evidence of loose flakes or crumbly rock. If it's a surface bolt, look for badly weathered rock as well. I said bedrock limestone just now. You'll find that trying to put a bolt in flowstone is usually next to impossible. Besides it's a very questionable conservation practice, as well being not very safe, because a lot of flowstone is only a thin coating.

Tap the surface of the rock with your hammer and listen for solid sounding areas. While not 100 per cent reliable, rock sounds can be helpful to an experienced ear. Even a beginner can detect a hollow sounding section and know it's not suitable for a bolt. As mentioned earlier, try to place primary and back-up bolts in different bedding planes or sections of rock.

A bolt should be installed in wall or floor where the load will be at right angles to the bolt shaft. Most bolts are noticeably weaker if subjected to a straight-out pull along the axis of the bolt. That why ceilings aren't a good location. In walls, a slight (five degree) downward drift to the hole is a good idea. Then, if the bolt were to loosen, it won't fall out under a right angle load.

Hammer blows (Fig. 11.8) should be hard but not hard enough to fracture the rock around the hole. Rotate the drill about 120 degrees after each blow. The Petzl bolt driver is nice in this regard because it has a neat collapsible handle on

Fig. 11.9. Attaching Carabiner to Hanger. Begin with gate up as shown at top. Then rotate carabiner 180 degrees so that gate is down and away from the rock, as shown at bottom.

the side. Don't lubricate the drill with oil or water. Instead, blow out debris every few minutes, preferably with a small hose. Wear safety glasses or goggles to protect your eyes.

It usually takes 10 to 15 minutes to set a bolt, but it can take longer in especially hard limestone or marble. Keep drilling until you reach the break off groove on the tapered type or the top of the non-tapered ones is flush with the surface. Remove the shield from the hole and install the conical plug in the toothed end.

Replace the shield in the hole and drive it in with several sharp blows until the break off grove or top is again flush with the surface. Then with the tapered type, strike the holder with a sharp sideways blow, to snap off the tapered top. With the screw-in type, unscrew the driver. The anchor is now ready for use. (The snapped-off top can be removed from the holder by putting the chisel end of the turning handle in the lower hole of the holder and tapping the end of the handle sharply.)

Hole Depth and Hangers. Hole depth is critical and must allow the hanger to be flush with the surface. This is necessary to prevent any bending or levering of the anchor when the hanger is loaded. Never hammer or pry directly on a hanger because this can damage and weaken it. Watch for evidence of physical abuse on existing hangers, such as hammer blows or prying marks.

Hangers are of two types, flat mounting and angled or offset. I recommend the flat lying type because they appear to take a load without the possibility of levering out the bolt as the offset type can. These are available from SMC (as shown in Fig. 11.9), Petzl type P13, and Leeper (though I haven't seen the Leepers for a while, they may still be available or in use).

I'm not as comfortable with the the Petzl type P 04, which is an angled type, or the other angled hangers because of the possibility of loosening the anchor. The Petzl catalog shows four illustrations of how to install their P 04, three of which are wrong. Seems to me when you can do it wrong three times out of four, I'd rather try another type less subject to

Fig. 11.10 Rope pads protect rope at lip and other points of abrasion. These pads are leather pieces attached to anchor by separate cords. Other good rope pad materials are denim, canvas and slit blue jean legs.

installation eccentricities.

High-tensile strength (Grade 9) bolts should be used if you can locate them. These come with either a standard hex-head or an Allen-head. Be sure to bring the proper wrench to tighten them up. Stainless steel aircraft bolts Type 316 are also sometimes available and are a good choice. No matter what type you use, curb the impulse to over tighten, since that can needlessly stress the bolt. One or two turns with a wrench past finger tight is enough

With American manufactured anchors, don't use a bolt longer than one-half inch. A longer bolt can force itself against the back of the hole and loosen the shield.   With

Petzl anchors, use the bolt (16mm) supplied with the anchor or hanger to be certain of the right length.

When attaching the carabiner to the hanger, be sure that its final position is down and out--that is, with the gate down and away from the rock. This keeps it from opening if the rope or sling twists under load (Fig. 11.9).

After drilling the hole and installing a hanger, should you leave the hanger there or remove it? That decision really depends on the cave and its traffic. If you do decide to leave it in place, you can apply Locktite to the threads to prevent theft. Whether you leave it or not, it's a good idea to install a small metal tag stamped with the date of installation and your club's initials or other identification. By the way, if it's the practice in your area to remove hangers after each use, better be prepared with a supply of bolts and hangers of your own.

Inspecting Bolts. What if you find a bolt already installed? Is it safe to use? To find out, attach a rigging runner with a carabiner and load it with your full weight in all directions, including straight out. If the bolt or shield moves, better forget it. If it doesn't move it might be OK.

However, any bolt more than two or three years old should be viewed with suspicion and studied more carefully. First, take off the hanger and study the area right around the hole for cracks and damage done during installation. Then, look at the surrounding rock for cracks and fractures. Next look at the hanger for hairline cracks, bending, and damage from hammering or prying.

If it passes all these tests, it may be safe to use it. Nevertheless, it bears repeating that you should not rely on any single artificial anchor. Always back it up.

Rope Abrasion and Pads

To prevent rope abrasion, rope pads must be installed wherever the rope is subjected to pressure against a sharp or abrasive surface (see Fig. 11.10). The primary place will usually be up near the anchor. Note that the longer the drop

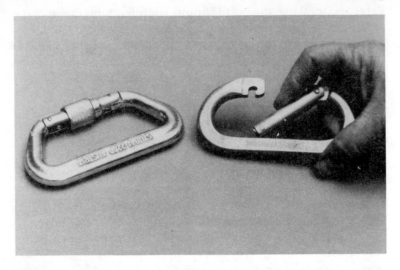

Fig.11.11. Locking and standard carabiners. Standard cara-biner gate has a pin which mates with a notched slot as shown. Newer locking carabiners have this construction also. Modern carabiners test at between 3000 and 6000 lbs

the greater the abrasion potential. Watch for places where the rope makes a sharp angle over an edge. This is more dangerous than where it only touches the wall.

Prusiking, with its constant up and down sawing motion, is potentially more damaging to ropes than rappelling, assuming a steady rappel rate. All cavers should learn to rappel smoothly and avoid the kind of Hollywood style jumping that pulls anchors loose and abrades ropes severely.

We routinely pad all drops with denim, canvas, or leather pads. Old blue-jeans legs, cut open at the seam, make good pads. Size should be about 12 inches wide and at least three feet long. As mentioned, for Dante's Descent in Arizona which has a basalt cap, we made up double thickness denim pads about 20 feet long and three feet wide. Leather wears really well, its only disadvantage is its high cost if you try to get a big enough piece for practical use.

Whatever you use, attach a 10 to 15 foot length of parachute cord, so the pad can be tied off and positioned properly. Don't tie the pad to the climbing rope itself unless there is absolutely no other possibility. In cloth pads, metal eyelets for threading this parachute cord are helpful to prevent tearing.

When passing the pad on the way down or up, carefully reposition the rope on the pad after going by. If there are several pads, for example at the top of the drop, it may be worth rigging a short tail of rope from the anchor so you can transfer to this and avoid the pads completely. This also makes it easier to cross the lip because you don't have the full weight of the rope below you. Don't forget to tie a figure-of-eight loop in the bottom of the rope tail, just as you do with a main rope, to keep from accidentally coming off the end.

European Re-Anchoring Practices. I might comment briefly on the apparently widespread practice in Europe of putting in additional anchors seemingly at any point where the rope touches a surface. These are called re-anchors or re-belays and an entire style of rappelling and prusiking has grown up around them. Presumably, this style works well for them and is the generally accepted practice in the type of caves they regularly explore.

It would seem that re-belaying is necessary because European caving ropes have a much lower abrasion resistance than ours. As indicated in Chapter 10, our vertical techniques grew up in parallel with the development of very strong, very abrasion resistant ropes of reasonable cost. We pad sharp and abrasive edges and surfaces, but not each and every point where the rope may touch something. And our abrasion resistant ropes (and our accident free record) show no evidence of damage from this style of rigging. Without

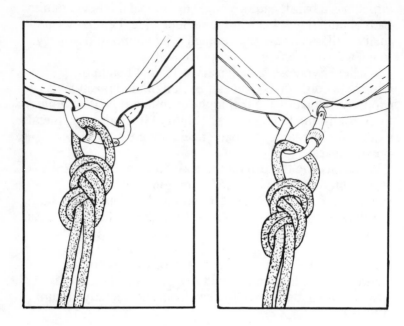

Fig. 11.12. Left, improper rigging showing load applied directly to gate, weakest point on carabiner. Right, slings and rope arranged correctly on long load bearing axis.

wanting to carp or criticize unfairly something that I haven't personally participated in, I would have to say that I've got some real problems with this practice of re-belaying.

In the first place, it means putting a whole lot more bolts in the cave. This is something I think most cavers on this side of the big pond would not be sympathetic to. It also requires what seems to be a very complicated and time consuming style of vertical caving. If I understand correctly, you may have to stop as often as every 10 or 15 feet and transfer yourself and your gear around another bolt. And every time you take yourself off and put yourself back on the line, it seems to me as if it's one more chance to make a mistake and have an accident.

I'm sure European cavers quickly become adept at this style of caving. And the slings and harnesses they use seem admirably well suited for it. But I guess my question is, is it worth it? Why not use a tougher rope to begin with and laugh at all those unused bolts and hangers as you smoothly glide on down the pit in a fraction of the time it must take to hook on all those cows tails and reconnect this and that.

I'm sure I'm going to get some static for this parochial viewpoint. But I know I'm expressing the opinions not just of myself but of many other seasoned American vertical cavers as well.

Carabiners

Carabiners are oval rings of special-alloy aluminum or steel. One side has a spring loaded, inward-opening gate (Fig. 11.11). Carabiners have a myriad of uses. Every caver should carry at least one locking carabiner with a piece of 12 foot webbing. Vertical cavers will need several more, of both the locking and unlocking types. The most important carabiner is the one for your seat harness. I suggest you get the strongest one you can. Be sure it's large enough to accept your descender and one or two slings for a Spelean Shunt and a safety Jumar (Chapters 13 and 14). .

Uses of Carabiners

- **Connecting rappel device to seat harness.**
- **Rigging to hangers, runners, and ropes.**
- **Tying to a line for a horizontal traverse.**
- **Attaching to a belay line.**
- **Lowering gear.**
- **Attaching equipment to packs.**

Carabiners have gotten much stronger over the years. They now test at from 3000 to 6000 pounds or more and cost anywhere from four to eight dollars. Large, heavy duty steel models suitable for rescue work can cost 15 to 20 dollars. Carabiners are designed so they can be opened under a nominal working load of about 200 pounds. This is an important characteristic, because you often need to open the gate and snap in a sling while sitting in your seat harness. Major brands seen at caving and mountaineering suppliers are: SMC, REI (made by SMC), Chouinard, Bonaiti , Stubai, Hiatt, and Clog, among others.

Carabiners are designed to be loaded on the long axis. Side loading strength is much lower, because the gate is unquestionably the weakest spot. When rigging you must be very careful that the load can't shift and be applied directly against the gate (Fig.11.12). Failure of a gate at a load as low as 300 pounds has been reported. Many carabiners have a locking sleeve to keep the gate closed. However, this sleeve doesn't add much strength to the carabiner. When a gate fails, test results suggest it is the hinge pin that most often breaks.

As indicated earlier, making a chain of three or more non-locking carabiners can be lethal. Twisting the chain will easily open one or more gates. Remember, too, that the gate should open downward and away from the rock. Like the boxer going for the long count, the final position is down and out.

Carabiners are easy to care for but aren't indestructible. Any carabiner that has been dropped some distance or bounced hard can develop invisible cracks and should be retired. To keep them clean, wash off mud with water or a solvent such as paint thinner. Lubricate the gate lightly with WD-40 or penetrating oil.

Rapid Links

A very strong (10,000 pound) rigging device for main ropes that shares several characteristics with the carabiner is the quick link or rapid link. It can be found in hardware, boating, and some auto supply stores. Most of these seem to be of French manufacture, the Maillon Rapide Link.

Unlike a carabiner, it derives a large part of its strength from its locking mechanism which in effect makes it into a continuous oval. Since it has no gate, it avoids the hinge pin, the weak point of a carabiner. Nevertheless, don't forget that the screw sleeve is integral to the design and function. The No. 9 size of the Maillon Rapide (about two-thirds the size of an SMC oval carabiner), tested to 10,000 pounds.

In the balance, I prefer carabiners to rapid links because they are more fail-safe. If you forget to lock a locking carabiner, you haven't lost any strength. You have given up the advantage of the gate being harder to open, but you're no worse off than if it was a nonlocking carabiner. But if you forget to lock a rapid link, the strength drops to one-ninth of what it is when locked. And if you load a rapid link with even a light load when it's not screwed shut, you may find—as I did—that it will never screw together again.

Pulleys

Pulleys are useful for hauling and rescue operations. The best types are rescue pulleys, consisting of a nylon or metal pulley wheel with two hinged flanges to protect the rope from abrasion. With the flanges hinged, you can put the pulley on the line anywhere and not have to thread the end through. Some of the best pulleys are the Russ Anderson brand manufactured by SMC.

When buying a pulley, be sure that the pulley wheel turns freely. If it binds, it can overheat and possible fuse nylon. Some can be disassembled for cleaning. Use Locktite when reassembling to secure the nut and take care that the wheel runs freely

12

Climbing and Belaying

> *Physical skills like chimneying, climbing, and belaying are just as important as technical vertical skills like rappelling and prusiking.*

To become a well rounded caver, you need certain physical climbing skills in addition to the technical ropes skills of rappelling and prusiking. Techniques like traversing, chimneying, free climbing, and belaying get you into the rest of the cave after you're dropped the entrance pit.

That's why we encourage you to practice and perfect your physical climbing skills, even though technical vertical work may seem more glamorous. Both types of skills must be in the arsenal of the complete caver who expects to explore all parts of the cave.

Traversing

Traversing is what you do on a narrow continuous ledge or on a series of foot holds that are located more or less in line

214

horizontally. An example is a narrow stream passage where you want to stay above the water. When the walls are close together, you can move sideways using chimneying techniques. Or if they're too far apart, you can straddle the span with one foot on each wall and the hands for balance. Often traverses are used to avoid climbing down to floor level and then back up again when it's clear that the passage simply dips down for a short distance. This is called staying high (and it has nothing to do with alcohol or mind altering substances).

Technique Tips. When you're on a ledge, a good technique is to move your feet in a shuffling motion . Don't try to cross one leg over the other, especially if you're facing the wall on a narrow ledge. Shuffling the feet helps keep you balanced, crossing the legs invites tripping.

If there's much exposure below you, you may want to belay folks across a traverse. Figure12.1 illustrates the infamous traverse across Passage Pit in Church Cave, California. (By the way, we almost always go to Church on Saturday, in case you were wondering.) Passage Pit can't be avoided if you're going to see the cave. It's either about one hour or seven hours inside Church depending on which way you're going on the circuit. The pit's about 25 feet across and 30 feet deep. It has a nice eight to 12 inch ledge for the feet and some friendly pendants for hand holds. But the pendants make you lean out over the pit and this makes some people nervous.

On the trip shown in Fig. 12.1, we tied a hand line into some existing bolts. You clip into the line with a sling from your seat harness and slide along, shuffling the feet in the approved manner. I have to admit that this is one time that the double cows-tail sling the Europeans use would be very handy. A cows tail is two short seat harness slings each with a carabiner to clip into a line on either side of a fixed anchor. Instead of a hand line, we sometimes belay the Passage Pit from both sides. The two-sides belay keeps the traverser from swinging like a pendulum in case of a fall.

In a project cave, where traffic along a certain route is

Fig.12.1 Caver clipped into hand line nears end of 25 foot
traverse across Church Cave's 30 foot deep Passage Pit.

heavy, it's not uncommon to rig a more or less permanent fixed line using bolts to speed traffic and minimize the danger. (Similarly, a fixed ladder and other aids may also be installed. These aids should be removed, however, when the situation changes.)

Chimneying

Chimneying is something you need to master early on because you'll come across a lot of chimneys in caves. A cave chimney may not always be your classic tubular pipe, the kind Santa comes down and the fireplace smoke goes up. Many are narrow vertical slots or fissures. Some are where two walls or large breakdown blocks come together. The techniques used for any of these is pretty much the same. The differences really come from how far apart the walls are rather than whether they're tubes or fissures. Traversing horizontally in a narrow passage uses similar techniques.

Back and Feet. Chimneying is strenuous, but doesn't require exceptional strength. Basically, it involves putting your back on one wall and your feet on the other and making like a spider. Try to choose the smoother wall for your back if you have a choice. This is not only easier on your spine, but knobs or ledges should be in front of you where they can be used for foot and hand holds.

In narrow chimneys of say 14 to 24 inches, chimneying down is fairly easy because gravity helps do the work and friction keeps you from falling (Fig. 12.2A). However, chimneys this narrow are quite a bit harder to climb up, since your legs can't do their job as well in such a narrow space.

Some chimneys are actually too narrow to be chimneyable at all. In that case, try this technique. Tie loops into a rope for footholds. Put your foot in a loop, brace yourself against the sides, and raise your foot as far as you can. At the same time, the others up above take up the slack in the line. Then you stand and raise your foot again and repeat the cycle. In this way you can often get up a chimney too tight for regular chimneying.

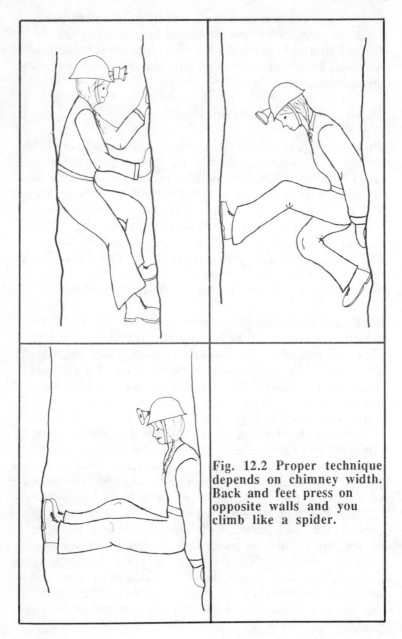

Fig. 12.2 Proper technique depends on chimney width. Back and feet press on opposite walls and you climb like a spider.

When a chimney widens to 24 inches and more (Fig. 12.2B), put one foot under your body on the back wall, and the other foot on the facing wall. This tends to require more downward pressure with your hands, but it's still fairly easy to do. Remember to brace firmly with your back against the wall, move your feet one at a time, then squirm up, down, or sideways with your back. For better control, try to keep your knees bent a little, if possible, like a skier or dancer, rather than straight out. Also, don't raise your knees above your waist or you may start slipping down. When you need to rest, put your feet a little below waist level.

In wider chimneys (Fig.12.2C), put both feet on one wall and your back on the other. Even though you can worm your way up completely smooth walls, a few good ledges and crannies sure make it easier. In fact, if you have a lot of good holds, you can go up with one foot on each side in a straddling motion which is faster and less strenuous than chimneying.

Belled Out Bottoms. A problem with cave chimneys is that many have a disconcerting habit of belling out near the bottom. With practice, you'll find that you can often shift gears and chimney sideways to a corner or a narrower spot to continue to the bottom. After you're down, study the pitch and try to remember how you did it. It will help you get started right when you come back later. Often when you chimney up, getting started is the hardest part. Sometimes a leg up from a fellow caver is the only way to do it, so don't be shy about asking.

One final point—because you usually have good support from the walls in a chimney, you can often lean forward or wiggle around to get a better angle on a hold. For example, some small ledges are too steep to hold your boot if you're standing vertically. But you can often twist yourself at a weird angle or lean way forward and use that hold after all. Sounds a little crazy, but as you learn to chimney, you'll see what I mean.

A modified chimneying technique can be used to slide down a smooth-floored slope if the roof is close to the floor

and irregular enough to offer some holds. By lying down
with your back on the floor and feet on the ceiling, you can
negotiate a difficult slope otherwise impossible to climb
without a hand line. A word of caution again—don't
descend headfirst in a slope because it may be impossible
to get back out.

Free Climbing

Free climbing—also called three-point-climbing or classic
rock climbing—is a skill that is best learned in practice
climbs above ground. Also, in case you haven't heard,
climbing can't be learned from a book. A book can describe
the principles, but the way to learn is under the guidance of
an experienced instructor. Incidentally, free climbing doesn't
mean climbing without a belay. It means without artificial
aids (etriers or hardware).   ·

Cave vs Rock Climbing. Cave climbing differs from
rock climbing in several ways. In the first place, caves go
down, mountains go up. Put another way, cavers usually
climb down to get into a cave and climb up to get back out.
With rock climbers, it's the other way around. This may
sound a little simple minded, but it helps to explain things if
you keep it in mind. Secondly, cavers climb in the dark. At
first glance this may seem harder, since the holds are more
difficult to see, but it has this benefit. You can't see how far
up you are. In rock climbing, this is called exposure—the
expanse of free air below you. In the dark, you can't see it
so you don't worry about it as much (it says here).
  Finally, rock climbing is generally more two-dimensional
than cave climbing. Classic rock climbing is often straight
up a sheer wall at a 90 degree angle or nearly so. Cave
climbing, on the other hand, is more often done not so much
on walls as in fissures, cracks, chimneys, and piles of
breakdown. There are times in caves where sheer walls must
be climbed, e.g, to push a high passage. Even so, I think
it's fair to characterize cave climbing as being more involved
with walls that are near each other than with sheer faces.

10 to 30 Foot Pitches. Cave climbing usually involves short pitches of 10 to 30 feet rather than the longer ascents found in mountain climbing. Depending on the skill of the group, short climbs of 10 or 12 feet in caves may or may not be belayed. However, if there is any doubt, rig a belay line and play it safe.

Climbing pitches in caves are commonly found in wide non-chimneyable pits or fissures, walls, large breakdown slabs and blocks, and steep slopes. Holds are usually large and muddy rather than small and dry as in rock climbing. Wide pits and walls are negotiated with a combination of chimneying and free climbing using ledges and holds. Breakdown blocks have sharp edges that are good for pulling yourself up and cracks between the blocks that a boot, knee, or shoulder can be jammed into.

Flowstone slopes (which shouldn't be climbed at all if likely to be damaged or dirtied), are made up of ascending ledges. These look like easy steps, but are sometimes too narrow or sloping to serve as good holds. Between the ledges, small ribs or knobby columns offer handholds or fingerholds for balance. Other useful flowstone holds are larger columns and stalagmites which can be hugged with both arms when swinging up onto a ledge.

Climbing Technique. In free climbing, you always strive for three points of contact   The feet and legs do the lifting. The hands take care of the balance. A climbing sequence might go like this. Starting with secure footholds and handholds, you probe upward with one of your hands to find a knob, ledge, or crack. When a good one is found, hold tight with both hands and look around for the next foothold. It helps a lot to lean out from the rock so you can see the holds better. You can always tell experienced climbers by the confident way they pull away from the face and look for holds. Once a good foothold is located, the weight is shifted upward and one of the hands starts probing again. Movement is smooth, sure, and graceful. Lunging or jumping are dangerous and counterproductive.

Fig. 12.3. Sequence of climbing moves up sandstone face. A jam hold for left foot in 12.3A is key to climb. By stepping up on left foot, right foot in 12.3B can now reach vertical bulge. In 12.3C, after pushing off with right foot, left foot is then jammed higher in crack for final move to upper ledge.

Plan the Route. Before starting a climb, plan the route, but allow for an alternate route if possible. Select footholds and handholds carefully, testing them before putting your full weight on them. Surprisingly enough, footholds so small as to be barely noticeable are used every day by experienced climbers.

For footholds, the side of the foot is better than the toe because toe holds put a greater strain on the leg muscles. When first placing the foot onto a foothold, flex the ankle a few times to be sure to get as much boot as possible on the hold. This helps you sense the hold with the sole of the boot. But don't shuffle around once the foot is positioned or traction may be lost. For balance, keep the knees bent slightly, and lean out to locate holds.

When no ledge or knob presents itself, a hold can sometimes be created by jamming the hand or foot into a crack (Fig 12.3). This is an important technique and is the only way some climbs can be made. For foot jams, insert the boot at an angle, then twist it into the crack. This makes it easier to get out after you put your full weight on it. Hand and fist jams are also very useful. Gloves are more comfortable for jam holds, although I always climb bare handed to feel the rock better.

Down Climbing. Generally, climbing up is easier than climbing down because you can see the holds better. When climbing down, try to face outward or sideways when it's relatively easy going so you can locate holds. When it's steeper, face in (as when climbing upward), get a firm grip and lean outward to find the holds.

When climbing down, always use a belay if there is real danger. On a tricky descent, you can ask for tension from the belayer so that you can lean out and look over your shoulder to find the next hold. Or, the belayer can hold you securely so you can probe around with your foot until you find the next one. Be sure the belayer understands what is happening before doing this.

Spotting Holds. As with any difficult situation, if you're at the bottom, you should talk the climber down the pitch, spot holds, and suggest how to make the next move. You can also help by shining your light on the holds to make them easier to see in the dark.

Down climbs in caves are usually limited to about 25 to 30 feet. If it's more than that, a rappel line is usually rigged, and the descent is made by rappelling instead. Similarly, if a particularly long upward climb is necessary, it will often be rigged for a ladder or prusik ascent.

Caution. Never climb up a pitch that you won't be able to climb back down easily. Sometimes it will run into a dead end and you'll have to climb back down. If it's not too long, it can sometimes be rigged for a hasty rappel, using a hand line or the caver slings carried by two or three cavers. One person in the group should always carry a 30 to 50 foot hand line when climbing and scrambling are expected.

Belaying

Belaying is a way to protect a climbing caver by means of a safety rope in case of a fall. It works like this—before starting your climb, you tie a rope around your waist or to a seat harness. A belayer situated above controls the rope so that if you start to fall, the belayer and the rope will stop you and keep you from getting hurt.

Belays are of two types—static and dynamic. A static belay is the one used in caving and a tight one at that. The belayer is located above the climbing caver and the rope is kept tight with very little slack. Thus the maximum amount you're likely to fall is only 1 or 2 feet before the belayer catches you. You may be climbing up or down, but the belayer is on top.

Dynamic belaying is different and is rarely ever used in caving. In rock climbing, however, the situation is reversed. A dynamic belay is given to protect the lead climber climbing above the belayer. High stretch dynamic ropes are now the order of the day. They give a soft stop that will not damage the climber, the belayer, or the anchor. The rope is left

Fig. 12.4. Sitting hip static belay. Belayer is tied with a slack-free sling to the anchor point coming from behind at right side. The direction of his pointing (right) hand and right leg are in the same direct line to the climber and the expected line of pull in case of a fall. Thus he will not be rotated out of position by a fall. There is no slack in the belay line, so the climber cannot fall for any distance and thereby overload the static rope.

Both feet are firmly anchored: the left against an adjacent surface, the right in a foot stirrup especially rigged from the anchor for that purpose because no natural surface was available in the direct line of climb. Note that the position of the anchor and especially the direction of the fall dictate which hand (the right) will be used as the pointing hand and which will be the braking hand (the left). Practice alternating hands so that you are proficient with both for either job. The rope is coiled loosely in a "messy" coil so that it can be drawn from the coil without snagging.

relatively loose or slack so the climber can climb freely and not be pulled off the face by the drag of the rope.

Since static belaying does not generate severe loads on the rope, low-stretch static caving ropes like Blue Water and PMI are used—with caution—for static belays on short drops of not more than 25 or 30 feet. However, as stated in Chapter 10, never use a static rope for a dynamic belay. That's a no no.

So if the cave entrance is a down climb, who belays the last person? What usually happens is that the an experienced

Fig. 12.5A. Taking up the slack from an ascending climber during a static belay calls for a repetitive sequence of hand movements. Vital point is to never let go of rope with braking hand (left hand in this case). Right or pointing hand is reaching forward as far as it can to begin drawing up the line.

climber does the belaying, then descends with a self-belay, such as a Gibbs ascender, after tying off the belay line up on top. Similarly, going back out, the best climber will climb the pitch with or without a self-belay depending on the difficulty, then belay the others up.

Sitting Hip Belay. For a static belay, the best and safest position—both for belayer and climber—is the sitting hip belay (Fig. 12.4). The first requirement is to tie yourself to a secure, slack-free anchor. Why is this so important?

Fig. 12.5B. Left or braking hand has pulled rope (just taken up by right hand) around body until hands meet. Here, right hand grasps both ropes together for a moment to allow left hand to slide smoothly along rope back to waist position. Thus left hand never leaves the line, but keeps hold of it, ever alert for a fall.

Without a good anchor, the pit could as easily claim two
victims instead of one if the climber falls. To attach yourself
to the anchor, you can tie-in directly to your waist using a
bowline on a coil. It's even better if you have a seat harness
to tie or clip into.

The rope tying you to the anchor can be a separate sling.
Or a tail in the belay rope can be brought back out from the
anchor and a Figure 8 Loop tied for you to clip into.
Regardless of the tie-in used, leave as little slack as possible
in the line so as not to put a sudden load on the anchor in a

**Fig. 12.5C.To hold a fall, left hand has been drawn
quicky across chest so that friction around entire
torso is applied to help the arrest. Legs tense and
apply pressure to braced feet.**

fall. After tying in, inch forward a bit to take any remaining slack out of the tie-in line.

Rotating Out of Position. When choosing your belay position, an important but little understood consideration is the possibility of being rotated out of position by the force of a falling climber. This reduces the wrap around the body and could result in the rope being torn right out of your pointing hand. Ideally, the anchor should be in the center of the belayer's back. Then the belayer's pointing hand (the

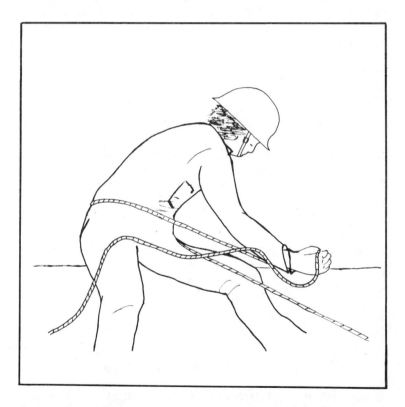

Fig 12.5D. Final step (as taught by the Mountain School, Renton, Washington) has belayer twisting body further to allow pinning the braking hand against the ground to get even more braking action.

right hand in Fig. 12.5A) and the climbing caver should be lined up in a straight line. Unfortunately, you're not always that lucky and the anchor has to be one side or the other not in the center of your back. But if you've learned, as we recommend, to belay ambidextrously, then you can choose as the pointing hand, the one that will line up on the side the anchor is on. Thus, if the anchor is on the right, choose the right hand for the pointing hand and vice versa. Finally, also be sure to aim your pointing hand and body in the expected direction of the fall.

Some instructors recommend running the rope through a carabiner on the pointing hand side of your seat harness. This also helps prevent you from rotating out of position or dropping the rope.

Belaying Position. Choose a position (Fig.12.4) where you can sit back from the edge of the drop with legs spread apart somewhat, knees flexed but not locked, and feet braced against a solid object like a wall, ledge, rock, or in a crack. Alternatively, as shown in 12.4, one of the feet can be rigged with a foot sling if no ledge is convenient.

Be sure to wear gloves. If you see someone belaying without gloves, you can be pretty sure that they don't really expect to hold a fall. You only hold a real fall without gloves once to become a believer.

Sloppy Rope Pile. Arrange the rope on your braking hand side (left hand in 12.4, right hand in 12.5D) in a loose, sloppy coil, free enough so it doesn't snag during a descent. Similarly, when taking it up with an ascending caver, try to keep it from getting too snarled up. The line down to the caver is held by the pointing hand. The rope then passes around your back into the braking hand. Never let go of the rope with your braking hand, under any circumstance.

Rope above Tie Off Sling. Also, be sure the belay rope is on top of the sling tying you into the anchor. This way, the rope will not scoot under your behind in a fall, but will rise up and be locked under your arm pits. Running the rope through the carabiner on your seat harness mentioned above will also help keep the rope from getting away from you.

When belaying an ascending caver, keep tension in the rope so there is never more than a foot or two of slack in the line. Taking the rope up while never letting go of it with the braking hand requires attention and practice. See Fig. 12.5 for a description of the proper hand movements.

When you're belaying a down climb, feed the rope out slowly. Keep the rope snug but not too tight unless the caver requests more tension. Develop a feel for the rate of climb so that the caver isn't held back, yet there is no slack. Don't make the caver pull the rope around your body.

Stopping a Fall. To stop a fall, the braking hand is brought quickly across the body and if necessary, all the way down to the ground on the opposite side, as in Fig. 12.5D. At the same time, both hands squeeze the rope. However, squeezing the rope is less important than the much greater friction you get from wrapping the rope tightly against your torso.

Surprisingly, even a small caver weighing only 125 lbs or so can safely stop the fall of a caver weighing 200 lbs or more. After you have stopped the fall, hold the person tight to allow them to regain a secure footing or slowly lower them back to the bottom.

Sound complicated? It can be learned in one or two afternoon sessions with instructors that don't mind coming off the wall yelling **Falling** (or falling unexpectedly later in the afternoon). But you'll need to belay regularly or practice it at least quarterly to keep the skill in top shape.

Tying into the Middle. If you have a long enough rope, there is some advantage to tying into the middle to be be-layed rather than the end. That way, the rope doesn't have to be thrown back down (and be subject to snagging). Instead, it can be pulled back down by the next climber using the free end at the bottom. Try it sometime. It works.

Climbing Signals

Climbing signals are a kind of verbal shorthand that simplifies communication. Signals differ a bit in different areas. Here are the ones I have found successful.

When you're tied in, your first signals will likely be:

Up Rope, if there's a lot of slack in the line, then:.

Ready on belay.

The belayer answers when ready, and not before:

Belay is on.

It's possible that seconds or minutes may pass before the belayer is ready to give the **Belay On** signal. However, under no circumstances should you assume that you're being belayed until you hear the return call. Be patient.

Then, if you're all set, you move over into the climbing position and call:

Ready to climb.

The belayer often answers,

Is That You? meaning is that you I'm feeling on the rope or is the rope caught.

If your answer is yes, the belayer will probably say

Climb, and off you go.

These initial calls are often shortened to **Ready to Climb** on your part meaning you are ready on belay and ready to climb, and **Climb** on the part of the belayer if all is well.

Other important signals to indicate your condition once underway are:

Falling, when you're doing that or expect to.

Tension, when you want the rope tighter.

Slack, when you want the rope looser.

Don't say Take up Slack when you want **Tension**, because the belayer will probably only hear **Slack**. Also don't use **Up Rope** for **Tension**. **Up Rope** is to take up the excess rope at the beginning or end or when hauling packs and gear.

At the end of the climb, when you are completely safe and preferably sitting down, call:

Off Belay, to tell the belayer to relax.

Finally the belayer calls:

Belay is Off, to indicate you are no longer protected.

After untying, the next call is:

Off Rope, meaning the rope is free for the next person.

Three other calls are useful not only for belaying, but for rigging and other situations too.

Before lowering a rope or ladder down a drop, ask:

Clear? meaning is the drop area clear?

If clear, the answer will be yes or silence if no one is there. Then, just before you slowly lower the rope or ladder, call

Rope! before you actually do it.

Finally, don't forget to yell:

Rock! any time you dislodge any object into the drop.

SUMMARY OF COMMON
   CLIMBING CALLS

Climber	Ready on belay.
Belayer	Belay is on.
Climber	Ready to climb.
Belayer	Is that you?
Climber	That's me, or yes
Belayer	Climb.
Climber	Tension.
Climber	Slack.
Climber	Falling!
Climber	Off belay
Belayer	Belay is off.

Fig. 12.6. Common climbing calls. These are calls I have found successful. Many local variations exist in different areas.

13

Rappelling

Rappelling is the technique for dropping pits. Techniques for short and medium pits are similar, but deep pits have some special requirements.

Before getting into the subject of rappelling, I'd like to make some general comments about American vertical caving techniques (called SRT or Single Rope Techniques in other parts of the world).

Over the past 25 years, American cavers have developed a style of vertical caving that has proven itself safe, simple, and versatile. It has allowed us to penetrate many new or previously unexplored pits and cave systems in the United States, Mexico, and other countries.

Vertical systems for many of us began with carabiner brake bars and Prusik slings of 5/16 inch (8mm) manila rope. The cable ladder was also widely used for short 30 to 60 foot climbs, and occasionally even for longer ones too. Rope for many years was mainly the old standby, 7/16 inch three-strand Goldline. It spun you around horribly and had

to be knotted together for really deep pits. Later, the first
kernmantle ropes came into use. Eventually these evolved
into today's superb quality static caving ropes with very high
strength, very high abrasion resistance, low stretch, freedom
from spin, and reasonable cost.

  During the two and a half decades of development and field
use, American vertical systems have achieved an enviable
safety record. Our systems are simple to use and relatively
simple to assemble. Moreover, they are multipurpose and
have shown their value under a wide variety of different
caving conditions.

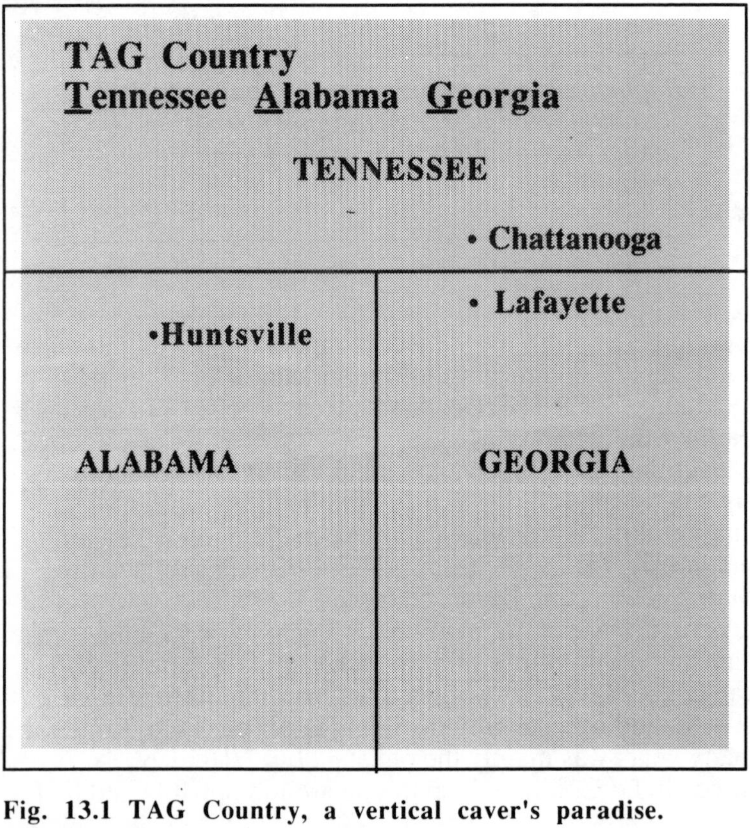

TAG Country
Tennessee Alabama Georgia

TENNESSEE

• **Chattanooga**

• **Lafayette**

•**Huntsville**

ALABAMA   **GEORGIA**

Fig. 13.1 TAG Country, a vertical caver's paradise.

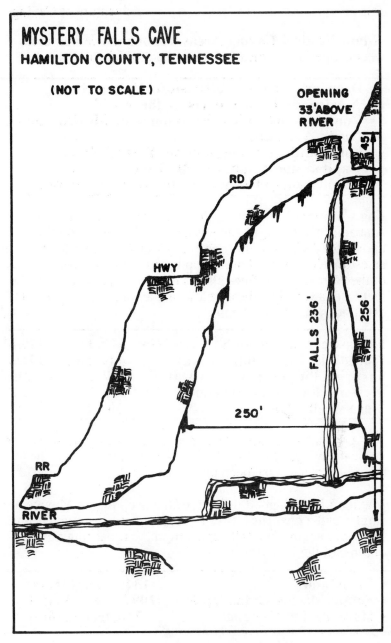

Fig. 13.2 Mystery Falls Cave, Chattanooga, Tennessee.

Main Vertical Caving Areas. Among the caving areas
where American vertical techniques are widely used are the:

- **Deep pits of the southeastern United States**
  Mexico, and other parts of the world
- **Complex multi-pit cave systems of Mexico and**
  North America.
- **Long outdoor drops such as Yosemite's El**
  Capitan and Canada's Mt. Thor.
- **Smaller pits of other North American caves.**

Tag Country. In the three southeastern states of Tennessee,
Alabama, and Georgia, there is a vertical caver's paradise
known as TAG Country (See Fig. 13.1). Concentrated here are
an estimated thousand or more pits. As a rule, the best known
of these are open-air free-fall pits that bottom out at 150 to 180
feet. But a few, like these below, are among the wonderful
exceptions that prove the rule.

Fantastic Pit, Ellison's Cave (Ga)	**510 feet**	**(155m)**
Incredible Pit, Ellison's Cave	**440 feet**	**(134m)**
Surprise Pit, Fern Cave (Ala)	**437 feet**	**(133m)**
Mystery Falls Cave (Tenn)	**316 feet**	**(96m)**
Mega Well (Ala)	**308 feet**	**(94m)**

TAG country has been described as one of the birthplaces of
vertical caving. (See Fig. 13.2, Mystery Falls Cave.) The
other birthplace is the deep pits of Mexico.

Mexican Pits. A good number of the deep pits in Mexico are
similar to the open air pits in TAG Country—but much deeper.
For example, the free fall depths from the usual rigging points
of three of the best known are:

• **El Sotano**	**1345 feet**	**(410m)**
• **Sotano de las Golandrinas**	**1094 feet**	**(334m)**
• **Hoya de las Guaguas**	**710 feet**	**(216m)**

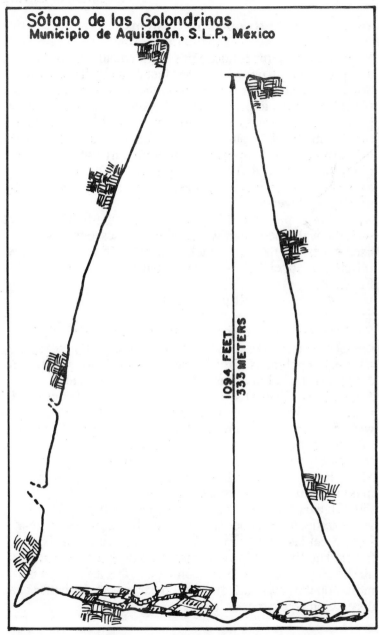

Fig. 13.3. Sotano de las Golandrinas (Pit of the
Swallows), near the city of Cuidad Valles, Mexico.

Rappelling Systems

Rappelling systems for deep pits work equally as well in any pit ranging from 50 to 1,000 feet or more. The key to doing really deep pits is a sewn (fail-safe) seat harness (see Chapter 10) to provide a secure, comfortable resting position. Seat harnesses are worn by 87% of NSS Vertical Section members (from a survey taken in January 1986.) To this seat harness, a rappel rack (preferred by 96% for deep pits) is attached with a high strength locking carabiner. A Spelean Shunt (see below) is used by many, but its use is by no means universal.

For shorter pits from 15 to 50 feet, particularly if in contact with the wall, the lighter weight Figure 8 descender is often used instead of the rappel rack. Past 50 to 75 feet, especially if free, the rappel rack is a more popular choice than the Figure 8.

Rappel Rack

For both medium and deep pits (50 to 1000 feet plus), the rappel rack is the descender most often used, as indicated above. Rappel racks (Fig13.5) are essentially long U-shaped devices with six brake bars. A five bar model is also available, but doesn't seem as popular. One of the legs ends in an eye, which is coiled, wrapped around the leg, or welded depending on brand. With the coiled type, be sure the coil continues clear around in a full circle. Most racks available today (mid 1986) are made by Blue Water and SMC. Rating of the welded eye SMC rack is 10,000 lbs, making it suitable for rescue applications.

Brake bars for rappel racks are of various types. Aluminum dissipates heat better, but leaves black marks on your rope. Steel lasts longer and doesn't leave marks, but is faster. The final choice is yours. I would guess, judging by all the black streaks I've seen on ropes, that aluminum is more popular, especialy for the top bar, where the better heat dissipation recommends it over steel.

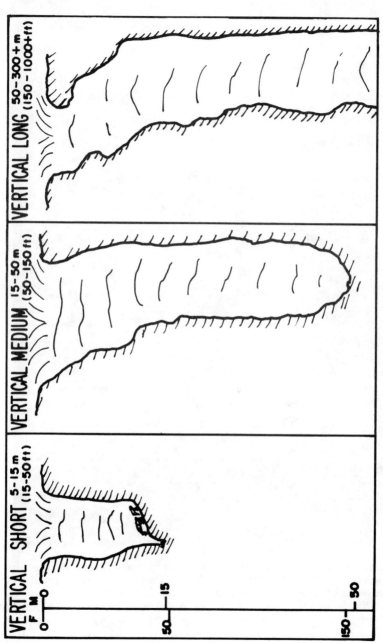

Figure 13.4. Vertical pits classed by depth.

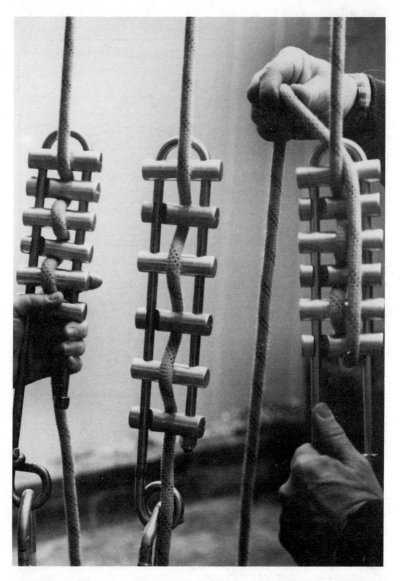

Fig. 13.5. Rappel racks. At left, bars have been shoved up tightly to stop descent. In middle, they are spread to allow movement (hand would normally be cradling rack, removed to show weaving in and out of rope on back of brake bars). At left, rope is being put between rope and rack to lock off rack for resting position. It is then brought down and wrapped around open leg of rack with hitches.

Types of Brake Bars

- Grooved or training, usually aluminum.
- Straight slot, aluminum or steel.
- Slanted or angled slot, aluminum or steel.
- Hollow steel, carbon or stainless.

When you buy a rack it may or may not have the bars already installed. If not (or if you want to change it around), here is the order of bars as recommended by SMC and others.

Recommended Order of Brake Bars

- Top bar: Grooved aluminum to route rope properly and dissipate heat better.

- Second bar: Straight slotted (aluminum or steel, grooved or not), to tell immediately if you've rigged it backwards (in a suicide rig).

- Third through sixth bars: Slanted slot, either aluminum or steel.

It's usually better to put the bars on the long leg rather than the short. This makes it easier to keep the fifth and sixth bars out of the way if you disengage them at the beginning of a very long drop. For a right handed person, the open side or short leg is normally on the right side, and visa versa for a lefty. Reason for this is it's better for the free end of the rope to exit on whichever side your lower hand will be on. The other hand cradles the rack.

Descent is best controlled by shifting the bars up and down with the left or cradling hand (if you're right handed), the other hand holding onto the rope at some point below the rack. This hand, can also control descent by pressing the rope against the hip, as with other rappelling devices. A third way to control descent is by adding and subtracting bars.

When you're learning, I don't especially recommend this

until you see how the rack feels with your own weight and
your own choice of bars. You'll find that except for really
long drops—300 feet plus—most average weight people will
need all six bars all the time. Over 300 feet, you often will
have to start with only four bars because of the weight of the
rope.

First Wrap Over Brake Bar. Note that the rope must
always be threaded so it passes over the top bar, not between
the steel rack and the top bar. This is important, because the
heat dissipating ability of aluminum is much better than steel
and where the rope first contacts the descender is where it's
hottest. Also, if you do it the wrong way, when you lock
the rack by wrapping the rope up over the oval end, the
standing part of the rope will pinch the overlapped end,
making it nearly impossible to unlock the rack.

   Heating of the first two bars can be a problem on long
drops (150 to 1000 feet). One good solution is to add two
3/4-inch aluminum tubing spacers to the rack frame between
bars one and two to keep the bars separated.

No Twist. An important footnote on the rack—it doesn't
put a twist in the rope the way a Figure 8 does. This is a real
plus if you have a lot of extra rope at the bottom of the drop.

Figure-8 Descender

For short and medium drops (less than 150 feet) the
lightweight Figure-8 has now captured a large share of the
market. These are available from many manufacturers: Russ
Anderson, CMI, Clog, and SMC among others. The Figure
8 is usually rigged with a single wrap. If this doesn't
provide enough friction, it can be rotated one or two full 360
degree turns to the left or right before clipping into the
carabiner. It can also be rigged with a second wrap for more
friction. (See Fig.13.5).

   A disadvantage of the Figure 8 is that it must be unclipped
from your carabiner to thread, which raises the possibility of
dropping it down the pit. Take care when rigging a Figure 8

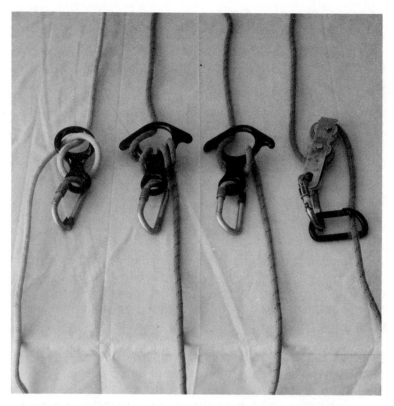

Figure 13.6. From left to right: 1. Figure 8 Descender in locked off position. 2. Figure 8 Descender with two wraps for added friction. 3. Figure 8 Descender with normal single wrap. 4. Petzl Descender with recommended second carabiner.

and don't forget to yell **Rock** if you're unfortunate enough to drop it.

A Figure 8 can be locked off by bringing the rope up over the top (again see Fig. 13.5). This isn't as easy as with a rack, but will give you a secure resting position. Further security can be provided by tying an overhand knot around the main line. You can also lock off a Figure 8 or any descender by wrapping the rope below the descender around your leg.

Rigging for the Twist. Another usually minor
disadvantage of the Figure 8—it puts a twist in the rope
below you. This won't usually be a problem if the rope only
had a few extra feet at the bottom. But if you have a lot of
excess length, you'd better leave it on the top when you rig if
you're doing a Figure 8 rappel. Otherwise, in a really
extreme case, you can get hung up some feet off the floor
and may have to have someone on the bottom unsnarl the
rope before you can continue. As indicated, the rack (and the
Petzl descender described next) don't suffer from this
malady.

Petzl Descender

A descender of quite different design is made by the French
caving outfitter Petzl. While widely used in Europe and
elsewhere, my January 1986 survey of the NSS Vertical
Section turned up only a single regular user of this
descender.

Actually, I guess I'm an irregular user. I bought one
several years ago for testing and evaluation and can
recommend it as a viable alternative to the Figure 8, if and
only if it is rigged with a second carabiner to add friction. I
say this because I had one unfortunate early incident when I
made the mistake of rigging it the way the instructions said
instead of asking an experienced user how to do it. Figure
13.6 shows it rigged properly with a second carabiner.
However, I am compelled to add that even today (mid 1986)
I still see drawings and photos in catalogs where it is rigged
without this safety carabiner.

Some may think this descender looks a little flimsy at first
glance (a characteristic many feel it shares with other Petzl
gear), but on closer examination it seems really well made. It
provides friction by two fixed capstans mounted between
vertical sides. One side swivels, so you can install it on the
rope. Note that the rope goes over the bottom capstan first
and exits from the top one. It's at that point that the second
carabiner is installed to add friction.

Actually, the Petzl has one major advantage over the Figure 8. It doesn't twist the rope. The version usually sold here has a hinged gate in one side so you can rig it without taking it off the line, another advantage over the Figure 8. An alternate self-locking version is fitted with a brake handle. All you do is let go and it stops you. It can also be disabled with a carabiner if you need that hand free.

My unfortunate incident was on a 110 foot rappel in Pinnacles National Monument where some California grottos have regular vertical training practice. I rigged it according to directions without routing the rope through the second carabiner shown in Figure 13.6. After stepping off the lip, I immediately found myself zipping down the face at a very rapid clip. I had taken the precaution of putting a spelean shunt on the line for this first rappel with a new device. So I locked it off, and came to a sudden stop. I still didn't know about the second carabiner rigging point, so the rest of my descent was interrupted several times by locking off the shunt to keep from going too fast.

Based on that experience and subsequent use of the Petzl, I can recommend it only if the second carabiner is installed.

Double Brake Bars.

One of the earliest rappelling devices was a pair of carabiners with brake bars. This set up is not widely used by cavers anymore because it has some real safety problems. The main one is that it loads the carabiners across the gate, their weakest part.

So I can't endorse carabiner break bars even for short drops. If you're ever in a situation where you have to use this descender, at least use the double version with two carabiners and bars, never a single carabiner brake bar. You're stacking the odds against yourself if you do this.

Spelean Shunt—Rappel Safety Device

The spelean shunt is an ingenious safety device invented by two Australian cavers. It uses standard and readily available

Fig 13.7. A 7 or 8mm sling or webbing loop attaches shunt to seat harness (and chest sling if worn), after first being threaded through hole in Gibbs cam. Carabiner also goes through cam. Sling should be long enough so shunt rides comfortably on top of descender. Weight of carabiner keeps cam from locking. After locking, shunt is released by pulling down on carabiner. For more leverage, a second short sling can be attached to outside end of carabiner as a pull cord.

Fig. 13.8. To install shunt, rope is first snapped through carabiner. Then Gibbs shell is slid onto rope and down through carabiner into its regular position over cam. Finally, quick-release pin is inserted so that non-gated (long) side of the carabiner rests on pin.

gear, a Gibbs ascender and a carabiner. It has answered a real
need for a backup during rappelling. You'll like the spelean
shunt for medium and deep drops. I would question whether
it's worth carrying it for short 20 to 50 foot pits, unless you
want to have it as a spare Gibbs ascender.

In the early days of cave rappelling (late 1950s and early
1960s), we sometimes used a separate belay line to safety the
rappeller. However, we soon found that a second line could
easily get tangled up and could be more hazardous than going
it alone.

Then several cavers (including me) started using the
so-called Prusik safety—a Prusik knot on the line with the
sling's other end attached to the seat harness. Problem here is
that unless you're close to the wall, you can get stranded in
mid air. With your full weight on the Prusik knot, there is
virtually no way to free it (for a person of average strength)
unless you have ascending gear to make a changeover.
Furthermore, if you're dangling from a chest sling or waist
loop (instead of a seat harness), the pressure on your internal
organs will literally kill you within about 30 minutes if the
squeezing isn't relieved.

Then along came the spelean shunt with a Gibbs and
carabiner in about 1977 (Fig. 12.7). Purpose of the
carabiner is to pivot on the Gibbs pin and provide the leverage
to release the Gibbs after the shunt has locked. It's simple
and it works. It does, however, take some practice to get
used to fitting it on the line until you've done it a few times.
See Fig 12.8 for specifics. A steel or heavy aluminum
carabiner is better because its weight will help keep the shunt
from locking. Additional weight may be why some people
also recommend a locking carabiner, but I have always used
standard carabiners.

Rides on Rack. In normal use, the shunt will ride above
your descender. If you were to pass out or get hit by a rock, it
will lock automatically. If you want to lock it yourself in an
emergency or to rest, just grab the Gibbs housing or the
carabiner and it will lock. Also be aware that the shunt may
lock unexpectedly near the top of the drop, if you jerk the line
suddenly or if it hits the wall when you have to squeeze

through a tight spot.

Be sure the sling is short enough so the shunt won't be out of your reach. To release, it helps if you can take your weight off the shunt for an instant, then pull down on the carabiner. If you're near the wall and have any kind of foothold, you can push up with your feet. You can also try wrapping the trailing line around your foot to step up for an instant. If you're free, you can bounce on the rope, though you may want to be really comfortable with your rappelling system and the shunt before you try this. If you can't relieve your full weight or have a lot of rope below you, you may need to attach a pull cord to get more purchase on the carabiner. This is a 12-inch diameter loop of 7 or 8 mm cord.

Rappelling Techniques

For short, long, and in between rappels—in other words all rappels— gloves are a necessity on both hands to prevent rope burn. To begin a rappel, stay well back from the edge of the drop and clip your descender into the locking carabiner on your seat harness. Face the anchor point with your back to the drop and the rope on your right side (or left side, if you are left-handed). Now, reach down, pick up the rope, and place a loop up through the descender (Practice the correct configuration in Figures 13.5 and 13.6 before you try this for real.)

This is a good time to check your rig. Start with the locking carabiner. Make sure you remembered to screw it finger-tight. Next, you should check the descender to be sure it's threaded right, particularly the brake bars in a rack. Watch out for the Suicide Rig with the rope on the wrong side of the bars. A sharp tug upward will usually ferret out this rigging error and should accompany your visual inspection.

Having checked these, you can move over to the edge of the drop. Here you should check again before stepping over the edge. It's surprisingly easy for the rappel line to loosen when you're moving around at the top of the drop and you

Figure 13.9. Rappelling against the wall with feet spread apart for balance. Rappeller looks over left shoulder to plan route down. Left hand is braking hand, right hand is above Figure 8 Descender for balance. Seat harness is from REI.

may lose tension. During the rappel, the pressure of the rope keeps everything in place. However it's also smart to check the rig on the way down, particularly, if stops are made on ledges.

Besides being a good safety practice, checking your rig at the top will increase your confidence and help stave off edge fright. Make no mistake about it, everybody suffers edge fright the first few times they rappel. But after practice, you learn to believe in your gear and the rope, and stepping over the edge becomes second nature.

On a rappel, be careful that the rappel rope doesn't run against your seat harness. The friction could fuse the nylon and cut right through it. Also check to be sure that hair, beard, clothing, and lamp wires are tucked away and won't get caught in the descender. This happens often with beginners and can be very dangerous and painful.

Over the Lip. Here are some specific hints for stepping out over the edge. With the rope taut between anchor point and your seat harness, step backwards with your legs spread as far apart as possible for comfort and balance. Then--and this is the hard part--just lean back and literally walk down backwards with your feet firmly planted on the rock face. As long as you're touching the wall it's not too bad after you get over the initial edge fright (Fig. 13.9)

But many cave drops are overhung. After a few feet, you suddenly find yourself some distance from the wall and must change to a free rappel.

As you start over the edge, lean back at a 45 degree or lower angle (Fig.13.10). Move down slowly to where the wall drops away, then plant your feet firmly and lean back further and further until the seat of your pants is slightly below your feet. When you first do this, you'll feel like you're hanging out there naked in the cold night air. Just go slowly, and trust your equipment. The next move is to flex your knees and gently let go with your feet. You will swing in slightly but only for a few feet if you have done it right. Don't push off hard and pendulum down in a big bouncy jump like they do in the movies. It puts huge loads on the

rope and anchor and begs for accidents to happen. Always
rappel slowly and steadily.

Avoid Sliding Sideways. When rappelling on a slope
or against the wall, resist the urge to slide or walk sideways
when you come to a ledge or overhang. Sliding sideways
can easily dislodge rocks and abrade the rope, negating the
purpose of rope pads. If you must move sideways, do it
with great caution.

Figure 8 Rappels. After inserting the rappel rope into a
Figure 8 or Petzl descender, tuck it against your right hip,
grasping it tightly in your right hand (left hip and hand, if
you're left-handed). The other hand rides slightly above the
descender—at chest or head height—and is used for balance,
not control. The hand on your hip is the braking hand and
must never let go of the rope. (The rappeller bracelet
described below can help prevent dropping.) Downward
movement is stopped quickly by bringing pressure with your
hand against the hip.

To get more friction, some cavers run the rope over the
shoulder and across the back to the opposite hip.
Alternatively , the rope can be run around the back to the
opposite hip. However, depending on your weight and the
length of rope, this may add too much friction and be less
comfortable.

There is also a safety problem with the opposite-hip
rigging. If you accidentally drop the rope it will tend to
return to the other side and may be out of reach of your
braking hand. This can happen with a same side rigging too.
A solution to this problem is the rappeller's bracelet. This is
a snug piece of elastic bungy cord worn around the wrist of
your braking hand with a carabiner snapped into it. The
rappel rope is run through this carabiner. Then, if your
braking hand drops the line, the bracelet keeps it within easy
reach. We have used this for years.

Rack Rappels. With a rack, the right hand can stay in
front near the descender since most of the control comes

Figure 13.10. To negotiate an overhang, brace feet firmly
and lower body until seat is even with or below feet.
Then gently flex knees and let go with feet. This puts
far less strain on rope and anchor than flashy jumping
and bouncing.

from the left hand fine tuning the bars up and down. Start
out with all six bars unless it's a drop of over 300 feet. If so
start with four bars and be sure you use a spelean shunt.
About half way down when you seem to be sailing along a
little too fast, lock off the shunt, pull up some rope, and
snap bars five and six into the rack. You can also lock off
the rack as shown in Figure 13.5 or by wrapping the trailing
rope around one leg.

At the beginning of the deep rappel, you may move so
slowly that you have to push the rope through the rack with
your right hand. If so, be sure to return your hand to its
normal position as soon as possible.

Also, during long rappels (over 300 feet), you may find
your legs going to sleep. To keep them awake, move them
in a bicycling or swinging motion. Or you can use foot
stirrups to support your feet and ankles and stand up once in
a while, like those shown in Fig. 13.11.

Figure 8 Loop Stopper Knot. On drops into pits of
unknown depth, put a knot in the end, in case the rope
doesn't reach the bottom. The best knot is a Figure 8 Loop
which will provide a convenient standing loop if you need to
rerig into a prusik to climb back up.

Bottom Belay. A very effective rappel belay can be run
from below by having someone hold the bottom of the rope.
In case of an accident, they can stop you by simply pulling
the rope taut. The natural straightening of the rope increases
the tension through the descender and will bring you to a
safe stop quite easily. However, belayer shouldn't stand
directly below the rappeller because of the danger of falling
rocks.

Changing over. What do you do if you get to the bottom
of the line and it's not the bottom of the drop? If you've
followed our advice so far you will come to a handy Figure
8 Loop in the end of the rope and step into it to take stock of
the situation.

Fig. 13.11. For drops of 300 to 1000 feet, foot stirrups help keep legs awake by giving feet something to push against and occasionally step up into to restore circulation. These stirrups are simply a Texas prusik system harness.

Dropping into pits of unknown depth is always risky business. The way to approach them is to be prepared. This means carrying your full vertical pack with you down the drop and using a spelean shunt or Jumar and sling to provide an easy resting position. It may even be expedient to wear your ascending gear on the way down so you can quickly change over to the other mode.

To make a changeover from rappel to prusik, the first step is to transfer your weight to your seat sling from your descender. If you are wearing a spelean shunt, this will already be attached to your seat sling, in the proper position above the descender. If not, take a safety loop sling (Chapter 10) from your bag of tricks and attach it above the descender with a Prusik knot. If you're a Jumar fan, you will probably prefer to attach your right Jumar to the line above the descender. For the moment, it is probably best not to derig the descender.

Next, attach your ascenders to the line, beginning with the bottom one, and stand up. This will allow you to derig the descender and begin ascending. If you are using a Gibbs as the top ascender or a chest box, the safety loop or spelean shunt will probably ride right above it.

Crossing a Knot. What happens when you have to cross a knot? First of all, we have to assume that the knot isn't going to come as a surprise. The reason a main rope has a knot in it is that it isn't long enough, so two ropes have to be tied together. This is an unusual enough occurrence that you're sure to have heard about it and are going to be ready for it. If you use ropes of different lengths, put the long rope at the top so the knot will be closer to the bottom. This reduces the weight of rope that has to pulled up during the crossing procedure.

To cross a knot when rappelling, you need to change over to your prusik gear, at least partially, prusik down past the knot, then change back over to rappel again. Obviously, it's easiest if you wear your prusiking gear on the way down, so you'll be all set. You may not have to use all your ascenders, but you'll have to at least partially changeover so you can get your weight transferred properly and not get hung up in midair.

The procedure differs slightly with Jumar and Gibbs systems and people of different heights. With Gibbs it's harder because you have to reach down and pull up the rope to put the bottom ascender on the line. This may be difficult if there much rope below you. It's easier with the Mitchell system, because the Jumars are right to hand. For that reason, you may want to choose the Mitchell system for pits where you have to use a knotted rope.

Fig. 13.12. Crossing a knot during rappel. I am attaching Figure 8 to seat carabiner after derigging rack, sitting in Jumar with short etrier, and attaching bottom Gibbs ascender to line. Next I will stand up on Gibbs to release Jumar and transfer weight to Figure 8 to continue rappel.

Fig 13.13. Body or hot seat rappel. Rope passes between legs, across hip and chest to opposite shoulder, then across back to right or braking hand. To stop, bring right hand against hip (and try not to scream too loudly from the pain). OK for against the wall and not more than 20 feet or so.

Essentially, what you do is to stop about a body length above the knot. This leaves you room to put on one or more ascenders and detach your rappel device (see Fig. 13.12). Then you slowly descend on your ascender(s), and one by one, pass them and the rack or Figure 8 below the knot. You can sit on your spelean shunt or a Jumar and sling while transferring the equipment below the knot.

Then, you step up on one of the ascenders, to release the shunt or Jumar and transfer your weight back to the descender. I suggest that you also change from rack to Figure 8 descender when crossing a knot. It's a lot easier to put a Figure 8 back on the line and to step up and release the shunt or Jumar above it than it is with a rack. If you can manage to have the knot closer to the bottom than the top, the Figure 8 should not overheat during the rest of the rappel

Though it sounds complicated, it really isn't all that hard if you carry a spare Jumar, spelean shunt, or some safety loops. You just have to go through the steps in a certain order. Needless to say, above ground is where you iron out the wrinkles.

The Body Rappel. I left for last the hot seat or body rappel (Fig. 13.13). Ancient though it may be, you should still learn how to do it for use in emergencies (if mechanical devices fail), or for short pitches where it's too much trouble to get rigged up. A body rappel is often done with a doubled rope since it is assumed the drop is short, and the doubled line will be used as a hand line on the way out. You can do a body rappel with a single rope too, but it's even more uncomfortable.

The reason for the discomfort, as can be seen by Fig. 13.13,   is that the rope contacts the body directly in four rather sensitive places: the crotch, the right rear cheek, the chest, and the left shoulder. Because of the resulting friction, not too many cavers would voluntarily choose the body rappel except in a real pinch. But learn it anyway, it's easy and not too bad if you stay against the wall.

———————

14

Ascending

Ascending is coming back up the rope using one of the three prusiking techniques described in this chapter.

During the growth of vertical caving over the past two and a half decades, prusiking equipment and systems have gone through any number of permutations and combinations. In case you're keeping score, three systems now seem to have emerged as the most popular on this side of the Atlantic:

- **Mitchell Jumar system for great versatility.**

- **Gibbs Ropewalker for long free drops.**

- **Texas Jumar system for short drops.**

By a happy coincidence, these are the three systems I regularly use and, as you might have guessed, that I use for the very same applications listed above. Before describing

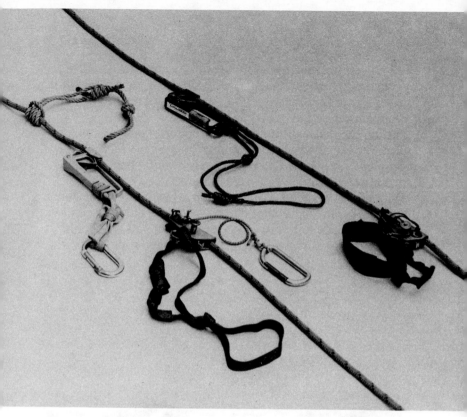

Fig. 14.1. Ascenders: Right hand rope, bottom: Gibbs ascender, attached to two inch stirrup for right foot with sewn-on chicken loop. Top: CMI-5000 ascender with 7 millimeter Perlon cord. Left hand rope, bottom: Gibbs ascender with sling for left foot and elastic bungy cord with carabiner to float ascender. Middle: Old type gray Jumar with properly tied sling (see also Fig. 14.2). Top: Prusik knot in 3/8 inch polypropylene.

the systems themselves, let's take a fast look at the gear that makes these systems possible.

Mechanical Ascenders

In the beginning, as they say, it was knots. At one point there were more than 16 different variations of the   simple Prusik knot vying for the affections of vertical cavers. Today, knot prusiking is still around, but mostly for contests and emergency use. It continues to be taught by the NSS Vertical Section at its annual workshop, because many of us believe it's a skill that every fully trained vertical caver needs to be familiar with.

But in the real world of the unlit underground, I think it would be fair to say that mechanical ascenders have completely replaced Prusik knots for coming back up the rope to see the light of day once more.

Modern ascenders fall into two broad categories: the Jumar ascender—plus its several clones—and the Gibbs ascender (Fig. 14.1). Despite differences in design, all ascenders share the common attribute of sliding up the rope easily, then

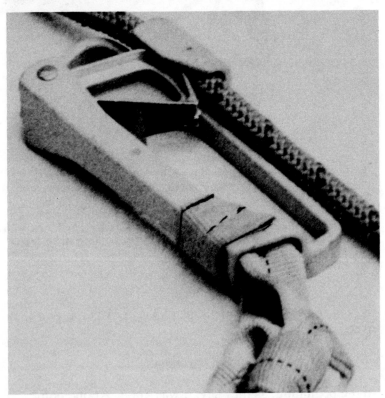

Fig. 14.2 Old type gray Jumar with sling properly threaded around back (strongest part) of frame then down through hole in bottom. Carabiner is attached to sling not directly to Jumar bottom brace.

gripping it securely when weight is applied. As you are aware, this is the same action as the Prusik knot.

Jumar Ascenders

Jumars were the first mechanical ascenders and remain very popular with climbers and cavers. They consist of a cast-aluminum frame and a steel spring-loaded cam. One side of the frame forms a convenient handle, useful not only for shoving them skyward, but also as a hand hold on the rope. The Jumar's big advantage over the Gibbs is they are much easier to put on and take off the line. With a little practice, you can do it one-handed.

This is a real plus when you need to come up over a lip, pass a knot, or have to deal with multiple drops. To help keep the ascender on the line, a plastic safety catch is provided. Always be sure this is in the locked position before applying your weight. Be especially careful when grasping the Jumar handle that you don't accidentally unlock the safety catch.

Another benefit of Jumars is that if you have to go back down the rope a few steps, it's a lot easier with a Jumar than a Gibbs. You often need to do this, and while it can be done with a Gibbs too if you practice it, it's simpler with a handled ascender. Jumars are designed to work on ropes from 6 to 13 mm. They are sold singly in right and left hand versions and in pairs, at a cost of about sixty to sixty five dollars per pair.

The Jumar available today is the yellow one. It's nearly twice as strong as the older gray model (1100 vs 660 lbs), and has an improved cam and safety catch. The tie off points at top and bottom were also strengthened and are now safe to tie into directly. These improvements take care of the very two problems with the gray one that I'm going to talk about in the Caution paragraphs next.

Caution: Sling tie off: If you're still using the older grey Jumars, there is an important safety precaution to be conscious of. Never attach a sling or carabiner directly to the bottom brace. On a gray Jumar, this brace is much weaker

than the main frame. It's also the spot most likely to be
damaged from a drop or sudden shock loading. Instead,
thread the sling up through the hole in the handle and around
the back as shown in Fig. 14.1 and14.2.

   Similarly, the top hole on the gray model is not strong
enough to support your full weight. It is OK, however,
for attaching the bungy cord in floating ascender rigs

Caution: Operating at an Angle. The second precaution with
the older gray Jumar is when it's operated
at an angle on the rope—as on a traverse or when ascending
a slope. At an angle, the gray Jumars occasionally may pop
off the line. You can counteract this very easily by clipping
a carabiner between the bottom of the Jumar and the rope on
traverses or slope. The safety clip on new yellow Jumar and
the other handled ascenders seems to take care of this bad
habit that the gray model has.

   A final safety note while we're at it. Be especially careful
not to drop a Jumar, gray or yellow. The cast aluminum
frame is somewhat brittle and could develop hairline cracks
if dropped any distance.

Safety Jumar. Because they're so easy to put on the rope,
many vertical cavers carry a Jumar—called a safety
Jumar—for difficult maneuvers like nasty lips, changeovers,
or crossing knots. A safety Jumar is equipped with a sling or
etrier which is normally clipped to the seat harness, the
Jumar itself either dangling below or nestled in a handy
pocket. Needless to say, any of the handled ascenders can
fill this role in addition to the Jumar itself.

Other Handled Ascenders. Several Jumar type ascenders
have made their appearance in recent years. One of the first
was the CMI ascender (latest model, the CMI 5003) from
Colorado Mountain Industries. Made from machined
aluminum alloy, it's often touted for rescue applications,
since it tests at 5000 lbs. Three strong tie-off points are
provided, two on the bottom and one on top. A trifle heavier

and priced at about seventy dollars per pair, they compete directly with Jumars.

Three other handle type ascenders are the Clog Expedition Ascender, the Petzl Handled Ascender, and the Bonaiti Ascender. All three, but particularly the Clog, are big enough to operate with gloves or mittens. The Bonaiti (see Figure 14.3) is the newest entry into the handled ascender sweepstakes. It features a swiveling mechanism on the handle side that applies your weight to lock the cam much like a Gibbs does. I have now converted my Mitchell system

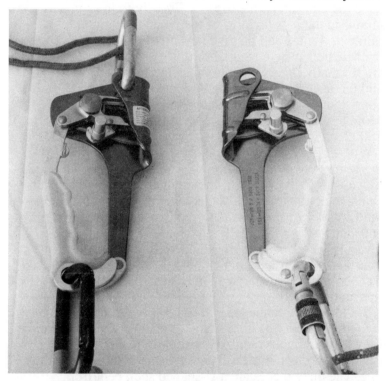

Figure 14.3 Bonaiti ascenders with swiveling handle assembly which holds the cam against the rope by body weight (as does the Gibbs) rather than a spring tension for better reliability. Handles are florescent material. Attached slings are for my Mitchell system.

to Bonaitis, and so far they seem to work out very well. The handles are phosphorescent by the way, which is helpful until the mud takes over.

Gibbs Ascenders

Gibbs ascenders were first introduced in the late 1960's, and have become very popular with cavers (and rescue teams) in North America because they offer several advantages.

Probably the stellar attraction of the Gibbs is that it doesn't have to be raised up the rope. It literally follows you as you climb, so the legs do most of the work. (Although in fairness, I must add that the legs do most of the work with the Mitchell system too). For this reason, Gibbs ascenders are for many cavers the most comfortable, the least tiring, and the fastest way to go up a rope. Gibbs systems consistently win the climbing contests at NSS conventions. More to the point, for really long drops from say 300 to 1000 feet, the Gibbs ropewalker is generally the favorite.

With a Gibbs, your feet and chest are attached directly to the cams. As you raise them, the cam comes up with them. Since your body weight, rather than a spring, operates the cams, the Gibbs will almost never slip, even on wet, muddy, or icy rope. Furthermore, wear on both the rope and cams is less, because there is no drag from spring pressure on the rope as they're moved upward. Also, since your hands are free from the duty of raising ascenders, you have both hands available to push away from the wall   at lips and overhangs.

But like everything else in life, you give something to get something. With the Gibbs, you give up ease of installation for a less strenuous climb. Because of the three piece construction, you must use both hands to put them on the line. The three pieces are a U-shaped shell bent from aluminum plate or optionally stainless steel, a cast aluminum or optionally forged cam, and a stainless steel quick release pin. (An earlier model with a very iffy wire spring on the outside has been discontinued). All three pieces are attached together (in the current models), so you aren't in any danger of dropping them.

Prices for a pair of Gibbs start at about forty-five dollars. They work with ropes up to one half inch in diameter and are individually tested to 1000 lbs at the factory.

Chest Ascender Boxes. Ascender boxes are now widely used with Mitchell and ropewalker systems because they make a big improvement in your climbing efficiency (See Fig. 14.4). They do this by keeping your body as nearly upright and as close to the line as possible. The Simmons roller functions the same way. Believe me, climbing a rope with and without a box is like night and day.

Just so we all understand—any energy you have to use to pull yourself back up (or back over) to the line is wasted energy. Put another way, any energy expenditure that doesn't contribute to taking you straight up the rope cuts your climbing efficiency.

Boxes have two sections: the main rope goes through one slot and keeps you snugged up tight against it. The other slot is for the upper Jumar sling of the Mitchell system. It routes the sling from the top Jumar down through the box to the right foot. This also keeps helps keep you tight against the line. The Simmons roller is for ropewalker systems and has a single channel for the main rope.

Besides the single-channel Simmons roller, the only two-channel box currently available commercially, is the Gossett (about thirty to thirty five dollars). It's ruggedly made of aluminum with four brass locking screws and nylon rollers. Another box, from Blue Water has been out of production for some time. A new chest box, made by John Blum of Portland Oregon, is still in the prototype stage. Its lighter weight and quick release operation have promise of making it a contender to the Gossett.

Speaking of operating, here's a tip for the Gossett box. I always tighten the knurled knobs finger tight, then back them off about a quarter to a half turn. This helps to keep the aluminum from seizing, and makes the screws much easier to open at the top of the drop or when loaded.

Chicken Loops. Chicken or security loops for your boots are needed for all vertical systems (see FIg. 14.8). I prefer one inch tubular nylon sewn in loops 6 to 7 inches long[1], but have also used 6 millimeter Perlon tied in a loop with a grapevine knot. They should be big enough to fit over the ankle of your boot snugly.

---

1. All loop lengths quoted are linear lengths measured end to end, after the sling has been doubled, then tied or sewn.

Fig 14.4. Chest boxes keep you close to the rope and increase climbing efficiency. At left, Gossett Box has four nylon rollers tightened by knurled knobs. At right, prototype of a lighter weight box made by John Blum with single quick release pin.

Besides holding the ascender slings in place, chicken loops have an important safety function. They keep you attached to the loop and the line if you should turn upside down. That's why you don't want to use bungy cord or rubber strips cut from an inner tube. I always leave my chicken loops inside my boots. That' s the only way I can be sure of finding the blasted things when I need them.

Mechanical Ascender Systems

Of the many ascending systems, the three described here have stood the test of time and have evolved into safe, versatile climbing aids. These are the Mitchell, Double Bungy Gibbs (both cams floating), and the Texas. Try each out for yourself if you can before deciding which is best for you. Almost everybody ends up modifying a basic system one way or another. So consider what's presented here not as the final word, but as a starting point for your system.

Mitchell System

In my view, the Mitchell is probably the most versatile system in the world for vertical caving. You can use it for long, short, or medium pits, and anything in between. For really long drops, it's almost as good as the Gibbs ropewalker. In fact, even though the two systems are configured very differently, the actual climbing motions are very similar. In both, your body remains nearly upright and you literally walk up the rope.

If you use both systems as I do, you can sometimes absentmindedly forget which one you're rigged into. That is, until you suddenly realize you have to shove up the Jumars to get going. Just raising your feet doesn't do it. And it's this added exertion of raising the ascenders that makes the Mitchell more taxing than a Gibbs system for some cavers—especially those who only do free pits or don't need the versatility of the Mitchell.

And for the complex multi-drop/multi-swim river systems of Mexico and North America, the Mitchell is the choice for many cavers. Finally, if you have a short drop where you need to be away from the rope (like in a water fall), you can convert the Mitchell into the Texas system right on the spot (see below for the specifics).

Basic System. In its basic form, the Mitchell is a two Jumar system with a chest box (Fig.14.5). My present system is two Bonaiti ascenders with a Gossett box . The climbing rope and right foot-sling go through separate left and right channels in the box. As a third ascender, I tie my safety loop in a Prusik knot above the box where it just rides along. Many cavers put their spelean shunt above the box to perform the same duty. When I want to rest, I shove up the Prusik knot, and sit in my seat harness.

For added safety, I link the the top hole of the lower ascender to my seat harness with a short 13 inch loop. In action, I usually end up raising the ascender with this cord rather than its handle, which is very convenient.

My slings are doubled 6mm Perlon cord. I put the right foot on the upper ascender, but it could be the left, it's all the same. The right sling wants to be just long enough to keep the upper Jumar above the chest harness when you're standing on the floor with both feet. I also have a separate Perlon cord (6mm) from the upper ascender to my seat sling. I can also rest on this sling by sliding the top ascender up high. The lower or left sling should place the Jumar as low as you can reach comfortably.

For your information in making your own slings, mine are doubled 6mm Perlon tied into loops with a Grapevine knot. The longer loop is 62 inches long. That's after knotting, so you need twice that plus another 18 inches for the knot. The loop for the lower ascender is 27 inches long. This means you should start with about 20 feet total if you're about 5 feet 8 inches as I am.

Walls and Lips. Climbing with the Mitchell when you're up against the wall can be difficult if the Jumars jam into the

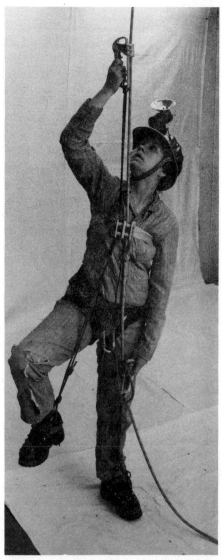

Fig. 14.5. My daughter Molly demonstrates the fine points of her Mitchell system (although it was a single bungy Gibbs she used for Guaguas). It has two Jumar ascenders and a Gossett box. Seat harness is REI. Short sling from seat harness to bottom Jumar adds safety and convenient pull cord. For additional safety and a resting position, Molly adds Spelean shunt above box to system shown here.

rock. A relatively easy way to solve this is to put your shoulder against the wall and turn a little sideways when you first contact the wall. You can also fend off the wall with one hand and move the ascenders up with the other.

At lips and overhangs, the chest box keeps you tight up against the rock. (The strategies given below are equally useful for a ropewalker with a box or Simmons Roller). The secret here is to come out of the box one or two steps below the lip. Many beginners go too high and get bent over the lip (see Fig. 14.6A). If you're too high to maneuver, go back down one or two steps before you do anything else. To come out of your box safely, you need to first attach your safety Jumar onto the line above the lip. The Jumar should already be clipped into your seat harness before you reach the lip. I usually hook mine in at the bottom and let it (and my pack) hang below me.

With safety Jumar hooked in, the line can be taken out of the box (and the upper ascender cord, too, if you're secure). This done, you can push away from the lip with both hands, step up in your ascenders, and muscle on over. It's not quite as easy as it sounds until after you've practiced it a few times, but the technique is fundamental to vertical caving.

A minor difference between the performance of Mitchell and Gibbs systems at lips is worth mentioning here. Since both use a chest box, the strategy is the same at first. But after the box is safely off the line, it's a mite easier to climb with a Jumar system than a Gibbs—if there are footholds to climb with. This is because the feet, especially the right or lower foot, are not tied directly to the line with a Jumar system. They are freer to probe around and seek foot holds than the rope-bound Gibbs feet. This isn't a major consideration, but I have chosen the Mitchell over the Gibbs when I knew the lip called for some acrobatics with obscure foot holds at the top.

Rigging a Tail. To make this a real piece of cake, when rigging, I often put a ten or 15 foot tail of the main line down the drop complete with Jumar and sling (Fig.14.6B) . As a little nicety, I may tie a Figure 8 loop at the bottom of the

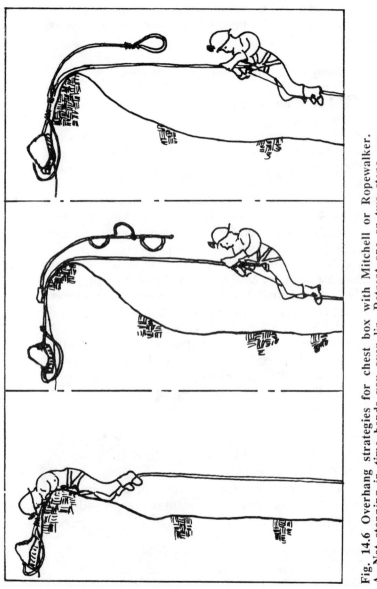

Fig. 14.6 Overhang strategies for chest box with Mitchell or Ropewalker.
A. Not stopping in time bends you over lip. Retreat one or two steps and attach safety Jumar for security before removing rope from chest box.
B. When rigging, leave tail and Jumar with etrier to clip seat harness into.
C. Tie loop in tail to attach pack, clip seat harness into, or use for foot hold.

tail. Then, if anyone needs help with a pack, they can hook it onto the tail, do the lip, and then pull up the pack (Fig. 14.6C). The loop can also be used as a foot hold to help get over the lip.

Double Bungy Floating Cams Gibbs System

Although the Mitchell system deserves high marks for long drops, the double bungy Gibbs system is the best I've ever used (Fig.14.7). Key element is the quarter-inch bungy cord that floats both Gibbs. It's attached to the shell of the lower Gibbs, then runs up through a pulley on the chest harness and back to the shell of the knee Gibbs.

With the tension of the bungy, the cams move up the rope smoothly and effortlessly with none of the kicking out or twisting of the feet required for non-floating systems. I use the standard quick release Gibbs, not the spring loaded version for this system. The chest box is a Gossett, serving double duty for both my Mitchell and Gibbs systems.

Instead of a box, some systems use a chest or shoulder mounted Gibbs. These work fine, but don't keep you quite as close to the line as a box, so they lose some efficiency.

I have used this rig for more than five years now, and it's the best I've ever had for long free drops. It was evolved by several of us in the NSS San Francisco Bay Chapter prior to and after Christmas trips to Mexico's deep pits in 1979 and 1980. Before this, I floated just the left or knee Gibbs. For the right foot, I had the cam sewn into a two inch foot stirrup (Fig. 14.8). I went to the double bungy because the single bungy still requires you to kick out with the right (lower) foot to lock the cam. I tried the spring loaded Gibbs for that foot, but it still slipped sometimes. The double bungy locks the cams every time, so you can concentrate on ascending, not your equipment's eccentricities.

Foot Mountings. For the right foot, the Gibbs is tied to the top of a two inch webbing stirrup with a four inch loop of 6mm Perlon tied with a Grapevine. This top mounting is more comfortable than the side mounting required when you have to kick out to lock a non-floating right Gibbs. A one inch webbing chicken loop with a buckle is sewn on the sides of the foot stirrup to secure it to the ankle.

The left or knee Gibbs is positioned at about knee level by a doubled length of one-inch webbing which when tied is about 18 inches long. Mine is made from about seven feet of webbing, first run through the eye of the Gibbs cam, then tied into a loop with a Water knot. To attach it to the boot, tie a Figure 8 Loop in the end, snug enough to fit tightly over your boot. A chicken loop (Fig. 14.8) keeps the sling secure on the boot just in case.

Bungy Cord. To attach the quarter-inch bungy cord to the Gibbs, I tied an overhand loop in the ends of the bungy. Then, in one of the small holes already drilled in the side at the top of the Gibbs, I put a mini-Rapid Link. These are about 1 1/4 inches long and can be found in hardware and auto supply stores. I don't know how strong they are, but I've never had one break.

While I was at it, I replaced the metal chain connecting the quick release pin to the shell with a nylon cord about 1/8 inch in diameter. It connects to the mini-Rapid Link also with an overhand loop in the end. The metal chain is too short anyway, so by substituting a longer cord, you can put the pin in on either side of the shell. This is a godsend and worth doing even if you don't float the Gibbs. Finally, with a 1/4 inch countersink in an electric drill, I beveled the edges of the cam holes on both sides of the cam (the hole the quick release pin goes through) in both Gibbs. This makes it much less of a struggle to install the pin when the whole assembly is at some weird angle, which it often is.

Top Ascender. For my top ascender I use a Prusik knot or a spelean shunt just like with my Mitchell set up. Either one just rides above the Gossett box until needed for resting. This third ascender is highly recommended to give you better odds in case of equipment failures.

Fig. 14.7. Double bungy Gibbs System floats both cams. From left bottom: right foot stirrup has sewn chicken loop around ankle and short Perlon loop to foot Gibbs; Bungy cord from foot Gibbs goes up through pulley below chest harness and back down to knee Gibbs. Knee Gibbs floats above left foot by 18 inch webbing sling secured by chicken loop on left ankle. Rope (10mm PMI) goes through Gossett box. Prusik knot to seat harness rides above box for safety and resting.

Ascending Techniques. Now that you've got yourself
lashed to the line, how do you get off the ground? It's
simple. Just walk up the rope. At the bottom, it's helpful to
have someone give tension on the end of the rope. If you're
last, however, you need another strategy. Many people give
themselves self-start tension by making a big loop in the rope
and pulling it tight under the left boot. A new wrinkle of
mine is to route the rope up through a carabiner attached

**Fig. 14.8 At right, floating knee Gibbs sling around sole of boot
secured by Chicken loop around ankle. At left, side mounting Gibbs
stirrup with sewn-in cam as used in a single bungy system.**

to your chest harness (see Fig. 14.9). This makes it much less strenuous to keep the loop tight under your left boot. After you get up 15 or 20 feet, the weight of the rope is usually enough to give your ascenders the right tension— usually, but not always. So don't drop the end of the rope completely until you're sure.

Lips. To get over lips the procedure is very much like the Mitchell system, because both use a chest box. See Fig. 14. and accompanying discussion for some hints on overhang strategies.

Texas System

For short pits in the range of 20 to 50 feet, many people swear by the Texas system (Fig. 14.10 and 14.11). This is a sit-stand system, similar to what the Europeans call the frog system because of the two stage amphibian like motions. It requires a minimum of equipment and is easy to learn. Sling lengths are not as critical as with some other systems, so the Texas is often chosen for group use or training.

Some cavers can use it successfully for much longer drops. But I find it far too strenuous beyond 50 feet or so. Although it has an automatic resting position half of the time—you just stay sitting when you want to rest—it does make you raise yourself up completely from a sitting position every cycle. This is far more tiring and less efficient than the Mitchell or Gibbs systems where you remain upright, glued to the rope.

Two Jumars. The Texas calls only for a seat harness with locking carabiner, two Jumars and two simple slings. The top Jumar attaches to your seat harness with a loop about 12 to 15 inches long. I use a safety loop (Chapter 10) which, in case you've forgotten, is about five to six feet of 7mm Perlon tied with a Grapevine knot. To add a degree of safety and keep the bottom Jumar in tow, I connect it to my seat harness. For this, I shorten the safety loop with a Figure 8 knot about a third of the way down, making two loops out of it. Then I run the shorter loop from my seat carabiner over to the carabiner on the bottom Jumar (see Fig. 14.10).

For the feet, I tie webbing into a dual foot sling. A locking carabiner attaches the lower Jumar to the sling. Many people are happy with a single foot sling, tied in webbing, like the 12 foot caver's sling I suggest you carry. A single loop is fine for really short drops. Or for longer ones, you can switch feet if the first foot gets tired.

To tie the dual foot sling, I use about 12 feet of one inch tubular webbing. First double it and tie the doubled part at the top into a double Figure 8 Loop. Put a locking carabiner in this loop for the lower Jumar. Then tie the lower corners of the sling with Figure 8 loops big enough to fit over your boots snugly (see Fig. 14.9).

To add an additional measure of safety to the Texas system—especially for deeper pits of 50 to 150 feet— a third ascender can be included. A Gibbs, positioned above the top ascender, will ride there and should hardly be noticed. A good way to attach it is via a chest sling which in turn is doubled down to the seat sling.

Converting from the Mitchell System. This conversion between ascending systems can be made in the field, as the military manuals used to say. In cave talk, that means at the bottom of a 30 foot waterfall drop where you need a system that won't keep you against the rope (and in the water all the time), like the Mitchell would.

This is a simple conversion, but as with everything else, it's best to try it above ground in the light of day, not 14 hours into the cave.

For most people, the short Mitchell sling for the left foot can stay just where it is. Or if you don't have it on, it can be installed the same way as for the Mitchell or you can put it on the right foot if you prefer. If it seems a little long, just tie a Figure 8 knot in it to temporarily shorten it.

The longer right-foot Mitchell sling needs to be shortened and attached to your seat harness carabiner. It plays the sitting role in your sit-stand drama, so be sure the Jumar isn't out of reach from your sitting position. I simply tie a Figure 8 knot about half way down on the long sling and

Figure 14.9. Self start technique runs rope under left boot and up through carabiner on chest harness. Carabiner helps maintain constant pressure on under-boot loop and keeps tension on ascenders.

clip the seat harness in there. Mine works out to be about 20 inches from Jumar to REI seat harness. Yours is bound to be different, but try a knot half way as a starting point and adjust to fit.

Special Techniques

Both these special techniques—changing over and crossing a knot—have to be learned by actually doing them. The best way, is in practice sessions above ground beginning with a demonstration by an instructor. Then, you need to get on the rope with your own rig and go through the steps yourself. The words below will familiarize you with the steps, but on-the-rope practice is the only way to really learn them.

Changing Over. To change from going up to going down, the key element is a safe comfortable resting position so you can thrash around with no danger of falling. This could be a safety loop tied off above the chest box or ascender with a Prusik knot, a safety Jumar, or a spelean shunt if you have one riding above your box. As with a rappel to prusik changeover, the first thing you do is to shift your weight to the seat harness via the upper tie off at the Prusik knot, Jumar, or shunt.

To get slack to rig the descender when you're in a Gibbs rig, remove the rope from the box (or upper Gibbs from the line) and bring some rope up through the foot and knee Gibbs. Don't take them off the line yet. If you're in a Mitchell rig, pull some rope up through the lower Jumar.

Next attach your rappel device to your seat carabiner (if it's not already there). I might add that this procedure is a whole lot easier with a Figure 8 or Petzl descender than with a rack, because a rack is so much longer it takes up a lot of the rope between seat harness and upper tie off.

Then, use the slack to rig in the descender as high as possible below the upper tie off at the Prusik knot, Jumar, or shunt. Step up on the lower ascender, loosen the upper tie off, and shift your weight onto the descender. Don't remove the upper tie off yet. Just leave it on the line for a minute more until you're sure all is well.

Transferring your weight to the descender should be easy if you have gotten the descender as high as possible when you rigged it a moment before. If not, sit back down and rig it over again, being sure to remove all of the upper slack below the tie off. Just be careful you don't jam it up tight against it.

When your weight is successfully transferred to the rappel device, you can take the lower ascender(s) off the line. Be sure to loosen the Prusik knot or remove the Jumar. If you've been using a spelean shunt, it will just come along for the ride on the way back down. Be especially careful not to lock the Prusik or Jumar when you're moving around or you may get trapped in midair. If so you'll have to put a lower ascender back on the line and stand up again.

Changing Over—Prusik to Rappel

1. **Attach safety Jumar (upper tie off) and sit in seat harness.**

2. **Loosen ascenders to get slack for descender.**

3. **Rig descender as high as possible below upper tie off and attach to seat harness.**

4. **Step up in lower ascender and loosen upper tie off.**

5. **Transfer weight to descender.**

6. **Remove ascenders and upper tie off from line and begin rappel.**

Crossing Knots. Crossing a knot in the rope while ascending is relatively easy with Jumar systems, but can be a struggle with Gibbs if there is considerable weight of rope below you. With that in mind, it's worth saying again here, that if you are going to be knotting two ropes of different lengths, give yourself a break and put the knot closer to the

Figure 14.10. Texas System, easy to rig and learn, but tiring for drops over 50 feet. Sitting position of sit-stand system shows Molly McClurg holding rope below lower ascender to aid in raising it. Note safety features: Chicken loops on boots, lower ascender looped to seat harness, tied seat sling instead of diaper sling, locking carabiners to CMI 5000 ascenders.

Fig. 14.11. Standing position of Texas sit-stand system. As she stands, Molly raises upper ascender attached to seat harness at same time.

bottom than to the top. That way, there will be less rope to haul up and rethread through ascenders and descenders and what all.

When you encounter a knot with Jumars, since they're well within reach of the center of your body, you pretty much move them one at a time past the knot and continue on. A separate Jumar safety may prove valuable for a third point on the line or to rest.

With Gibbs, the first step is to put a Jumar (or Prusik knot or spelean shunt) above the knot so you have a secure sitting position. Then you can walk up a bit, remove and reset your chest box or upper Gibbs, followed by your knee Gibbs, above the knot.

The bottom Gibbs will be harder because it's down low and if there's much rope weight below you, it may be a fight. Practice this above ground with weights on the rope until you're proficient so you don't get hung up in a cave.

If you're climbing in tandem on a long drop with someone else on the line below you, you probably won't be able to loosen the lower Gibbs. In this case, the person below can prusik up to you, remove your bottom Gibbs, and reset it for you above the knot. Just what that person will do about the knot is problematical, unless it's a Jumar user. If so, be sure the Gibbs caver is on top and the Jumar caver below.

Crossing a Knot When Ascending

1. Stop 12-18 inches below knot and attach safety Jumar above knot.

2. Ascend one or two steps.

3. Reset box and upper ascender above knot.

4. Sit in seat harness.

5. Pull up rope, reset lower ascender above knot.

6. Bon Voyage.

Emergency Systems. In a pinch,how many ascenders do you need to get up the line? If you have only two ascenders of any type, you can try the Texas System. Start from the sitting position. If one of the two ascenders you have is a Gibbs, put it on the seat sling. The handled Jumar type is better for above as an assist in standing up.

If you have only one ascender, what can you do? Put the ascender on the seat sling. Use the rope itself as a foot loop by wrapping it around your foot. Then stand up, raise your seat sling (or let it ride up if it's a Gibbs), and make another foot loop. If you have no ascenders, try taking a bight of the rope, attach it back up on itself with a Prusik knot and clip that into your seat sling. Make the end a foot loop as above.

You have no protection with any of these, but in a real emergency they sure beat trying to climb hand-over-hand.

Special Hints for Long Drops

Hanging on a single cord of nylon hundreds of feet above the floor and from the nearest wall—talk about being lonely. This is where training and practice pay off. So if it's lonely going down, what about coming up. It's more so. Here are some specifics to get ready for the big ones.

First of all, you need to get used to the weight of a long rope on your rack and ascending system. At a convenient short drop of 20 or 30 feet, attach a couple of spare tires or other weights equaling about 40 or 50 lbs. You'll see that you'll have to start with only four bars or you won't move at all. About half way down, have someone cut the weight in half, and try to put the two other bars back on the rack. It's not as easy as you thought. A spelean shunt is a help here to get the weight off the rack.

Then put on your prusik gear, proceed up the line, and try to get over the lip with the full weight on the bottom. If you don't succeed, try putting down a short tail and transfer your weight to the tail via a safety Jumar to your seat harness. Also, do a changeover and cross a knot with the weight on the line. Try this routine once a week during the long winter months until you get used to the extra weight.

To avoid fighting rope weight at the lip of a deep pit, put a short line (100 feet or so) down the drop. Don't forget to tie a Figure 8 Loop in the end as a stopper knot. Then rappel down to about ten feet above the knot and transfer to the longer line to finish the descent. First put your spelean shunt on the other line, transfer your weight to it, then pull up some slack in the main line and transfer your descender. Release the shunt, and you're on your way. When you come back up, transfer back to the shorter line and use that to cross the lip without such a heavy weight below you.

Counting your Steps. Pacing yourself is very important on deep drops. When coming up a long drop, I take very short steps of six to eight inches. I try to climb for 100 steps, then rest for a count of 60. After five or six cycles, I may not be able to do 100 steps every time and have to settle for 75 or 80. The routine of counting gives you something to think about. After you leave the bottom, there is a long lonely time when it doesn't seem as if you're making any progress. Counting helps break it up. Then suddenly, the walls get closer and the top seems a reality at last.

Practicing Prusiking. To practice ascending, a rig with a rescue pulley mounted 15 to 30 feet above the ground is often used. Select a climbing rope of anywhere from 150 to 1200 feet. From the pulley, run the short end of the rope down to the climber. On the other side of the pulley, run the rope through a rack so that another person can give tension and assure a steady flow of rope. Attach the rack to a fixed point (like a tree or a strong wall fixture in a gym) with a sling and carabiner. Be sure the main body of rope is coiled very loosely or set in long, lazy bights on the floor so it won't tangle. A third person (or the second person after some practice) is needed to give tension below the climber for the ascenders to grip the rope, and to take up the slack as the climber ascends.

Fig. 14.12. Crossing a double Sheetbend knot while prusiking with Gibbs system, I have already attached safety Jumar to line and moved chest box above knot. I am now resetting knee Gibbs above knot. Next step will be to pull up line and reset lower Gibbs above knot.

Knot Prusiking

The original technique of prusiking was developed in Austria
by Karl Prusik and written up in the Austrian Alpine Journal in
1931. It was intended as a means of self-rescue for a climber
who had fallen into a crevice. The knot he devised for this
purpose still bears his name, as does the general technique of
ascending ropes with knots or mechanical ascenders.

Three Knot Prusik System. Today climbing with Prusik knots
is becoming rare except for contests and emergency use. But
the technique is easy to learn and I think every serious vertical
caver should be familiar with it. The system I'm going to
describe is the basic three knot version. Since it doesn't
include a seat harness, there isn't a good resting position.
Anyone interested in using knots as a primary system for
longer drops will need to attach the upper knot to a seat
harness through a chest sling or not as preferred.

For a chest loop, I use about eight feet of webbing tied into a
chest sling with a carabiner in front (Fig.10.10). The loop that
attaches to the chest sling is about 22 inches long. The right or
middle foot loop (you can reverse these if you want) is about
64 inches long. The left foot or lower loop is about 57 inches.
(These lengths are for the finished slings which have been
shortened by the length of rope needed to tie a Grapevine and
Figure 8 knot.)

Prusik sling lengths are fairly critical so be prepared to
fiddle around with them until they're comfortable. Start with
about 12 or 13 feet for each foot, plus about four feet for the
chest, for a total of about 30 feet. Use 5/16 or 3/8 inch
Skyline (three strand laid), Perlon cord, or polypropylene.

To secure the slings to your feet, a snug Figure 8 Loop is
tied in the bottom of the foot slings. A chicken loop of 1 inch
tubular webbing is run around your ankle to secure the slings.
Some folks add foot stirrups of 1 or 2 inch webbing.

To begin, you stand astride the rope, raise the chest knot as high as possible, followed by one of the foot knots--the right with this system, but always the one attached to the middle knot and the longer foot sling (Fig. 14.13. Then the weight is shifted onto the right foot. Next, the left foot and sling are raised and tucked under the body.   Finally you stand up on both feet, sliding the chest sling as high as possible at the same time to start a new cycle.

This system works for free ascents of not much more than 25 feet. Beyond that the pressure on the chest sling begins to take its toll. Up against a wall, however, you can go 50 or 60 feet without chest problems because you can lean against the wall to relieve pressure.

Ladders

Do cavers still use cable ladders? Well, the answer used to be yes, but now it's more like, once in a great while. Thirty feet is about as far as anyone will climb today on a ladder. Ladders are still found in one-pit caves where it's easier for everyone to climb out on a ladder than to take the time to put on ascending gear. Even in this case, most people will rappel down. Cavers rarely climb down ladders, since rappelling is easier and a lot more fun.

 Cable ladders are made of high-grade aircraft cable (standard or stainless) with rungs of aluminum alloy measuring about 5 inches wide. The ends have metal eyes for attachment to anchors. Length is usually 33 feet, with a spacing of about 10 to 15 inches between rungs.

A ladder is best carried in a cloth sack or cave pack to protect it from damage and abrasion. Lower it gently down the pit to protect it and keep it from snagging.

After use, wash the mud off and inspect it when it's dry for loose cable strands and other signs of wear. To test it before use, rig it to a solid anchor, stand on the bottom rung, and bounce on it with your full weight a few times. For storage and transport, coil a ladder by twisting each of the rungs in the opposite direction to form a crisscross pattern in the cable (Fig. 14.15)

Fig. 14.13. Three knot Prusik system. Chest knot had been raised as high as possible and right foot knot is just being raised. Next step is to raise left foot and left knot, then again raise chest knot as high as possible and repeat cycle. Note chicken loops of 6mm perlon around ankles to keep slings on. For serious knot prusiking, a seat harness for resting would be needed.

Fig. 14.14. Climbing a cable ladder, a somewhat younger Molly McClurg alternates feet on front and back of ladder. Both hands are on back. Belay rope is tied around waist with Bowline on a coil.

Climbing a Ladder Just about anyone can learn to climb a ladder on the second or third try. The first thing you have to do is convince yourself that this fragile-looking item will really support your weight. Admittedly, at first glance it doesn't inspire a lot of confidence with its spindly cables and thin, narrow rungs.

The trick to cable ladder climbing is to place one foot behind the ladder and the next one on the front to keep your feet from pushing out from underneath (See Fig 14.14). You

Fig. 14.15. For carrying and storage, roll up a ladder and twist in alternate direction as shown at every rung. Tie with short length of sling or cord.

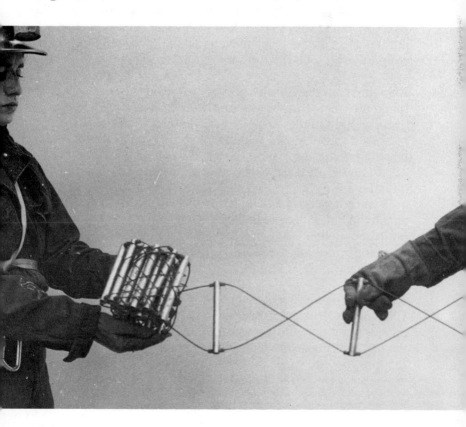

must also climb with your legs not your arms or you'll get tired immediately. Both hands can go on the back side or they can be alternated front and back. To get started, stand on the first rung with the hands on the rungs above the head and shift your weight onto that rung. Next, put the other foot around on the back side on the second rung, the next on the front, and so on up to the top. Don't try to put both feet on one rung. They're made only one boot wide.

This technique of alternating the feet on the front and back works well when the ladder is hanging free. However, when the ladder is pressed tightly against an overhang or wall, you need to force the ladder away from the wall, so the hands and feet can get at the rungs. One way to do this is to turn the ladder slightly on its side. This takes a bit of strength, but is easy to maintain once done. You can also put both feet on the front side and push the ladder away from the wall with the toes of your boots.

Belaying Ladder Climbs. Climbing a ladder is easy, but still inherently dangerous, particularly when wetness, muddy gloves, and fatigue come into the picture. For these reasons, I must caution you to never climb a ladder without a belay no matter how short the pitch It's also possible to fall off if you tire or if it's slippery. See Chapter 12 for details on belaying.

If you're the last person up a ladder, it is a good idea to attach the bottom of the ladder to your seat harness or a tail on the belay line. This way the ladder will follow you up as you climb, making it easier to unsnag from rocks or overhangs.

Rigging. For rigging and anchoring suggestions, see Chapter 11. When rigging a ladder, be sure to select an anchor point that allows two or three rungs to remain above the lip This makes it far simpler to get off when you reach the top. As with ropes, lower—don't throw—a ladder down the drop, so it won't get snarled on an overhang.

Appendix 1

Caving Skills Self-Tests

•Basic
•Intermediate/Advanced
•Technical Vertical

Here are three self-tests that all cavers, beginning or advanced, can use to compare their progress toward becoming fully competent cave explorers. Each test contains specific details and dimensions, such as the size of a crawlway to be negotiated or the depth of a pit to be dropped.

To assess your conservation awareness, see Chapter 2.

Caution: Even though these are self tests, many of them must be done with at least two other cavers for safety reasons. Since most are done underground, the same rule about not caving alone applies during a test as with any other cave trip. The long drop vertical tests may have to done above ground if you don't have deep pits in your area. But here again, it would be unsafe to try these alone without other cavers present in case of an emergency.

Basic Skills

Knots. Tie the five basic caving knots blindfdolded or in total darkness, including backup overhand knots where required:

1) Bowline and Bowline on a coil.
2) Water Knot
3) Grapevine Knot
4) Figure 8 Loop
5) Prusik Knot.

Carbide Lamp. If using a carbide lamp, extinguish it in total darkness and immediately find and light your secondary source of light. Then, find the cause of the following troubles and correct them. (Another caver could purposely introduce some of these troubles in your lamp or in a test lamp.) This test assumes you are carrying extra water, carbide, and a spare parts kit at all times in the cave, plus your two other sources of light.

• Lamp won't light. No water or carbide, clogged tip, wet felt, bad gasket, loose bottom. Refill lamp with water and carbide. Put the used carbide in a suitable container for removal from the cave.

• Lamp burns irregularly. Same causes as above. Dismantle lamp and replace felt and tip.

• Flame around gasket. Bad gasket or thread seat, loose bottom.

• Flame around tip. Bad or loose tip, bad tip seat.

• Water spurts from tip, bubbles out of water filler cap, or flame is several inches long. Too much water; decrease flow and wait before lighting. Felt may also be soaked.

Electric Lamp. Turn the lamp out. Find and light secondary source of light. Then determine the cause and repair the following troubles. It is assumed that you have spare bulbs and batteries at all times as well as two other sources of light.

• No light. Bad bulb, dead batteries, loose connection. Take lamp apart and tighten or replace bulb and batteries.

• Irregular light. Symptoms as above.

• Dim light. Check batteries for corroded or loose connections.

• Cable catches on obstructions. Reroute cable from battery to lamp. Also demonstrate ability to remove lamp from helmet or disconnect cable quickly when it snags in a tight spot.

Crawling. Crawl through a low passage, averaging 14 inches or less in height, 2 feet or less in width, and 10 feet or more in length.

Scrambling. In a breakdown area scramble up and down over some good-sized blocks—10 x 10 x 20 feet—using walls and ceiling, if available.

Slopes and Slots (down). Slide downward on a slope (using walls and ceiling if possible), a semi-vertical passage (less than 45 degrees), or a fissure, for at least 10 feet in total depth. (This assumes the landing below has previously been explored and is known to be a safe stopping place.)

Slopes and Slots (up). Similarly, climb, crawl, or chimney back up this or a comparable passage.

Tilted Slots (down). Slide down a tilted slot or fissure of similar dimensions as above, so that you slide not straight down but at an angle.

Tilted Slots (up). Similarly, climb or clamber back through this or a similar slanting passage.

Intermediate and Advanced Skills

Tight Crawling. Crawl through a tight passage 12 inches or less in height with at least one S curve that requires turning over or crawling on your side, with one shoulder ahead of you, and pushing hard hat and gear ahead of you.

Verbal Climbing Signals. Demonstrate the proper verbal signals and use them in each test.

Rigging. Find and rig a satisfactory anchor and backup anchor for a belay line and the belayer.

Static Belaying. Using the sitting hip position, belay a 150 to 200 pound caver on both an ascent and a descent in a cave, Successfully hold an unannounced fall by both an ascending and a descending climber.

Traversing. Make a horizontal traverse while on belay, using three-point rock climbing skills and, if the walls are close together, chimneying.

Chimneying Down. Chimney down a vertical or semi-vertical pit (more than 45 degrees), that is wider than 2 feet on the average, and at least 15 feet deep. Use a belay if the chimney bells out, is slippery, or is otherwise dangerous.

Chimneying Up. Chimney up the same or a similar pit.

Free Climbing. Using three-point climbing technique, climb up and down while on belay, a 20 to 30 foot vertical pit or wall that is too wide for chimneying and too steep for scrambling, using handholds and footholds.

Technical Vertical Skills

Rappelling

Find and rig a good high anchor and backup anchor for a rappel line inside a cave or at a cave entrance.

• Rappel into a tight fissure or pit where you are against the wall most of the way. Drop must be at least 40 to 50 feet.
• Rappel into a medium-width fissure or pit where you have contact and free rappelling. Drop should be at least 40 to 50 feet.
• Rappel into a wide fissure or room where you are mostly free from the wall. Drop must be at least 40 to 50 feet.
• Rappel down into one of these pits, perform a changeover, then ascend back to the top.
• Rappel down a long drop, in a cave or outdoors, of at least 150 feet and preferable 200 feet or more. Demonstrate your ability to handle the weight of the free hanging rope—from 10 to 30 pounds or more—by adding and removing bars from your rack, locking off and unlocking the rack, and locking and unlocking your spelean shunt or other

dynamic safety device. (A Prusik knot is not recommended for this because of the difficulty of freeing it under load.)
• Rappel down a line to a knot or obstruction. Then transfer to an adjacent line and continue on down.
• Rappel down a line with two knots and successfully pass them both. Then continue on down.

Prusiking

Rigging a Prusik Line. Find and rig a good high anchor and backup anchor inside a cave or at a cave entrance for a prusik line. (This can be the rappel test anchor.)

Prusiking
• Prusik up the three separate types of drops—narrow, medium, and wide— required for the rappel test (in the same or a different cave).
• Prusik up a pit at least 150 to 200 feet deep of any type, using a three-ascender system and a seat-sling resting position.
• Prusik up in one of these drops and perform a changeover to rappel. Then rappel back down.
• Prusik up to a knot or obstruction, then transfer to an adjacent line and continue up.
• Prusik up a line that has two knots and successfully cross them. Continue on up.

Rigging a Ladder. Find and rig a satisfactory anchor and back up anchor for a cable ladder, a belay line, and the belayer.

Ladder Climbing
• Climb down and up a 30 foot cable ladder with a proper static belay from a separate belayer.
• Climb down and up a 30 foot ladder using a self-belay on a fixed line with a Gibbs ascender or Prusik knot.

Summary of Vertical Equipment Required

This is a run-down on the vertical gear I take along on cave trips. For caves with known vertical pits, I carry a separate pack for vertical gear in addition to a cave pack.

Horizontal Caves—No pits expected. Caver's sling (12 feet of 1-inch webbing), and locking carabiner (we always carry this sling).

Intermediate Caves—Small drops (25 or 30 feet) or a new cave with unknown but expected vertical extent.

50-foot 8 mm hand line
Figure-8 or Petzl descender
Caver's sling and locking carabiner
Mitchell System with Gossett chest box
9/16-inch mini-etrier (attach with Jumar to line)
Safety loop (20-inch diameter) 7-mmm Perlon; 2 carabiners

Advanced Caves--Short and medium pits (25 to150 feet).
Figure-8 or Petzl descender
Spelean shunt
Chest sling, homemade 2-inch, with Gossett chest box
Seat harness attached to chest harness
Double bungy Gibbs system with two ascenders, safety
    loop on line for third point , OR
Mitchell system with Gossett box if multiple drops, water
    hazards, or other technical problems.
One-inch etrier with Jumar, plus 9/16-inch mini-etrier
Two extra safety loops, 4 carabiners
Spare Gibbs (part of spelean shunt)

Really Big Ones--Deep vertical pits 150 to 1000 feet +.
  Rappel rack plus high strength carabiner.
  Spelean shunt
  Chest and seat harnesses as above
  Double bungy Gibbs as above, floating both knee and foot
  Gibbs and Gossett box.
  Spare Gibbs (part of spelean shunt)
  Jumar and 1-inch etrier, plus 9/16-inch mini-etrier
  Three extra safety loops, four carabiners

Appendix 2

Sources of Further Information

Publications, Publishers, Bookstores

Association for Mexican Cave Studies, P.O. Box 7672 UT
    Station, Austin, TX 78712. AMCS activities newsletter
    contains accounts of what many call the most interesting
    caving anywhere.
The Canadian Caver, P.O. Box 275, McMaster
    University Hamilton, Ontario L8P 1JP, Canada.
Cave Research Foundation, Cave Books, 901 Buford Place,
    Nashville,   TN 37204. Excellent training manual and
    maps of MammothCave and Carlsbad. Caverns.
Caves and Caving, British Cave Research Association,
30 Main Road, Westonzoyland, Bridgewater, Somerset,
England. A British caving magazine.
Descent, Ambit Publications, 13-11 Stroud Rd.
    Gloucester, GL1-5AA, England, Great Britain.
Journal of Spelean History, Jack H. Speece, 711 East
Atlantic Ave., Altoona, PA 16602.
NSS Bookstore, Cave Avenue, Huntsville, AL 35810.
    Supplier of caving books and NSS puablications. .
NSS Bulletin, Cave Avenue, Huntsville, AL 35810.
Quarterly scientific and technical journal.
NSS NEWS, Cave Avenue, Huntsville, AL 35810.
    Monthly news and feature magazine.
Nylon Highway, Bruce Smith, Ed. 1822 Mountain Bay
Drive, Chatanooga TN 37343. Vertical Section
Publication..
Speleobooks, P.O. Box 333, Wilbraham, MA 01005.
    Large selection caving books and periodicals.
Summit, a mountaineering magazine, P.O. Box 1889, Big
    Bear Lake, CA 92315.

Equipment Suppliers

Blue Water, Ltd., 209 Lavvorn Rd, Carrollton, GA 30117
California Mountain Co., Ltd., PO Box 6602, Santa Barbara,
    CA 93160
Caves Unlimited, 4956 Asbury Circle, Dubuque, IA 52001.
Custom Cave Gear, Box 7351, Chalottesville, VA 22906.
Eastern Mountain Sports, Vose Farm Road, Peterborough,
    NH 03458. Stores in northeast, St. Paul, Denver.
Grotto Store, 26519 Oak Ridge Dr., Wind Lake, WI 53185.
L&S Sporting Goods, Box 176, Phillipi, WV 26416.
Pathfinder Sports, 5214 E. Pima St., Tucson, AZ 85711.
Pigeon Mountain Industries, Box 803 Lafayette, GA 30728
Recreational Equipment Inc.,Box C88125 Seattle, WA
    98188.Stores in west,Salt Lake City, Denver,Minneapolis.
The SpeleoShoppe, P.O. Box 297, Fairdale, KY 40118.
SpeleoSports Ltd. Star Rte. Box 57A, Tijeras, NM 87050.
J.E. Weinel, Inc., Box 213, Valencia, PA 16059.

Organizations

American Cave Conservation   Association, P. O. Box
7017, Richmond, VA 23221. Protection and preservation of
cave resources through management, education and training
programs, and cooperation with other organizations.
Publishes a newsletter on cave management, conservation
projects, and related matters.
Cave Research Foundation, P.O. Box 443, Yellow
Springs, OH 45387. Supports research and exploration
projects in Mammoth Cave (Kentucky), Carlsbad Caverns
(New Mexico), Lilburn Cave (California), and other locations.
National Speleological Society, Cave Aveneue,
Huntsville, AL 35810. Nonprofit educational and conservation
organization affiliatedwith the American Association for the
Advancement of Science. About 6,500 members and over 100
chapters (grottos). Write for membership information and
name of the chapter nearest to you.Please include a self-
addressed envelope. Publishes a monthly magazine and a

twice a year scientific bulletin. Has an extensive library and
operates a bookstore.
British Cave Research Association. Membership:
J.R.Woodridge, Assistant Secretary, 9 Chelsea Court,
Abdon Ave., Birmingham 29, England. Publications: 30
Main Road, Westonzoyland, Bridgewater, Somerset,
England.Issues monthly bulletin and quarterly transaction.

Recommended Reading and References

Cave Exploration

Bedford, B.L. 1975. *Challenge Underground.*
Teaneck, NJ: Zephyrus Press. Bedford's adventures
and survey of British caving make interesting reading.
Casteret, N. 1938. *Ten Years Under the Earth.*
London: The Greystone Press. Casteret, a pioneer cave
explorer, recounts many of his underground adventures in
this fascinating series of books.
------------. 1947. *My Caves.* London: J.M.Dent & Sons.
------------. 1951. *Cave Men, New and Old.* London.
Dent.
------------. 1954. *The Darkness Under the Earth.*, NY:
Holt
------------. 1956. *Descent of Pierre Saint Martin.* New York:
Philosophical Library.
------------. *More Years Under the Earth.* London:
Neville Spearman.
Chevalier, P. 1951/1976. *Subterranean Climbers.*
Teaneck, N.J.:Zephyrus Press. Twelve years in the
world's deepest caves in. Reprinted in 1976 with a new
introduction by the author.
Conn, H. and J. 1977. *The Jewel Cave Adventure.*
Teaneck, NJ: Zephyrus Press. The exciting story of
twenty years of discovery in this 50-mile-long cave in
the Black Hills of South Dakota. As much a story of
dedication to a monumental task as it is the unfolding of
an intricate maze.

de Joly, R. 1975. *Memoirs of a Speleologist.*
Teaneck, NJ: Zephyrus Press. Pioneer French cave
explorer, along with Casteret, and inventor of the cable
ladder, narrates his lifetime career as a cave explorer.
Eyre, J. 1981. *The Cave Explorers.* Entertaining
tales of 30 years of caving in England, Europe, and
Mexico.
Farr, M. 1980. *The Darkness Beckons.* London:
Diadem Books.Fascinating account of the development
of cave diving.
----------. 1984. The Great Caving Adventure. Sparkford,
England. Both caving and cave diving are covered in this
equally fascinating second volume.
Folsom, F. 1962. *Exploring American Caves.* New
York: Collier. Interesting stories of famous caves,
including some coverage of the formation of caves, cave
animals, and techniques. Recommended.
Gurnee, R. and J. 1974. *Discovery at the Rio Camuy.*
New York: Crown. Exploration and discovery of a
major cave system in Puerto Rico. Fascinating reading.
Gurnee, R.H. 1978. *Discovery of Luray Caverns,*
Virginia. Closter, NJ: R.H. Gurnee. One of America's
premier show caves, Luray Caverns has a story to equal
its beauty. Excellently retold by Russ Gurnee, a lifelong
caver and former president of the NSS.
Halliday, W.R. 1959. *Adventure is Underground.*
New York: Harper & Row. Once described as the
"spokesman for speleolgy" because Halliday was one of
the first active cavers to publish his and other cavers'
underground adventures. His books are recommended
reading for every caver, even though his lofty style and
egocentric tone tend to be aggravating to some readers.
This, his earlier book, covers western caves and cavers.
--------. 1966, 1976. Depths of the Earth. New York:
 Harper & Row. An updated and expanded volume.
Hovey, H.C. 1896, 1970. *Celebrated American
Caverns.* New York and London: Johnson Reprint
Service. Originally published in 1896 and long out of
print, this fascinating survey of 19th century caves is

available in a beautiful new edition.

Jackson, D. 1982. *Underground Worlds*. Alexandria, VA: Time Life Books. Beautiful, glossy presentation, a must book. (I am compelled to mention, however the unattributed redrawing on page 116 of a photo from my *Exploring Caves* . This photo also appears on p.225 of this book).

Judson, D. 1973. *Ghar Parau.* New York: Macmillan. Fascinating story of 1972-73 British expedition to "the big one" in Iran, some 3000 feet deep, in 26 small to medium, sized pitches.

Lawrence, Joe, Jr.; and Brucker, R.W. 1955 and 1975.*The Caves Beyond.* Teaneck, NJ: Zephyrus Press. A very welcome second edition includes a new introduction and the entire text of theoriginal edition. One of the best cave "adventure" books, the one many of us cut our teeth on in the 1950s.

Mercer, H.C. 1896 and 1975. *The Hill Caves of Yucatan.* Teaneck, NJ: Zephyrus Press. Searching for evidence of human antiquity in Central American caverns

Miller, S. 1942 and 1978. *"Why Floyd Collins Couldn't Be Rescued."*Louisville Courier-Journal, reprinted in Journal of Spelean History 4, no. 4, April/June 1978.

Mohr, C., and Sloane, H.N. eds. 1955. *Celebrated American Caves.* New Brunswick, NJ: Rutgers University Press. Stories of famous caves and cavers.

Murray, R and Brucker, R. 1979. *Trapped.* New York: Putnam. Modern analysis of the Floyd Collin's story. Beautifully researched and told.

 Nymeyer, R.1978. *Carlsbad, Caves, and a Camera.* Beautiful photos and interesting text about the early days around Carlsbad, New Mexico.

Sloane, B., Ed. 1977. *Cavers, Caves and Caving.* New Brunswick, NJ; Rutgers University Press. Excellent anthology covering the exploration, history, science, and adventure of caves. Recommended.

Tazieff, H. 1953. *Caves of Adventure.* New York:

Viking.First hand account , 2000 foot descent, Pyrenees.
Waltham, A.C. 1975. *Caves*. New York: Putnam.
Beautiful color and black and white pictures with
excellent supporting text Waltham is a geologist and
active caver. In many instances, he writes from his own
experience. Recommended.
----------. 1976. *The World of Caves*. New York:
Putnam.Waltham's second book is in an oversize format
with many color pictures. World wide in scope.

Cave Sciences

Bauer, E. 1971. *The Mysterious World of Caves*.
York: Watts.An International Library of Science books
for young people. Beautiful color illustrations and
authoritative text by a German university professor.
Translated from German.
Bogli, A., and Franke, H.W. 1968. *Luminous
Darkness*. Berne: Kummerly and Frey. Science of
speleology written in lay terms by two eminent Swiss
speleologists and beautifully illustrated with their
photos--many in color and full page in size--of Hollock in
Switzerland and other European caves.
Cullingford, C.H.D., Ed. 1962. *British Caving--An
Introduction to Speleology*. 2nd rev. ed. London:
Routledge and Kegan Paul. Written by members of the
British Cave Research Association. Basic science text
oriented to British caves and cavers. Some material on
Griffin, D.R. 1958. *Listening in the Dark*. New
Haven, CT: Yale University Press. Acoustics and sonar
used by bats to avoid bumping into walls and each other.
Mohr, C.E., and Poulson, T. 1966. *The Life of the
Cave*. New York: McGraw Hill. Cave life and ecology.A
fascinating introduction to the subject. Beautifully illustrated.
Moore, G.W., and Sullivan, G.N. 1978. *Speleology,
The Study of Caves*. Teaneck, NJ: Zephyrus Press.Revised,
second edition of this very readable general text on cave
sciences. Highly recommended.

Techniques and Equipment

Aleith, R.C. 1975. *Bergsteigen: Basic Rock Climbing*. New York: Scribner Well written and illustrated text covering all aspects of rock climbing. More comprehensive than Robbins.

Anderson, J. 1974. *Cave Exploring*. New York: Association Press. Concise treatment, nicely illustrated by the author, but now dated. Her recommendations for brake bar rappels and diaper slings without a backup waist loop are not in step with current safety practices. In addition, bowline appears to be tied with the end on the outside of the loop making it only half as strong. Also, two essential knots--the Water knot and Grapevine—are omitted. Belaying and knot prussiking are well documented, but mechanical ascenders and systems, now overwhelmingly preferred to knots, are only mentioned in passing.

Blackshaw, A. 1965, 1977. *Mountaineering: From Hill Walking to Alpine Climbing*. Harmondsworth, England and New York: Penguin Books. More or less a British equivalent to the next lising. Very complete and well illustrated.

Ferber, P. ed. 1977. *Mountaineering: The Freedom of the Hills*. Seattle: The Mountaineers. Third edition of this comprehensive text covering all aspects of mountain travel including excellent treatment of climbing, belaying, and rappeling. Jumar as shown in figure 121 (p. 211) is dangerous. It should run up around stronger vertical brace.

Halliday, W.., M.D. 1974. *American Caves and Caving*. New York: Harper and Row. This is Bill Halliday's technique book written in the same lofty "spokesman for

speleology" style found in his other books. Reasonably
comprehensive treatment, with especially good sections
in cave medicine and first aid, and a good introduction to
cave search and rescue. Vertical sections are generally all
right but are now somewhat outdated. Halliday's
curious insistence that tennis shoes and manila ropes are
suitable and even safe for cave use is certainly outside the
mainstream of caving and has frequently been criticized.
His very weak conservation and safety messages have
also brought him justifiable heat from reviewers.

Judson, David and Charles, ed. 1984. *Manual of Caving
Practice and Equipment.* London. Anthology of
British techniques. Complete and authoritative. Vertical
techniques are now up to date at least as far as European
practice are concerned.

Lyon, Ben.1983. *Venturing Underground.* Wakefield,
England: EP Publishing. A generally excellent book
except for some curious opinions on American vertical
techniques.

Kahrau, W. 1972. *Australian Caves and Caving.*
Periwinkle Books. Beautifully illustrated, this is a good
short introduction to the caves and cave techniques of the
land down under.

Livesay, P. 1978. *Rock Climbing.* Seattle: The
Mountaineers. Excellent beginners volume by a well
known British climber and climbing instructor.

Montgomery, N.R. 1977. *Single Rope Techniques.*
Sydney, Australia: Sydney Speleological Society
Occasional Paper No. 7. Covers ropes, knots, rigging,
descending, and ascending. My only serious disagree-
ment is his statement that gloves may not be desirable on short
rappels. I recommend gloves for all rappels. Reasonably
complete, but doesn't mention belaying.

Robbins, R. 1971. *Basic Rockcraft.* Glendale, CA: La
Siesta Press A concise but good introduction to rock
climbing by one of the Yosemite "big wall" climbers. A
must for all serious cavers.

--------. 1973. *Advanced Rockcraft*. Glendale, CA: LaSiesta Press. Companion to above. However, avoid tying to bottom brace of a Jumar as shown on page 45.
Thrun, R. 1971. *Prusiking*. Huntsville, AL: National Speleological Society. Detailed descriptions of knot and mechanical ascender systems. Now dated, but of interest to vertical cavers.

Glossary

ABSEILING. British term for rappelling.

ANCHOR. A secure point (rock projection, breakdown block, tree, expansion bolt) to which a caving rope, ladder, or belayer can be safely attached. A secondary or backup anchor is suggested unless physically impossible. Called a belay in Britain.

ANDERSON, RUSS. Designer of rescue pulleys and other hardware.

ARAGONITE. A less common form of calcium carbonate found in caves (the more common is calcite), often in the form of needle-like crystals.

BACON OR BACON RIND. Speleothem made up of a thin sheet of calcite with alternating bands of color. The brown or darker bands are usually caused by iron oxide.

BASALT. A common type of lava, in which lava tubes form.

BASE LEVEL, see water table.

BEDDING PLANE. The surface or boundary that divides two adjacent beds of sedimentary rock (such as limestone).

BELAY. A method of protecting a climber in case of a fall. A rope is tied or clipped to a harness on the first caver (the climber), so that a second caver (the belayer), who is securely anchored, can stop a fall. In Britain, this is sometimes known as safetying or life lining. A belay in Britain is what we all an anchor.

BELAY-IS-ON. The call used by the belayer to tell the climber that the belayer is ready to belay and the climber is now protected.

BELAY-IS-OFF. After a climber has reached a safe spot, and has called off-belay, the belayer relaxes and indicates protection has ended by answering belay is off.

BINER. Colloquial for carabiner. The British slang term is krab.

BLOWING CAVE. A cave that has large air currents moving in or out for extended periods. Changes in barometric pressure are believed to be the cause.

BLUE WATER, Ltd. (Carrollton, Georgia). Manufacturer of static caving ropes

BONAITI. Italian manufacturer of carabiners, ascenders, and other hardware.

BOXWORK. Honeycomb-like speleothem of calcite projecting from a cave wall or ceiling.

BOWLINE. A knot used to form a nonslipping loop; one of the basic knots any caver should know. See knots.

BREAKDOWN. Large piles of rocks and boulders that have fallen from the ceiling or walls at an earlier time in the cave's geologic history.

BUNGY CORD. Flexible cord made of rubber strands covered by fabric sheath. Used for Gibbs ropewalker prusik systems to keep tension on ascender cams.

CMI. Colorado Mountain Industies, manufacturer of clilmbing and caving hardware.

CABLE LADDER. See ladder.

CALCITE. The most common cave mineral, a crystalline form of calcium carbonate.

CANYON HOPPING. See straddling.

CARABINER. An oval-shaped, aluminum-alloy or steel link with a spring-loaded gate in one side, used in climbing and rappelling. Sometimes equipped with a locking sleeve and called a locking carabiner (or, in Britain, a screwgate carabiner). Often spelled karabiner in Britain. Slang terms are biner in America, krab in Britain.

CARABINER BRAKE BARS. A formerly widely used descender using two carabiners each with a bar installed crosswise. Loading of the gates, the weakest part of a carabiner, is considered questionable. Now supplanted by the Figure 8 Descender or Rappel Rack.

CARBIDE LAMP. A miner's lamp used by cavers. Acetylene gas produced by mixing water with carbide is ignited and burns at a jet positioned in a reflector.

CARBONIC ACID. A weak acid made from carbon dioxide and rain or soil water that slowly dissolves limestone to form caves.

CAVE. A natural void beneath the earth, usually made up of several rooms and passages.

CAVE FORMATION. See speleothem.

CAVE ICE. Year round ice formed in some caves with small entrances, especially lava tubes.

CAVE SPRING. See resurgence.

CHIMNEY. 1. A vertical or near-vertical shaft, either tubular or simply where two walls come close together; 2. Climbing up or down such a shaft by means of pressure on both surfaces by back and feet.

CLEAR-OF-THE-DROP? A question shouted down a drop before lowering a rope or beginning a rappel.

CLIMBING. Caving movement used in pits, fissures, and cave walls. Involves three points of contact and other classic rock climbing techniques.

Also, the call climbing is used by a climber to indicate that a climb has actually begun so the belayer can pay out or take in the belay rope.

CLIMBING CALLS. Signals used between cavers during climbing, and to a smaller extent during technical rope work (rappelling and prusiking), such as belay-is-on, is that you, climbing, tension, and so forth. The ones listed here are only suggested. Many local variations are in common use.

CLOG. British company manufacturing carabiners, ascenders, Figure 8 descenders, and other hardware.

COLUMN. A speleothem formed where a hanging stalactite and a rising stalagmite have grown together.

CORKSCREW PASSAGE. A twisting passage, often a tight crawlway or fissure, either horizontal or vertical.

CRAWL OR CRAWLWAY. A passage lower than about three feet requiring and knees or belly crawling. Often preceded by adjectives like miserable, wet, long, or uncomfortable.

CREVICE. A narrow opening or fissure in the floor of a cave, often 10 to 50 feet or more deep; also a high, narrow passage.

DEAD CAVE. A cave in which the speleothems have stopped growing because water is no longer reaching them.

DIAPER SLING. Formerly a commonly used, but unsafe, sling for rappelling usually made of one inch nylon webbing. A separate, redundant waist loop can add the necessary safety factor in case the diaper might break and unwind. Sewn harnesses are now preferred.

DIG. An attempt to gain entrance to a cave or a new area of a known cave by excavation, or in some cases, by blasting, though the latter is controversial in many areas.

DOLINE. See sinkhole.

DOLOMITE. A sedimentary rock similar to but less common than limestone in which caves can occur.

DOMEPIT. A large, dome-shaped cavity above a room or passage, created by solution, not by breakdown. Often close to the surface.

DRAPERY. A thin, curtain-shaped speleothem caused by a sheet of dripping water rather than a single series of drops.

DRIPSTONE. Any of several calcite deposits caused by dripping water, including stalactites, stalagmites, and flowstone.

DROP. A descending slope, pitch, or pit.

DUCKUNDER. A lowered ceiling in a stream passage or lake room where the ceiling and water meet causing a caver to duck under for a few feet. Extremely hazardous and not for beginners. Also called a siphon.

EXPANSION BOLT. A type of anchor for ropes and ladders. It is placed into a predrilled hole and expands when driven in. If installed properly, a 3/8 inch bolt has a working load (25 percent of test load) of about 1550 pounds in concrete.

EXPOSURE. See hypothermia.

FALLING! An emergency cry for help from climber to belayer.

FALSE FLOOR. A thin floor made of calcite or lava under which dirt or gravel has been worked away.

FIGURE 8 DESCENDER. A light weight friction device for rappellling down a fix rope. Has pretty much replaced the much less safe carabiner break bar dsescender.

FIGURE 8 KNOT. A versatile knot with several forms. Loop version, Figure 8 Loop, has become almost as popular as the bowline for modern nylon ropes. Recommended knot for tying a loop in the middle of the rope as well as several other applications.

FILL. Clay, mud, rock, or other material found on the floor of a cave.

FISSURE. A narrow crack, break, or fracture. Body size fissures (and crevices) are usually negotiated by chimneying or traversing movements.

FREE OR FREE CLIMBING. Term used by rock climbers to signify climbing without artificial aids such as slings (runners) or etriers. However, rock climbers are usually belayed on all but the simplest climbs, whether free or aided by hardware.

FLOWSTONE. A coating of calcite deposited by flowing water.

FORREST MOUNTAINEERING, LTD. (Denver, Colo), manufactturer of seat harnesses and climbing hareware.

FLUTE, STREAM. Scallop-like ripples in a cave wall caused by stream action.

FORMATION. See speleothem.

GIBBS ASCENDER. A device used for prusiking up a rope, in a technique called rope walking. Also used for hauling and rescue applications.

GRAPEVINE KNOT. Recommended knot for tying Perlon slings into a loop. Also called the double fisherman's knot.

GROTTO. A small room or chamber opening off of a larger one. Also, a local chapter of the National Speleological Society.

GUANO. In cave terminology, bat dung. A very rich fertilizer, also formerly used for gunpowder.

GYPSUM. A sedimentary rock (primarily calcium sulphate), which is softer and more soluble than limestone. Sizable caves can occur in gypsum.

GYPSUM FLOWERS and HAIR. Varieties of delicate gypsum speleothems, often of great beauty.

HARNESS. See seat harness.

HAND LINE. A short 30 to 50 foot fixed rope (tied at the top) used for climbing or scrambling on steep pitches when holds are scarce.

HAWSER ROPE. British term for laid or three-strand rope.

HELECTITE. A beautiful, twisting speleothem that seems to grow in defiance of the laws of gravity.

HOLD, HAND or FOOT. Small ledge, knob, or crevice that can provide assistance in climbing, scrambling, or chimneying.

HYDROLOGY. Scientific study of underground and surface water.

HYPOTHERMIA. A dangerous condition caused by wet and cold where body heat is being lost rapidly. Lack of food can accelerate the effects. Can kill if not checked. Sometimes known as exposure.

ICE CAVE. A type of cave, usually in lava, which contains ice all year.

IS THAT YOU? Climbing call meaning Is the pull I feel on the rope really you or is it just caught on something? Important so as to keep a tight belay.

JOINT. A crack, usually formed at right angles to the bedding plane in limestone.

JUMAR ASCENDER. A device for prusiking up a rope. Slides up easily, locks when weight is applied.

JUNCTION. A place where two or more passages come together.

KARST. Terrain with many sinkholes, disappearing streams, underground drainage, and caves. See Slovenian karst.

KARABINER. British spelling of carabiner.

KERNMANTEL. The most common type of nylon climbing rope. Made of a core (kern) of straight, twisted, or braided nylon filament covered by an outer sheath (mantel) of braided nylon.

KEYHOLE. A keyhole shaped passage, usually tight.

KNOTS. The basic recommended caving knots are: Bowline, Figure-of 8 Loop, Grapevine, Prusik, and Water Knot.

KRAB. British slang term for carabiner.

LADDER. Caving ladders, made of aircraft cable and aluminum rungs, are used for climbing out of 10 to 30 foot pits. Deeper pits are more commonly pusiked now.

LAID ROPE. Made of three main strands of continuous filament nylon. Now less common than kernmantel ropes. Called hawser in Britain.

LAVA TUBE. A type of cave formed in lava as it cools. Often nearly circular in cross section.

LEAD. A side passage, often small or obscure, hopefully leading to more cave.

LIVE CAVE. A cave with speleothems still being developed by water.

LIMESTONE. A rock composed primarily of calcium carbonate and readily dissolved by carbonic acid. Most caves are formed in limestone.

LOST RIVER. A stream that runs underground for some of its length.

MARBLE. Limesone later subjected to heat and pressure. Many caves occur in marble.

MOON MILK. Whitish, puttylike form of flowstone.

MOVE. During a climb, an individual movement or step progressing to the next position.

NSS. See National Speleological Society.

NATIONAL SPELEOLOGICAL SOCIETY. An organization headquartered in Huntsville, Alabama, with about 6,500 members and more than a hundred local chapters or grottos, including a few in Canada.

NUT, CLIMBING. See wedge.

ON-BELAY. See ready-on-belay.

ON-RAPPEL. Call made when beginning a roped descent.

OFF-BELAY. A climber uses this call to tell the belayer that a safe position has been reached. Belayer will usually answer belay-is-off.

OFF-ROPE. Call or shout made up or down the drop indicating the rope is free for the next person. Don't yell off rope until both you and your gear are completely unattached from the rope.

PMI, Pigeon Mountain Industies (Lafayette, Goergia), manufacturer of static caving rope.

PERLON ACCESSORY CORD. Four to eight mm kernmantel rope for slings. Perlon is a European generic term for a type of nylon.

PETZL. French manufacturer of caving equipment.

PINCH-OUT. In caver talk, a passage that tapers down and becomes too small to penetrate.

PIT. A vertical hole, more or less tubular. Also loosely applied to crevices and fissures. A number of caves have pit entrances resulting from breakdown, dome pit solution, or stream action.

PITCH. A steep ascent or descent. A long climb is frequently divided into several pitches.

PITON. Used in rock climbing (but rarely in caving), a flat spikelike device driven into a crack with a carabiner eye in one end. Also called pins or, in Britain, pegs.

PRUSIK KNOT. A basic caving knot used primarily for climbing up a fixed rope. Easily moved upward, but holds fast.when weight or tension is applied.

PRUSIKING. Method of climbing out of a pit on a fixed rope using Prusik knots or mechanical ascenders with slings attached to feet and chest. Used for pits from 20 to 1000 feet or more.

RAPPELLING. Method of safely sliding down a fixed rope using a descender like a Figure-8 or a rappel rack. Today, cavers usually rappel into a pit, then come out by prusiking, or in short drops, on a ladder.

RAPPEL RACK. A multi-carabiner descending device of adjustable friction, primarily for medium and long drops.

READY-ON-BELAY. Call used by climber to tell the belayer that he or she is tied into the belay rope and ready to be belayed. Often shortened to on-belay. The belayer answers, when ready, with belay-is-on.

READY-TO-CLIMB. Call used by climber after belayer has indicated that belay-is-on and climber is protected. Also shortened to climbing.

RESURGENCE. Point where a cave stream reappears on the surface.

ROCK. Shout this loud and clear the instant you dislodge anything down a pit or drop.

ROPE. Before lowering a rope (or ladder), ask if the drop is clear, then shout rope!

RIMSTONE. A Crusty calcite deposit at the edge of a lake or series of pools.

RUNNER. A sling used to attach a rope or ladder to an anchor.

SMC. Seattle Manufacturing Corporation, manufacturer of caranibers, rappel racks, and other hardware.

SAFETY. See belay.

SCRAMBLE. A half-crawling, half-climbing movement used to negotiate steep or muddy slopes.

SEA CAVE. A void or cavity in rock along a shore caused by wave action.

SEAT HARNESS. A fail safe sewn harness used for rappelling, prusiking, and belays. Usually made of 2 inch webbing with a waistband and sewn leg loops. The first piece of vertical gear a
vertical caver should get is a comfortable seat harness.

SHELTER CAVE. A cavity in any kind of rock offering shelter from the weather.

SINK or SINKHOLE. A depression, often 30 to 100 feet or more across, usually caused by collapse of a cave passage below the surface of the ground. Also called a doline.

SIPHON. See duckunder.

SLACK. Call used by a climber to have the belay rope loosened somewhat.

SLOVENIAN KARST. Area around Postonja in northern Yugoslavia, the so-called "Mother Karst," where most of the original scientific studies of cave development were done. Many geologic terms come from Slovenian, such as karst and doline.

SLING. Short (8 to 25 foot) piece of nylon webbing (or 7 to 9 millimeter Perlon cord), used to attach ropes and ladders to anchors, or to attach safety lines, rappelling devices, and ascenders to cavers.

SODA STRAW. A thin, hollow form of stalactite from which water drips and deposits calcite at the tip.

SOLUTION TUBE. Type of passage developed by dissoving action. Usually of nearly tubular proportions unless modified by stream action at the bottom.

SQUEEZE. An extremely tight passage. Also squeezeway.

SPELEOGENESIS. The origin and development of caves.

SPELEOTHEM. Generic name for cave deposits of calcite, aragonite and gypsum. Includes stalactites, stalagmites, columns, drapery, flowstone, rimstone, gypsum flowers, helectites, and others caused by deposition.

SPELUNKER. A term used mostly by non-cavers to describe a caver. Not generally used by cavers except humorously.

STALACTITE. A hanging speleothem formed by calcite in dripping water.

STALAGMITE. A calcite deposit built upward from the floor by dripping water. The largest are over 100 feet high.

STRADDLING. Bridging across a narrow canyon or pit with arms and legs on opposite walls.

SWALLET OR SWALLOW HOLE. The point where a stream disappears in karst country.

SWAMI SEAT. A seat harness. tied with knots, rather than sewn, to provide separate waist and leg loops. Complcated to tie and not as comfortable as a two inch sewn harness, but safer than an unsecured diaper sling or unsewn Texas seat.

TALUS CAVE. An underground cavity formed by falling rock or where soil has been washed away between large boulders. Can be quite extensive.

TAPE. British term for nylon webbing.

TENSION. Call used when climber wants the belay rope tighter. say

TEXAS SEAT SLING. An easily adjusted seat harness often made from two-inch nylon webbing. Leg loops are formed by metal clips. Reasonably comfortable, it lacks sewn joints, so could unravel if it broke (as can a diaper sling).

TROGLODYTE. An animal, including the human, who lives in a cave.

TRAVERTINE. A course type of flowstone, formed by calcite in water flowing over a surface.

TUBE. See solution tube and lava tube.

UIAA. International Alpine Association, a standards and rating organization for rock climbing and mountaineering.

UP-ROPE. Call used at beginning of a climb to indicate extra rope is ready to be pulled up. Tension is used when a tighter belay is wanted during the climb

WALK-IN CAVE. A cave with a large entrance. Usually but not always, with large walking passages inside.

WATER KNOT. Recommended knot for tying webbing into a loop or tying two pieces of webbing together. Also called webbing knot, sling knot, and tape knot.

WATER TABLE. Top or highest level of underground water in a given area. Also called base level. Below this level, cavities and voids may be flooded.

WEBBING. Tubular nylon, usually the one inch size, used for slings and runners. Called tape in Britain.
WEDGE, CLIMBING. A type of easy-to-place and easy-to-remove rope anchor used by rock climbers (and only rarely by cavers). Most have a hole to attach a rope or sling. Also called a climbing nut or chock.

WILD CAVE. An undeveloped cave in its natural state, in contrast to a commercial cave where lighting and paths have been added.

WINDOW. A hole in the ceiling of a cave. In a lava tube, usually from bubbling or pressure of the lava. In a limestone cave, usually from

Index

Numbers in bold type
indicate illustrations and captions